Flying Naked

Books by Michael Bleriot
Memories of an Emerald World
The Jungle Express
Wings of Blue
Flying Naked
Flying Naked 2

Flying Naked

An American Pilot in the Amazon Jungle

MICHAEL BLERIOT

MacGregor Books

Washington DC MMXV

To the Pilots, Crews, and Mechanics
of the C-27

Contents

Forward. i

1   Hearts of Green 1

2   Colombia 17

3   Venezuela 29

4   Myths. 91

5   Elves 105

6   The State of the Union 197

7   Naked 279

The List. 349

Glossary. 351

FORWARD

THE C-27A SPARTAN WAS a twin-engine turboprop cargo plane used by the U.S. military in Central and South America during the 1990s. Modified from the Italian G-222, it was large enough to carry several tons of cargo and people but small enough to get into most of the airstrips scattered around the jungles of the region. That mission was called tactical airlift. For ten years the C-27 filled an essential tactical airlift niche by supplying locations too remote for helicopters to reach and too small for bigger aircraft to land.

The C-27 wasn't sleek: a bulbous nose and squat fuselage made it look chubby – some compared it to a baby seal. But it was rugged enough to pound down onto rutted clearings carved into the forest and durable enough to bounce through thunderstorms over the Andes mountains. Crews routinely mistreated the airframe and engines by carrying too much, landing too hard, or driving it like an off-road vehicle through grass, gravel, sand, or mud to get where they were going. Many of the crews flying the "Mighty Chuck," as it was affectionately called, amplified their harsh treatment by being inexperienced. Others came to the plane with lots of hours in the air – and then misapplied lessons learned in other aircraft. Yet the C-27 never complained and always persevered. In a decade of operations it rarely broke, never crashed, and won accolades from those who had the privilege to fly aboard – in both the cockpit and the cabin.

The C-27 had one home, Howard Air Base in Panama. Crews also staged temporary operations from satellite fields in Honduras and Peru. From these locations they reached sites as far north as Guatemala and as far south as Bolivia, from the Pacific coast to the jungles of Brazil.

The C-27 fleet left Panama in 1999 when the United States gave the Canal Zone and its military bases to the country of Panama. The Air Force retired the planes shortly thereafter.

Flying
Naked

1. Hearts of Green

THE FIRST PLACE THE Air Force sent me was Hondo, Texas.

Hondo was a dustbowl on the plains outside of San Antonio where the Air Force housed its flight screening program. Flight screening was just that, a three-week haze of intense flight instruction designed to weed out guys who probably wouldn't make it through the formal course later. If you wanted to survive you had to learn fast, keep your mouth shut, and ignore the stress.

And there was stress. I arrived with fifteen other pilot wannabes and we all assumed the only way to survive was to make sure someone else failed first. Though we didn't stab each other in the back we didn't help each other, either, and whenever someone stumbled the rest of us rushed to distance ourselves for fear of being weak by association.

Then there were our instructor pilots. It was a screening program so the IPs were supposed to be tough but ours were particularly harsh because they didn't want to be there in the first place. They were all first-assignment guys, FAIPS, pilots only a couple of years older than us who believed they should be flying fighters somewhere instead of coddling students. Every time they looked at us they were reminded that – assuming we made it through the program – we would probably get to a real cockpit before they did. That fed their resentment and encouraged them to yell ever louder. We had to leap to our feet when they approached, say "Sir" five times in every sentence, and jump at their every order, but still they hated us.

Lastly there was the plane. It was the Marchetti SF-260, a test aircraft the Air Force was thinking of buying as a new trainer. "Test" meant that no one we knew had flown it yet, which meant there was no inside gouge to help us through the program. It was faster than the Cessna that most pilots trained in and unlike the Cessna it was fully aerobatic. We wore parachutes in case we screwed up so badly that we had to bail out.

In sum, we students were nervous, the instructors were bitter, and the planes were unlike anything we had ever seen. After three weeks only eight of us were left.

Beyond the stress, though, two things about Hondo stuck in my mind long afterward. The first was the taste of lemon drops. South Texas is hot and the Marchetti's cockpit was small so the first guys to go up and twirl around the sky ended up puking their guts out. Yakking was embarrassing but if you kept doing it you could wash out of the program – as two guys found out. So airsickness was a big deal. We all worried about it and wondered how to avoid falling victim. When one of the IPs casually mentioned that lemon drops would keep our stomachs under control we all ran out and bought bags of the stuff. I sucked on more hard candy that month than I ever have before or since. Who knows if it worked? I passed the course, that's all that mattered.

The other thing I remember was the conflict between Captain Simpson and Hollywood. Simpson was my instructor. He was a dead-ringer for Alan Arkin but unless the actor was wound tighter than a catapult spring the resemblance stopped there. Simpson was a captain who hated the Marchetti, hated being at Hondo, and hated being an instructor. Like Erich Fetterman down in Panama, he was a screamer. From the start of every sortie he was angry about something: he beat on the dash, yelled at the tower, or smacked me on the head when I did something wrong. "Trim, trim, *trim!*" he would scream as we entered the pattern. If I strayed off altitude his hand flew across the cockpit, making me see stars. If I didn't stray but he thought I might, the hand rose and hovered in anticipation of violence.

Hollywood was a guy from California who showed up at the course with all the wrong priorities. "Hey, dudes, any of you ever surf Texas?" he asked on our second day in the barracks. He asked

the question while standing in the doorway holding a surf board and then announced his intention to head to Corpus Christi for the weekend
in pursuit of waves. The rest of us were buried in
books trying to memorize aircraft systems: Hollywood was in search of a curl.

When Simpson and Hollywood met it was like
The Great Santini encountering a yoga class. Simpson screamed and screamed; Hollywood shrugged
and smiled. Simpson yelled until he was hoarse;
Hollywood gazed back through half-lidded eyes.
Simpson despised Hollywood because he didn't
try. Hollywood tried even less because he didn't
like being ordered around. He enjoyed making
Simpson mad. That only escalated matters and
doomed his flying career before it started.

Hollywood might have lasted had he been a natural flyer but he wasn't, which meant that Simpson
quickly accumulated enough in-flight evidence of
ineptitude to back up his natural loathing of our
beach-loving colleague. Not that evidence was
needed. Hollywood's attitude was his own rope.
The situation erupted for good when during a
post-flight debrief Hollywood tired of Captain
Simpson's criticism and said, "Hold on, dude. You
can't say that. You don't know what I can and can't
do. You don't *know* me."

Simpson leaped to his feet.

"*Dude?!* Did you call me *dude?*!"

Hollywood was gone within hours.

I've thought of him and Simpson ma
in the years since Hondo. Each in his own way
represented a broader category of people that I
encountered in one assignment or another, at one
base or another, during my career. They were both
in a situation where they didn't belong, doing
something they didn't really want to do, and they
were stuck. Maybe they got there because someone expected it of them, or because they thought
it was a path to better things, or because they had
simply ended up there and now didn't know how
to get out. There are plenty of people like that in
the Air Force including some in flight suits. They
became pilots because it was a way to advance in
rank or to attract women or to make money later
in the airlines. They might have been successful
and productive in another profession but they
weren't in another profession. They were here,
they were now – in Simpson's case, instructing; in
Hollywood's case, trying to fly – and pride or greed
or a misplaced vision kept driving them forward.

Little things brought them to mind. Years after
Hondo I was in Ecuador and happened to join a
crowd at a Guayaquil park to watch city officials feed
cabbage to a troop of green iguanas. The iguanas
lived in the park and were highly territorial but tol-
erated the staring of humans so long as we stayed
off the grass and gave them their space. That we

did. But the lizards weren't the only animals on display. Some folks were there to coo over a simple cottontail rabbit who was the iguanas' companion. The bunny, orphaned and isolated in the park, joined the troop out of loneliness and now despite the illogic and the danger considered itself one of them. It followed the iguanas around, munched leaves, and basked in the sun. It answered the officials' dinner bell. It huddled with the reptiles at night. It bobbed its head as they did and even tried to climb trees. The rabbit worked way too hard for its food, exposed itself unnecessarily to predators, and its brown pelt was wholly out of place among the leathery jade hides of its companions. But it never left. When someone wondered aloud why, a street vendor near me chuckled.

"On the outside he is fur," the man explained. "But on the inside his heart is green."

So one day, thinking about Simpson and Hollywood and that lost little bunny, I realized that what they taught me could be boiled down to a simple truth. To wit: there are two kinds of pilots: Pilots, and pilots.

A Pilot with a capital 'P' is someone who flies for the love of flying, for the thrill of being airborne and the adventure of seeing new places, for the excitement of being away from the ground and all its encumbrances, and for the joy of being in control of life, nature, and the machine that's strapped to your butt. A Pilot feels his ultimate responsibility is to fulfill the dreams of earthbound ancestors who could only stare skyward and wish.

The other kind of pilot is the one spelled with a small 'p.' That kind flies for all the other reasons.

At the beginning of my stay in Panama the 155th Tactical Airlift Squadron could have been described as a bunch of pilots, those with the small 'p.' Early in the squadron's formation we all became bogged down in the routines necessary to build up a bureaucracy. We flew – but less and less. The schedules, manifests, meetings, ground training, paperwork – all had to exist or we would never get anything done. But that bureaucracy, that organization, and those daily routines became our existence.

In no time at all we built a cubicle city on the second floor of the hangar. Each of us took a desk and hunkered down into an "additional duty" like Awards & Decorations, or Supply, or Evaluations, that like everywhere in the Air Force soon defined our existence more than did our time in the cockpit. More and more we found ourselves sitting under fluorescent lights and staring at computer screens while receding from the reason we joined the Air Force in the first place: to get airborne, to experience spontaneity, freedom, and the sense of getting something done.

That's how our squadron in Panama started and how it could have continued. Absent a conscious re-direction, we were destined to lose sight of what mattered to us most. Every day that we spent at a desk was one not spent in the cockpit. We needed an opportunity to remind ourselves of who we were. We needed a call to put the capital P back where it belonged.

And we got one.

Of course it was Walt who directed the change. I say 'of course' but his selection as our leader in the quest was never fore-ordained. It came about simply because he was our most out-of-the-box thinker. Though he didn't call his superiors "dude," Walt was a pioneer in disregarding rules and exploring the horizons of aviation insurrection. Also, his wife was a heartfelt proponent of holistic medicine, New Age philosophy, and organic food. "Never give your heart and soul to something that has neither," she lectured me when I wondered aloud about making the Air Force a career. Together they formed the squadron epicenter for pushing the envelope on what was allowed, real, and normal. His outlook on life emphasized exploring the unknown; hers insisted that once he got to the unknown he must respect what he found.

Somehow their philosophies merged and caused him to dream one night of an old, old pilot. "Old" in the sense of long ago, a genuine World War I type with leather helmet and flowing scarf. The pilot took Walt flying high over the southern continent, high enough that he could see all the countries and mountains and jungles and rivers and oceans and forests and beaches and streams from the Mexican border right down to the Straits of Magellan. Together they circled and banked and soared to see how vast the world was and how green, and how much lay between the coasts of the lush, teardrop-shaped land beneath them.

Then someone reached up from below. Lots of someones. People, animals, plants – all stretched out their hands or limbs and offered Walt gifts. Except they weren't gifts. They were treasures, pieces of their respective cultures. They were objects significant and not, bits of an emerald world for him to accept and collect into a giant mosaic to preserve a moment in time. Walt didn't know the people, he didn't recognize the plants, he'd only heard of some of the animals; yet all reached forward to offer a memory and ensure they weren't forgotten.

The old pilot beckoned to indicate Walt had no choice. So he accepted the memories one by one. Then he awoke in a sweat and wrote it all down.

When he finished writing he had a list of 26 items he knew he had to find.

"I don't know," he shrugged when we asked him where he would look. "I don't know. Everything was green. Everything! It's one gigantic green continent, you know? That jungle is huge. And the mountains... Even the rocks seemed green. These little hands came up from everywhere and held things out. From villages, from forests, from the coasts. The people were so serious. I couldn't turn them down. I didn't have the heart. I couldn't tell them I know nothing about them or their culture. I just floated there and grabbed whatever they had."

"Maybe that's the point," I suggested. "Maybe it was all a guilt trip. You've been down here for months and haven't taken any interest in the locals."

"I do my job."

"Yeah, but that's all. You're supposed to be our out-of-the-box thinker. You're not doing that."

"Of course I am. So I occasionally toe the line – to think out of the box you have to know where the box is in the first place, you know."

"But you just said..."

"Who are these people to give me stuff? Why me?"

"That's what I'm saying. Maybe this dream was telling you to learn about them."

"Learn about who?"

"Whoever was giving you the stuff."

"But I don't know *who* was giving me the stuff! I don't know which hands held what. Most of the time I couldn't tell where they came from. I mean, general areas, yeah – countries, coasts, rivers. They were just there. The next thing I knew I had a list."

"You weren't sick?" Lowell demanded. "Or on drugs?"

"I don't do drugs."

"Your wife does weird stuff."

"Oh, please. She's a vegetarian."

"That's what I mean. How about something she fed you? That chai tea, maybe, or some of that stuff I saw growing in your refrigerator."

"That's grass."

"Ah-ha!"

"Not that kind of grass. Prairie grass. It's got an enzyme she says keeps the skin young. We eat it in salads."

"If you're beginning to graze maybe that'll cause bad dreams," I suggested.

Walt was unfazed.

"Look, I'm not a complex guy. I fly planes. Pull back on the stick, the houses get smaller. Push forward, they get bigger. All I know is that I had this dream, I woke up and wrote stuff down, and now I've got a list of things I don't know what I'm supposed to do with."

"What are you talking about?" Lowell sniffed. "It's obvious what you have to do."

"What?"

"What do you mean, what? Are you new? Go get them. Go pick up this stuff."

Walt perused his list with a dubious eye. "Where?"

Lowell laughed. "That's your problem. Just do it. If you don't, it'll eat away at your tiny, selfish, flight-hogging, trip-stealing heart. In fact, it'll eat away at mine now if you don't do something."

"He's right," I agreed. "You've got me curious. You should go collect this stuff."

Walt still looked doubtful. I read the piece of paper over his shoulder.

"A coconut, a cayuca...the branch of a carob tree?"

He shrugged.

"A rainstick, a Korubo warclub – oh, good luck on that! – a coat of arms... A coat of arms? This is South America, Walt, not merry old England."

"Yeah, that one confuses me," he admitted as though the other items made sense. "It's supposed to be here in Panama, too."

"A wareken...a ware...I can't pronounce this one."

"It's a bottle of some kind."

"Uh-huh. And what's this? Pilot wings? You have those."

"Yeah, but they're supposed to come from Costa Rica." He pointed to a notation on the list.

"You need a Costa Rican pilot's wings?"

He rubbed his temple. "I don't know."

"One monarch butterfly..." I kept reading, "...a flute, a basket of tagua nuts, a sisal – what's a sisal?"

"I don't know that, either."

"What do you mean, you don't know?"

"I mean, I don't know! I just wrote this stuff down!"

"Oh, come on," said Lowell. "Who are you, Joseph Smith? Is there an original version of this written on golden plates?"

"A pullover made from vicuña wool – dude, that'll be expensive if it's even legal. Didn't we have a Secretary of State once lose his job over one of those?"

"It gets better. The woman who held that up was reciting poetry."

"What's the significance of that?"

"You tell me."

Lowell started to say something and stopped himself. He looked at me instead and twirled a finger by his head.

"Two Brazilian lottery tickets," I continued. "That's not bad but we don't get to Brazil much; a petroglyph; a pizote; a skull. A skull, Walt?"

He threw up his hands. "I don't know!"

"Uh-huh. Well, now that we've decided you're going to get all this stuff, how are you going to do it?" I demanded. "I mean, some of them are way out there... Sheesh, a petroglyph... Is there a deadline? Are you just going to quit your job and walk the earth like Cain?"

Walt's leprechaun face pressed itself into a pout, innocence mixed with the tragedy of one forced to carry mankind's burden. He shook his head.

But of course the mood soon lifted. It didn't take long for someone in our band to remember that we were in the military and that in the military the best way to reduce a burden is to delegate it to others.

So Walt held a party to distribute the load. At first we signed up for individual items. Then we realized that some things on the list would be easier to find than others – a box of dirt from the *colpa de Guacamayos* in Peru, for example, was going to be tough but still a lot more accessible than a shrunken head. And T.J. and Steve already had an idea how to get a case of Chilean Kunstmann lager but nobody knew what to make of 'Vilcabamba's gold.' So Walt made copies of the list for everyone to carry. It was a mission, he assured us, just like any other, and he insisted that we prosecute it with appropriate seriousness and respect.

But seriousness and respect weren't our strong suits. We were Pilots, after all, and I wondered if we were up to the task. But whether we were or not we agreed not to let him take on the quest alone. If it would gnaw at his heart, we promised, it would gnaw at ours.

From then on we were all engaged in a transcontinental treasure hunt.

2. Colombia

GUYS JUMPED ON THE list at first. It became a contest to see who would be the first to find one of Walt's dream items. Mannie, our fanatically clean Academy grad, won that competition when he found an old cayuca floating in Lago Gatún and brought it in to the squadron. One down, only twenty-five to go. But that only encouraged us more. Even the mechanics over in Hangar 2 got involved when they heard about the treasure hunt, serious guys like Harry and Vince who normally occupied themselves with side-job business pursuits but who could always be counted on for an adventure.

It wasn't all fun and games, though. Work intervened as taskings came down from the Wing to support the DEA in Colombia and Peru. I got a few of those flights and because of some of the destinations I always took a mechanic with me.

Vince was aboard for example when we landed at Cartagena. We were glad he was, since on short final we sucked a pigeon down the #1 engine and knocked it out. It was poor timing. We were there to pick up people who really wanted to leave the country.

Somehow most of the pigeon got through the propeller and went down the intake when we were about thirty feet off the ground on our approach. The engine stalled. Mick was on the controls at the time. He cursed but we knew he stayed calm because his raspy Boston accent didn't get any thicker. He simply jammed in rudder and called, "Don't touch anything – we*ah* landing."

On the runway we shut down the left engine and taxied to an out of the way hangar at the west end of the field. There six gringos waited in the shade of an awning. Two wore jackets and ties, the others were dressed down. There were also two Colombians looking very Miami Vice-ish in pale suits and mirror-sunglasses, a Colombian policeman, and two local soldiers hanging out behind the crowd with automatic rifles cradled in their arms. The subject of all their attention stood squeezed in the middle. Colombian, medium-height, unshaven, undistinguished. His clothes were dirty and he looked like he hadn't slept in a while. He barely looked up as we taxied in. So close did the others stand around him it was hard to make out the handcuffs on his wrists.

Bird, our loadmaster, was responsible for everything in the back of the plane. He jumped from his seat and lowered the ramp to the outside. Vince was on the move as soon as I set the brakes. He dropped the crew entrance door and jumped out with a step ladder to take a look at the engine. There was no evidence of a fire but a foreboding rattle as the engine spun down suggested the bird knocked some compressor blades loose. If that happened the engine was done. Without an intact compressor, airflow to the combustion chamber is irregular and it's impossible to control the heat generated there. Worse, there's no telling where the missing blades have gone. Into the engine, most likely, where they would cause worse damage. It was amazing that a pigeon could bring down a million-dollar motor but it could and did.

"Toast," Vince said to me quietly as he came down the ladder. The #2 engine was still running. Mick still sat in the co-pilot's seat.

"Beautiful."

I expected nothing less. Our casual out-and-back sortie was in reality a rendition that many people back home were following. It was supposed to be a milk run but a stupid accident now threatened to bring the flight to a grinding halt.

Four of the agents, with their prisoner, hurried onto the plane. One of them poked his head back out the door, wondering at our delay. Vince turned so his back was to the man.

"What's their backup plan?" he whispered.

I thought about that. Even if they had a backup means of getting the prisoner out of Colombia, we were their first option. They would press us to do something. Our passengers never cared why we couldn't do the mission. All they knew was that we couldn't. Lt Col Rasmussen tried to counter that pressure by issuing a standing order never to do anything we felt unsafe about regardless of the rank of the passenger in back. But other factors were at work. Our egos, for example. When I got in a plane I wanted to do the mission whatever it was. So did Vince and so did Mick and so did every guy in the squadron.

"We can go," I said carefully. I wouldn't have suggested such a thing to just any crew chief but Vince didn't like giving up any more than I did. He would do anything to get a plane airborne.

Right now, for example, he raised an eyebrow listening to my idea. In the heat sweat trickled down his olive skin.

"Yeah, we can," he agreed. "I'll button 'er up."

I gave a thumbs-up to the agent in the door and waved him down the stairs. When I explained the situation he started to protest but backed off as I told him our plan. He looked at his watch, looked toward the gate they had come through, and nodded. He clearly thought we were trying to come up with an excuse *not* to leave. When I told him it was only an hour flight back to Panama, that was all he wanted to hear.

"So what ahh we doin'?" Mick asked when I jumped back into the seat.

"We're taking off," I said.

"Of course we are," he replied.

"You opposed?"

"Naww. I figured that's what you two were talkin' about."

"Any problem with it? Speak up if you think it's stupid."

"Of course, it's stupid!" he squawked, voice rasping like a Nantucket whaling captain who had discovered I was a member of Greenpeace. "It's absolutely stupid! But that doesn't mean I won't do it..."

Bird closed the ramp and jumped up to the seat. Vince filled him in. He looked the least enthusiastic of any of us but didn't say anything. Which was good because I'd been with him on other occasions where he *was* nervous enough to speak up and vote against a plan. If he was going along this time maybe my idea wasn't so bad.

What confidence I felt came from knowing where we were. We were on the coast, at sea level, in the middle of the day with cloudless skies and no mountains for fifty miles. We were light – even with passengers only at forty-six thousand pounds – we had a long runway, and we would be flying in clear weather which meant we could go as low or as high as we wanted. There would be no call to cross mountains, climb through storms, or race at top speed. And we were flying a C-27, whose engines – FOD notwithstanding – almost never failed. If ever there were prime conditions for single-engine flight, these were them.

So long as we didn't smack another pigeon.

"*Ground control, Shark 12 is ready to taxi.*"

"*Shark 12, taxi to holding point, Runway 07.*"

"*Shark 12, taxiing to Runway 07.*"

"Anything different?" Mick asked as we rolled down the parallel to the beginning of 07.

"Yes," I said. "You have only one engine and the plane is designed to fly with two."

"Aww, thanks. You got any *uthuh* great information for me?"

Ground handed us off to Tower, who told us to hold short of the runway for landing traffic. An Avianca 727 floated past us and pranged onto the thousand-foot markers. I began to feel obvious with only one propeller turning, the flushed warmth that comes when everyone in a room is looking at you. Did the 727 pilot notice?

We ran through our before-takeoff checklists.

"*Shark 12, you are cleared for take-off.*"

"*Shark 12, cleared for take-off.*" A huge relief.

Mick taxied us onto the runway and stopped to run up the #2 engine. He got the power lever halfway up before Tower called us back.

"*Shark 12! Are you having trouble?*"

We froze. Mick stopped moving the throttle. After a moment's hesitation, I pointed for him to continue and keyed the mike.

"Tower, uh, that's a negative. No trouble."

"Shark 12. One of your engines is not running. I can see the propeller not moving. Do you have a problem?"

Mick hesitated again on the throttle. I wondered how to tap dance this one and realized I should have thought of an excuse before. No airport in the world could legally allow a multi-engine air-craft to take off with one engine out.

"Uhhh, any suggestions?" I asked the others. "Vince?"

"No, sorry," Vince replied over my shoulder. "I didn't think he'd be able to see us from the tower. He must have binoculars."

I waited a few more seconds, the plane vibrating under the load from #2. Then, after another prompting from Tower, decided to go with the truth.

"Uh, sir, we've had to shut down one of our engines momentarily but it's not serious. We've decided we can continue."

There was a pause. For a moment I thought we might have pulled it off.

Then, *"Negative! Shark 12, your take-off clearance is cancelled. You cannot take-off without an engine. Taxi clear of the runway and return to parking."*

I ground my teeth. Which was worse, being denied clearance to take off or the shocked tone of the controller that implied I must be an idiot?

"Want to try the old 'I don't understand' trick?" Bird suggested.

I shrugged. Nothing else came to mind.

"Uh, roger, Tower," I tried as calmly as I could. *"Understand cleared for take-off."*

"Negative!!!" We cringed. *"Shark 12, negative!! You are not cleared for take-off! Taxi off the runway immediately!"*

In the distance, from the base of the tower which was located almost all the way on the other side of the field, two trucks drove onto the runway and stopped at intervals along its length, blocking our roll. Our bluff had been called. We had no choice but to taxi clear.

Back at the hangar a pick-up from airfield operations waited for us. I took some relief from that. The men inside weren't police or soldiers. They were just sent over by the tower to make sure we weren't up to anything suspicious. The agent I'd spoken to before jumped up to the cockpit and leaned over Bird's shoulder to look at the truck. His companions from earlier were gone from the hangar.

"You're screwing us," he said to all of us. "Every minute we delay here you are *screwing* us."

He kept looking at the gate adjacent to the hangar. I wondered what, or who, he was afraid might come through there.

I kept quiet. He was right.

"Engine shutdown," I called. "Vince?"

"Yeah?"

"I've got an idea. Tell me if it's dumb."

Vince met me outside under the dead prop. His eyes widened when I told him my idea.

"That's dumb."

"I thought so."

"But," he held up a finger, thinking, "it might work. Give me thirty minutes."

It took him fifty. Almost an hour during which the agents stayed out of sight in the gloom of the cabin, stirring only as they watched Vince run up and down the stairs grabbing tools from the hell-hole or hauling in pieces of the aircraft from outside. The one who yelled at me squeezed up next to Bird's seat and kept an eye out the front window. He made no secret of the fact that he was carrying two sidearms, one in a shoulder holster and the other stuck in his waistband. He didn't yell any more, preferring instead to let his angry silence speak for him. Even that dissolved a bit as it became obvious we were trying hard to do something. He didn't know what but we were hustling.

I struck a nonchalant attitude with the airfield representatives. For a while they watched Vince open up cowlings and turn wrenches. Then, convinced we were really going to fix our engine, they got bored and drove away.

Within an hour everyone was on board again and we were ready to make another try.

"Tower, Shark 12 is ready to taxi to runway 07."

"Shark 12, standby."

Mick and I exchanged anxious glances.

"Look good for the binoculars," I advised.

"Shark 12, you have both engines working? You have fixed your engine?"

"Yes, sir, that's affirmative, Tower," I lied. *"We apologize for the problem earlier. It was a minor engine malfunction and we did not want to delay. However, our problem is fixed now."*

Tower wouldn't have thought so if he could see how I was sweating. If we were caught in this lie, we would all surely be arrested. I wondered how long I would last in a Colombian prison.

"Shark 12, you cannot take off with a failed engine. That is true at any airport. Please remember that in the future when you come to Cartagena." Lecture concluded, a long pause. *"You are cleared to taxi, Shark 12, to runway 07. Hold and call when ready for take-off."*

Mick's sigh of relief was audible above the rumble of #2 engine.

"Okay," I pointed. "Taxi."

We rolled down the taxiway to Runway 07. All the time we were getting farther away from the tower but I could feel probing eyes on my back. Any second I expected to hear an accusing cry from the Tower that signaled the gig was up. Everyone else felt the same. Mick, for once, was quiet. Bird sat in the third seat sitting forward, hunched over and watching the inertial system record our ground speed. Vince stood on the steps behind Bird's seat, headset on. The agent stood next to him. He didn't have a headset but he watched all of us for any sign of alarm.

We rolled up to the hold-short line on the hammerhead, just outside the start of the runway.

"Heeeere's the tough part," I breathed into the mike.

"*Tower, Shark 12 is holding at 07, ready for take-off.*"

Another long pause. This one went on forever and I knew the binoculars were sweeping back and forth across our plane. I tried to breathe long, slow breaths as the sweat poured down my forehead.

"*Shark 12, you are cleared for take-off. Fly runway heading until 1000 feet, then left turn, climb on course.*"

"Go!" I said to Mick. "Go before they change their minds! We ignore any more calls! *Shark 12, cleared for take-off,*" I hurried to radio back.

Mick ran up the good engine and released the brakes. The C-27 accelerated slowly, pushing us to the left hard enough that I used the steering grip to keep us on centerline until 60 knots when Mick took over the controls. We rolled twice our normal distance before rotation but then lifted off cleanly, a lot of right rudder keeping the nose straight.

As we flew by the tower I half-expected to hear another call, something threatening, something to violate us, something to signal our trick had only half-worked. But nothing came. I looked over my right shoulder at the #2 engine. The seven-foot propeller blades there were spinning at their highest speed and virtually invisible. All you could make out clearly was the bullet-shaped black spinner in the middle, pointing forward into the slipstream.

I looked to our left. On the #1 engine the spinner looked just as normal, unencumbered though it was by any blades at all. The tower controller may have noticed a slight difference between the two wings from his vantage point but if so, he was still puzzling over it.

I looked back to offer a smile of gratitude to Vince, who stood just in front of where the blades were strapped down on the cabin floor. At four hundred feet he leaned up to offer me a high-five.

The drug agent, much relieved to be in the air, kept quiet. But he did shake Vince's hand.

3. Venezuela

IT WAS MONTHS BEFORE I finally found anything on Walt's list, and when I did it was by accident. Lt Col Rasmussen caught me in the hangar one day and asked, "Mike, how's your Spanish?"

Oh, boy. Not again. He had asked me that question the year before and back then I ended up spending two months living on the north coast building refugee camps for Cuban migrants.

"No, this time it's a good deal," he insisted, seeing my concern. "I need you to go to Venezuela. There's flying involved. Call it an exchange."

"A trip?" I asked, thinking that I had an overnight bag in my car.

"Not a short one. You'll be there a while."

"Yes, sir. Do I have time to run home for clothes?"

"Oh, sure. You don't leave until Monday."

"Alright, sir. I'll be ready."

He paused and then asked, "Don't you want to know why you're going?"

"Sir, you said there's flying involved?"

"Yes."

"Then no."

But I should have asked.

I should have asked because there are rules to flying. Rules that a good pilot doesn't deviate from. Two of them are never fly with anyone who won't drink with you, and never get in a cockpit with anyone braver than you. They aren't the eleventh and twelfth commandments, not as hard and fast, say, as making sure your number of landings equals the number of takeoffs, or lighting the afterburners only after you leave the chocks, but still they're good guidelines to live by.

The rule about drinking helped explain the unpopularity of guys in our squadron like Griswold Beckett who in addition to being a lousy pilot was also a teetotaler. But the rule about bravery was more complex: sometimes what looked like courage was just sheer stupidity.

I remember sitting in the cockpit on the Bogotá airport one night with Karl Masters, a long-time T-38 instructor who had finally given up waiting for a fighter assignment and instead accepted an offer to join us in the C-27. Lightning danced on the field around us and rain drove across the ramp in gales as one of the bigger thunderstorms I'd seen in South America played out its fury. For some reason a few of the commercial airliners still took off into the weather instead of waiting for it to clear. One by one they lined up on the runway a half-mile away, obscured by the rain with only their anti-collision beacons marking their position, then roared toward us and disappeared into the storm a hundred feet after getting airborne. Granted, they were local carriers, airlines like Fawcett and Taca and Andean Air, the kind you read about on Page 9 of the New York Times after they've smacked a hillside and killed 200 people. But it was still amazing to us that someone with a pilot's license would look at the brew Mother Nature had cooked up and think it was a good idea to go jump into it.

None of us thought much of the local pilots. By "local" we meant any pilot hailing from any country in our theater, be they military or commercial. We couldn't – they crashed too often. A dozen factors explained why: age of the equipment, maintenance practices, training, experience, culture, scheduling routines, etc. But we in the 155th didn't care why they crashed. We just knew they did and that often it was for really stupid reasons.

There was the 757 out of Lima that went down in the Pacific after the pilots failed to notice that a mechanic had taped over the plane's static air pressure ports while the aircraft was being painted. That caused every instrument from the altimeter to the airspeed gauge to give wildly inaccurate readings after takeoff. The pilots fought the controls, argued over what was wrong, and finally stalled and crashed.

There was the Uruguayan C-130 that ran out of gas – again over the ocean – because the engineer did his math wrong but was afraid to tell the pilot (who then shot the engineer after they ditched in the waves).

There was the DC-3 pilot over Cochabamba who couldn't fly instruments and tried to scud-run his way to the field, which worked until he met a hill three miles outside the city.

And my favorite was the Paraguayan Metroliner that collided with a Brazilian Casa outside of Asunción because *both* aircraft were at the wrong altitude and *both could see each other*, but neither one would give way to the other.

So we didn't think much of the local crews. It comforted me that the only time I needed to trust them at all was when I hopped a cheap flight on vacation.

The Venezuelan base that Lt Col Rasmussen sent me to was *El Libertador*, near the town of Maracay. It sat a hundred miles south of Caracas and the coast, separated from them by a mountain range and a whole lot of jungle. Caracas was the capital, Maracay was the sticks.

Charlie Manson came with me on the plane but he didn't stay. We flew down in the back of a Reserve C-130.

"I just want to say hi," he explained after we landed.

The C-130 crew took one look around the decrepit El Libertador airfield and decided it wasn't the kind of place they wanted to get stuck for the night so they left their engines running. Manson and I lugged my bag over to the grass and then walked in search of Group 6, *Grupo Seis.*

"To whom?"

He shrugged.

"To whoever's here. I called to set this thing up with their Group 6. It's a unit that flies planes like ours. There's a Lt Col Amodio in charge but I dealt with some major. Simi...Simano-something."

I looked around the airfield. The sky was overcast and made the already-quiet installation seem deserted. There wasn't a soul in sight, doors hung open on the hangers, and nobody had swept the taxiways in years. The place was a mess.

"If you set this up," I asked slowly, "why aren't you the one doing the exchange? You speak Spanish better than me."

"I also outrank you," he explained. "And I'm not stupid enough to do an exchange in a dump like this. I'll come down for a day, but two months? No."

We looked for a while and then he gave up and left. As I watched the C-130 take off I wondered if it would come back in three weeks as promised.

El Libertador was an all-purpose air base for the Venezuelans. There were F-16s, Mirage 50s, C-130s,

G-222s, DC-3s, a couple of Casas, an AS-332 helicop-
ter, some old O-1 Birddogs, and a scattering of civil
aircraft lying around the ramp. The ramp's con-
crete surface was broken and patchy, with enough
grass growing through it to feed a herd of cattle. I
knew that because there were cows grazing there.

The Venezuelan Air Force was in average shape
for a South American country, which meant it was
in lousy shape. There wasn't a lot of money available to keep the Air Force flying. What money the
government had it spent mostly on fighters. Venezuela had bought brand new F-16s from the U.S.
in the mid-1980s. I could see them parked a quarter-mile away on another ramp, gleaming like very
expensive toys. They were status symbols, like a
family buying a Porsche instead of a minivan. And
like all status symbols they must have sucked up a
lot of the Air Force's budget because everywhere
else on the field looked like the back lot of Dave's
Used Aircraft Emporium.

There are few things more depressing to a pilot
than an airplane that can't fly. A bathroom without
a mirror, maybe, or a bar with no women. But while
I waited for someone to show up I stood in the
doorway of the nearest hangar and grew depressed
gazing out on a landscape of battered, marooned
flying machines. I counted five motor-less fuselages
within range of a thrown crescent wrench. Three
were Shorts 360s, one was a C-47, and the fifth was

an F-5 that looked as though it had been mauled by a shark. Aircraft parts lay everywhere. The wing of a 707 lay just yards away. A pair of landing gear sat in the grass. The nose of something had been removed from its owner and leaned against a tree like an enormous clamshell. The noseless aircraft was nowhere to be seen.

I wondered what the carnage meant for me.

Charlie had said that Venezuela flew the same planes as we did. That was sort of true. Group 6 flew the G-222, which was a basic Italian airframe that U.S. mechanics had modified and turned into the C-27. The C-27 had stronger engines, beefed-up landing gear, and a completely overhauled bank of electronic equipment. But the two aircraft were close enough to make a comparison. They handled the same and parked together on a ramp would be obvious close relations.

So I was here to fly with Group 6. Why? On the flight down Manson called it 'Diplomacy of the Lowest Common Denominator.' Washington wanted to stay close to Venezuela and everyone in SOUTHCOM had to do their part. Our squadron's part was to sponsor a pilot exchange.

"Buen' día, capitán."

The voice came from behind me. I wasn't a captain but turned around anyway.

A tall major with a Tom Selleck-moustache and gold-rimmed RayBan knockoffs stood in the doorway to the squadron. Next to him was a short, round lieutenant colonel. The major wore a strained smile. His boss looked away. I hurried over.

"*Discúlpeme, major,*" I apologized, and saluted. "*Teniente Bleriot, a su servicio.*"

Major Semanoa's voice was rich, deep, and easy to understand. He had the tolerant face of someone used to disappointment and it was easy to see that he and the colonel both were disappointed at seeing me. First, I had arrived without sufficient notice that they could be there to meet me. Second, I wasn't higher ranking. For a moment I felt embarrassed. Then I realized what I had been doing when they interrupted me: looking at a decrepit airfield littered with tangible evidence of a failed state. To heck with them, I thought. I'm an American and my planes work

"*Dónde está Capitán Manson?*" Semanoa asked.

Running like a scared puppy, I wanted to answer. Instead I said, "He has already left."

Semanoa introduced his boss, Lt Col Amodio. Amodio offered a limp handshake with the enthusiasm of royalty meeting peasants. His sour look persisted through our small talk but it became clear he wasn't mad at me. He just didn't have much to be happy about. His flight suit had patches, his boots were worn to the thickness of slippers, his leadership was on the verge of a coup, and most of his aircraft didn't work. Now having a junior American officer to entertain was icing on his cake. Amodio was all-business in a world full of politics, corruption, and frustration. Lack of money, lack of parts, lack of training, and lack of time were the currency he traded in every day. He spent more time looking around the ramp in despair than I did.

If there was anyone else on the base worth meeting I didn't meet them. Instead the two men gave me a tour. Amodio insisted on it. We left my bag at their squadron and started walking.

"Why are you here?" Amodio asked me.

"Because my commander told me to come," I said.

He grimaced. "I appreciate your honesty. Your Spanish is good."

I noticed he didn't say 'very good' which meant he was honest, too.

"Where did you learn?"

"From television," I replied.

"Television?"

"When I found out how beautiful Latin women are I wanted to learn how to speak to them. So I started watching *telenovelas*." The story wasn't completely true but it was easy flattery. It broke the ice better than saying I took four years in high school because the alternative was Greek.

Semanoa chuckled and then tested me by asking which Latin soap operas I watched. I rattled off my favorites: the Mexican *Maria La del Barrio* and *Luz y Sombra*, then threw in the Venezuelan *Café con aroma de mujer* for good measure. Semanoa nodded and laughed again.

Amodio didn't laugh. His heavy-lidded eyes took me in as though his days just got better and better.

"Well," he grumbled, "If you can't fly, you can always come home and talk soap operas with my wife."

The next day I met everyone in their squadron. The day after that I studied with their copilots. On the third day we tried to fly but couldn't. None of their planes worked. Group 6 had eight G-222s but four were hard-broke, meaning they weren't going to be fixed anytime soon; one was a hangar queen, meaning it was used for spare parts; one was in phase, meaning it was undergoing an overhaul; and the remaining two worked intermittently but had more issues than National Geographic. The government was pressuring them to fly more to support a push against illegal mining so the maintenance troops were working hard: still, the outlook on most of the birds was mixed.

Major Semanoa had been confident they would have at least one plane in good enough condition to fly a few laps around the flagpole. When the maintenance chief, a senior enlisted man, reported to him that the airplane wasn't ready Semanoa's moustache quivered with fury. He did an admirable job of suppressing his anger so long as I was in the room but once I'd left he let loose on the mechanic like a dam giving way, the shouting audible down the hall. Regardless of country, the flying world is all the same: frustrated pilots vent at helpless mechanics as though the wrench-turners are deliberately trying to keep us on the ground.

The next day the story was the same. Amodio got involved this time but both of them yelling at the mechanics didn't make the planes work any better. Embarrassed, the colonel muttered something about a parts shipment being late.

Near the end of the week the maintainers reported we would definitely be able to fly. We scheduled a nine o'clock take-off, then slipped it to ten when the plane wasn't ready. Another slip followed, to eleven o'clock, and finally the chief mechanic came over to the ops building and said we might as well go to lunch. However, he promised, the plane would *definitely* be ready to fly by two that afternoon.

No one ever told me exactly what was broken on the plane. I didn't pry but still watched with apprehension as mechanic after mechanic rolled his tool cart out to the apron. There were so many doctors involved in the operation it looked doubtful the patient would ever recover. But the supervisor's mood was optimistic so the Venezuelans maintained their spirits. We went to lunch confident we would be airborne by mid-afternoon.

"Teniente, a tu primer vuelo con Grupo Seis!" Major Semanoa toasted me at lunch. He held his glass out over the table and the others joined him. They were all drinking wine.

"*Gracias,*" I replied, and lifted my own glass of water in thanks.

No one said anything until after the toast, then Semanoa asked pleasantly if I wouldn't like something stronger to drink. I declined.

"Nothing to calm your nerves?" he joked.

I held out my hand, palm down, to show my nerves were steady. "*Como hielo.* Like ice," I promised. "No fear!"

A captain by the name of Uribe choked on his wine.

"Then you haven't flown with the major!" he shouted.

The crowd laughed, the lieutenants not as freely as Uribe, who seemed comfortable enough around his superior that he could make the joke. One, a friendly fellow named Moreno, laughed a little too loud until Uribe slapped him. Another young guy, with mousy hair and an Adolph Menjou moustache, used his laugh to hide stealthy but frantic motions in my direction to indicate that yes, I had better drink some wine. A third lieuten-ant did the same. His nametag said Caraba but I'd already heard that his nickname was Coco.

"No, really," Semanoa offered again, passing me the bottle of wine.

"Thank you, no," I insisted.

"You don't drink?"

"Oh, I drink. Just not now."

"Why not?"

Give it up, already, I thought. I didn't want any wine. But I also didn't want to come out and say it was against U.S. Air Force regulations to drink alcohol before flying. If my commander found out I could lose my wings. Besides, flying inebriated was just plain stupid.

"I'm weak," I joked. "One glass of wine and I fall asleep."

That worked.

"At least you have an excuse!" Uribe laughed. "Moreno just flies like he's asleep!"

The aircraft was ready at two o'clock – mostly. But still there must have been thirty mechanics hovering around it when we returned from lunch. They swarmed like bees when we approached, making frantic last-minute adjustments that made me feel none too confident.

There was also a swarming of crew members. Because flying was so dependent on maintenance and their maintenance was so lacking, Group 6 did what we in the 155th would have done under similar circumstances: when a plane finally came up airworthy, they put as many crew members on board as possible to get the experience while they could. Therefore, the number of people who were going to tag along on my inaugural flight kept growing. On the first day it was supposed to be five. On the second day we grew to seven, then ten. By the time the mechanics were ready we were a group of fifteen, all of whom would be flying on a plane whose crew complement was three.

Semanoa barked orders.

"*Teniente!*" he called.

"Sir?"

"You'll fly later," he apologized. "I must get our co-pilots re-current first. It has been a long time since they have flown."

"Absolutely. Whenever it's convenient for you."

"We are going south to Angel Falls. You know them? They are the highest in the world. It will be a navigation practice for our young pilots."

Semanoa flew in the left seat with a lieutenant named Victoria. They ran up the engines and then shut down when fuel began to leak. The mechanics swarmed again, opening engine cowlings and positioning ladders under the wing so that all of them could try to fix it at once. After a ten-minute delay we started again and taxied to the runway. There the left gear strut collapsed, causing the left wing to dip within four feet of the ground. We turned around and taxied back to the chocks, listing like a torpedoed merchant ship. Maintenance was waiting and hooked up a compressor with the #1 blade still turning. In ten more minutes we were back on our way. This time we made it onto the runway before tower reported smoke coming from our right cowling. Another trip to parking, another swarming of the mechanics. A fitting had slipped and caused oil to leak onto the plating around the combustion chamber. Nothing serious, their chief of maintenance assured us. Thirty minutes this time and then we were on our way.

I sat in the cabin in a web seat. Lt Col Amodio sat across from me. With each delay he popped up and climbed into the cockpit, leaning over Rubin's shoulder to survey the situation for himself. After a discussion he would return to his seat looking frustrated the way only a thwarted pilot can.

Finally we took off and headed south. For an hour we droned. I had to give up my headset when one of the loadmasters had a problem with his so for a long while I had no clue what we were doing or where we were. When I looked out the window all I saw was jungle.

From time to time the younger co-pilots swapped out of the front seat. Victoria came back and sat down looking pleased, happy that he'd gotten to fly. There's your half-hour for the month, I thought in sympathy. It made me realize how lucky I was by comparison. I felt cheated if I didn't fly thirty hours in a month. By all rights I should look as happy as Victoria each time I got out of the cockpit.

"Mike!" someone shouted.

I looked up. It was Lt Col Amodio by the crew door. His intercom had gone out and he shouted above the engines.

"Sir?"

He pointed out the porthole window on the crew door and yelled something I couldn't make out. I looked outside.

We were flying parallel to a river, an inconspicuous waterway hemmed in by trees. It flowed in the direction we were flying, its gray surface mottled with shadows thrown by the afternoon sun. Nothing extraordinary. Amodio kept shouting something but he was losing the battle against the #1 engine only feet away on the other side of the fuselage. Occasionally I heard the word "*muerto*" (dead) but didn't apply it to anything. The only odd thing I saw about the river were twin lines of foam that flanked each shoreline just out of reach of the leaves.

In the end I never got to fly that day. The #2 engine started leaking oil again and we had to turn for home long before Angel Falls. Amodio got up into the co-pilot's seat and stayed there in case they had to shut the engine down. Semanoa apologized to me, clearly embarrassed. I told him not to worry about it. What else could I say? I didn't add that for me it would be a big plus if we just made it back to Maracay without crashing.

In Maracay I stayed in a hotel called the Alhambra. I had half-expected to spend my open-ended exchange living with a family of someone in Grupo Seis but nobody in the squadron ever mentioned that and I didn't know how to bring the issue up. On the first day Semanoa mentioned a hotel. He later dropped me at the Alhambra for no other reason than it was the closest one to the base. I stayed there a week until they offered up a barracks room on the airfield, which I accepted under the theory that it would make me "one of the guys" and earn their respect. The barracks turned out to be the kind of place Papillon spent years trying to escape: moldy walls, intermittent power, showers across the street, and the constant smell of urine. After another week I had to give up my room to incoming Army recruits and moved back to the hotel.

The Alhambra was nice enough. My top-floor room loomed over the south side of the city and gave me a glimpse of the air base five miles away. Most of the city was behind me out of sight. The lights below were spaced widely at night and every evening there were rolling blackouts. When that happened I sat by the window and listened to traffic. There were roaches but not that many and they always disappeared whenever the lights came back on.

"How is your hotel?" Major Semanoa asked one morning when he picked me up at the Alhambra. His automobile was an old diesel Volkswagen that had come up from Brazil. From the looks of it, it hadn't come on a boat.

"Nice," I lied. I started to make a joke about the roaches but stopped.

"Good," he nodded, stroking his moustache and looking like he wanted to say more. He was uncomfortable around me. Mostly it was because after six days in country I hadn't flown yet. Well, that wasn't completely true since I'd flown in the back of the G-222. But I hadn't *flown*. I'd only ridden in back. Semanoa was embarrassed by that.

He was also in an unusual spot because he'd been tapped by Amodio to be my sponsor, my chaperone. As a major he wasn't used to dealing with lieutenants as anything but subordinates. Now here I was his guest.

"Would you like to come to dinner in my home on Sunday?" he asked as we drove to the base. "I mentioned to my wife that we had an American visiting and she insisted you come to dinner. She was especially interested after I told her that you watched our soap operas."

He swerved around a pothole with practiced ease, concentrating on the road more than he needed to and making the invitation in an offhand way as though it was all his wife's idea and he didn't really care if I came to dinner or not.

"Well, sure," I replied. "Thank you. I would be honored to come."

A flatbed pickup carrying milk cans turned in front of us, much too close. Semanoa shouted an insult out the window.

"Hmm. Do not be offended if she makes you eat too much. She is one of those women who believe all men are starving and her job is to feed them." He waved his hand and grimaced as though he had tried to correct her but failed. "And when she learns you're single she'll probably try to marry you off as well."

"Well, more Venezuelan women win beauty pageants than any other country," I said with a smile. "If you have any hot single neighbors I wouldn't mind meeting them."

"Maybe," he agreed. "But remember: no matter how beautiful a woman is somewhere there is a man who is tired of putting up with her crap."

He caught me off-guard with that and I laughed. Semanoa laughed, too. For the first time in a week he relaxed.

"*Es un rio muerto,*" he said a few days later, pointing out the window of the cockpit. "That river is dead."

We were at five hundred feet in a left bank somewhere near the Colombian border. I looked across the cockpit to where he was pointing. A line of water the color of graphite snaked through the jungle parallel to the frontier. It was wide enough for a boat to transit but turned so often and so sharply that it was hard at our low altitude to see more than a quarter-mile of the water at a time. It looked like any other river to me.

"*Qué quiere decir?*" I asked. "What do you mean, *dead*? How can a river be dead?"

"I mean, dead. It is so polluted with mercury and arsenic that nothing can live. Look, you can see where it has started to affect the shoreline."

He pointed again at brown trees flanking a sand-bar. They stood out because nothing was brown in the jungle, at least not at tree-top level. Everything was an infinite green from wherever you stood to the far horizon.

"That much? That many chemicals come from the miners?"

"Of course."

Rubin was the engineer in the third seat. He nodded as Semanoa spoke. Both had the attitude that the truth was self-evident, that the situation was obvious. But I was coming from an Air Force whose enemies were foreign armies and drug smugglers, not environmental polluters. In the United States we had other agencies to deal with ecology problems. Looking for unlicensed gold and silver miners was outside my lane.

"This river comes from those hills up there," the major pointed again, jerking the nose up so that we ballooned. "It's nothing, just a small waterway. But to the south it joins with the Ocaña and that's how the miners get here. We'll follow it to the hills than come back again to the east."

We did that for two days, criss-crossing a vast oval of land between Lake Maracaibo and the border. Our aircraft, #384, kept working and after a few hiccups the maintainers got its sister ship #381 working as well so miracle of miracles two planes from the squadron were flying at once. Lt Col Amodio actually smiled when that happened. Morale around the flight line improved.

Morale had been low because of the maintenance troubles but also because of political battles in the capital. All the papers or the TV could talk about were that the president might step down, that this party or that faction was plotting against him, and that people were out of work and unhappy. The *bolivar* kept dropping. Money was tight and coup rumors increased.

I flew whenever something got in the air though I wasn't always in the seat. I made it clear that I wasn't there to steal anybody's hours and was just as happy to watch a mission from the cabin. When I wasn't flying I sat in the tiny office at the front of the squadron and helped the engineers translate technical manuals they had bought from the Italians. Sometimes I wrote lesson plans for their pilots based on what we did in Panama.

When I did fly, it was fun. The pilots of Grupo Seis learned early that I loved being in the air. That helped them relax. Not completely since I kept turning down drinks at lunch, but somewhat. I watched them like a hawk to see who knew how to fly and who didn't but they were watching me, too. Every time I touched the controls Major Semanoa noted how well I held altitude or rolled out of a turn or landed where I said I was going to. Sometimes he would take the controls and repeat a maneuver without saying a word, possibly to test himself but most likely to show me he was just as good. It was clear he didn't trust me completely because whenever anything was remotely tricky – a short runway, some rain showers in the vicinity – he always took the controls. But my feelings weren't hurt. The friendly competition was fun.

"*Usted vuela bien,*" he said offhand one day.

"*Gracias, major.* You sound surprised."

Semanoa leveled out and thought about his answer.

"You are American. Americans assume they do everything better than anyone else. Sometimes they do. But not always. You know, wherever you go in the world there are good pilots and bad pilots."

"Es verdad," I agreed.

"We have good pilots and bad pilots, the Colombians have good pilots and bad pilots, the Brazilians have good pilots and bad pilots. I am sure the American Air Force is the same way. Your nationality does not make you good all by itself."

"Of course not." I told him about Griswold Beckett, the only really bad pilot in our squadron and the one who had worried about a fly in the cockpit one night when he should have worried about the thunderstorm outside.

"Bwa-ha-haa!" Semanoa exploded in laughter. "You see? You have them, too."

"Yes, we do. That is why I try to fly only with good pilots."

"Ah-ha," he said. "But what is a good pilot?"

That was a good question. I hadn't tried to define the term before. It was easier to describe a bad pilot. But I tried anyway.

"A good pilot is one who always has the same number of landings as takeoffs," I told him.

The major waved a hand to indicate my explanation was incomplete.

"Un buen piloto," he offered, "is one who knows his limitations and does not try to impress fools."

"A good pilot never stops learning," I countered.

"A good pilot always makes a plan – but is always ready to make a new plan when the first one fails."

"A good pilot never jumps out of his own plane!"

"A good pilot must never let his ego get too big..." Semanoa said, laying a finger on the tip of his nose. Then he pointed at me. "But he must have a big ego."

"Agreed, sir."

"It is your turn."

I thought for a minute. I thought I was a good pilot but that didn't mean the sky didn't scare me sometimes. When did I get scared?

"A good pilot," I exclaimed, "knows that if he has a choice between betting on himself and betting on Mother Nature, he should always bet on Mother Nature."

Semanoa nodded vigorously.

"A good pilot," he announced, "always spends his time on the ground thinking of flying, and his time in the air thinking of women!"

"Are you thinking of women now?" I accused him. "Should I take the controls before we crash?"

"*Ha, Teniente!* In Venezuela we can control our women! That is another thing good pilots do!"

We went on like that for an hour.

One afternoon the strong sun of the morning gave way to scattered rain and an overcast layer of cloud. We were scud-running northwest of a town called Mérida when I asked Semanoa what happened when they found illegal miners. Semanoa demurred.

"We take appropriate action."

"What does that mean?"

"In the past we have made a report about the location of the miners. The naval marines – we call them riverines – then send a patrol out to investigate the matter."

"Do the marines arrest the miners?"

"No. Oh, no. By the time they get there the miners are almost always gone. They move, you see, all the time."

He explained how the miners worked. They looked for gold but also for other minerals such as silver, copper, or nickel. These elements existed in trace amounts in the sediment of the rivers; the challenge was to get to them.

The miners operated shallow-draft boats that were movable processing plants. Chugging their way up tributaries of the major rivers, they dropped anchor in backwaters or coves and went to work, dropping a diver over the side to position hoses along the bottom. With powerful vacuums the hoses would suck up the sediment and throw it into separating bins on the boat itself. Here the mulch was spread thin, cleaned, and leached and the minerals extracted. Any excess was dumped over the side, including the mercury and arsenic used in the leaching process. Huge quantities of toxins were thus thrown into the ecosystem from each illegal boat, the poison left to drift with the current down one tributary after another as the miners left to sell their product in town. In smaller rivers the toxins killed everything, leading to the "dead" zones Semanoa pointed out day after day. Dead fish washed up on beaches where the water itself once was potable. Animals that drank the water died or suffered. Entire species of insects, reptiles, and birds declined.

No tree-huggers themselves, the flyers of Grupo Seis still watched the destruction of parts of their country and took the affront personally. I heard it in their voices when they explained why much of their duty was devoted to "eco-poaching." Which brought me back to my original question.

"So what do you do with them?" I asked again. "Do you ever catch the smugglers?"

Semanoa remained elusive.

"Times are changing," was all he would say.

"Too bad you don't have guns on board," I lamented.

Semanoa gave me a hard stare. "Times are changing," he repeated.

That afternoon we found a boat. It was more of a barge than a boat, long enough that the skipper required a deft touch maneuvering around the river's hairpin turns. It was in full operation when we spotted it with three hoses leading off the decks at stern, midships, and bow. The half-dozen men on board looked up as we flew over.

Semanoa made a low pass while Coco took notes. The miners kept working, knowing that a government plane was just a nuisance and that actual troops on the ground were hours if not days away. After the third pass one decided to make a point, however, calmly fetching a rifle and making a show of standing in the open with it cradled in his arms. Semanoa muttered an epithet and turned us toward a wider orbit.

"There were no markings on the boat," I said, not sure what was the point of our efforts.

Semanoa shook his head. He passed me the controls and tried to contact the base at Maracay via the HF radio. It took him ten minutes to get through. When he did he inquired about the "Quick Reaction Force." The answer was almost half an hour in coming, during which time we cruised the northern stretches of the river and kept the barge in sight from a distance. No quick reaction force, Semanoa was told. Not today.

I began a turn back to the south but with a sigh he pointed for me to roll out.

"*Recto,*" he ordered. Straight ahead.

We flew home.

Two days after flying near Mérida we were supposed to return to the Ocaña area. At the last minute Semanoa changed our plans in order to take
food out to a mission in the Arauca River region.
It was actually a load of more than just food – at
Maracay half a dozen trucks contracted by some
diocese pulled out onto the ramp, each driver
wanting us to load his supplies first.

We had two planes that were working, 381 and
384, so we formed a line from each truck in turn
and passed boxes of clothes, classroom supplies,
toys, building materials, and the like from hand to
hand to the cabins of both aircraft. We didn't stop
loading until the trucks were empty and the planes
were full. It was only then that I realized nobody
had bothered to weigh anything.

I rode in the cabin on the trip out. Captain Uribe
and another captain by the name of Herrera flew
381 while Semanoa flew with two lieutenants. They
traded seat time as we flew first to a mission site
near where the Orinoco River flows out of Colombia, then to the primary destination farther east.

The first location looked like a mission. There
was a church made of logs with a thatch roof. It
sat on low ground a mile from the river and at
the edge of a village. The buildings in the village
were clay. The fields around them were flooded
from a recent storm, a slough behind them having
breached the smaller levees so that in places there

was an unbroken line of water leading all the way to the river. One field that was dry sat on a ridge behind the huts. That was where Semanoa landed our plane, steering between the downslopes on either side and trying to leave room for our wing-man. As we waited for 381 to touch down I watched a dozen naked children play in the water at the bottom of the hill.

"Are these Indians?" I asked no one in partic-ular. The kids were short and chubby with deep brown skin. They were engrossed in their play and paid no attention to us.

"*Sí*," Semanoa answered. "*Pemón.*"

Several people waited in the grass, standing by a pile of crates and burlap bags.

We stopped near the crates and waited for Uribe to set down. He circled us twice to make sure we were done taxiing, then landed toward us offset toward the river. I watched his approach with some anxiety, not mentioning what had to be obvious to everybody – that if something went wrong he had no go-around options except through us. But Uribe seemed to know what he was doing. 381 wobbled a bit on touchdown, the right wing dipping danger-ously low on the upside of the hill, but then settled into the mud. The soft earth helped the plane slow. They rolled out just behind our plane.

"What kind of mission is this?" I asked while the noise of 381's engines wound down.

Luna shrugged.

"*Católico*," he said.

The people waiting were all Venezuelans except for two. There was a tall American man in his mid- to late-fifties and a girl of about twenty who stuck close to him. Both were outfitted like L.L. Bean models. The man wasn't in charge but seemed familiar with everyone in his group and with the logistics of what needed to come off our planes and what to put on. The girl was quiet and just watched. That was fine with me because I was happy to watch her in turn. She was beautiful, an absolute stunner. Pale skin and shoulder-length black hair, a lithe body that even a denim shirt and cargo pants did justice to. She would have been a knockout anywhere but here in the austere Venezuelan Outback a mirage induced by malarial fever couldn't have been more pleasing. It goes without saying that she paid no attention to me.

A short fellow with a round face and big smile welcomed Major Semanoa. Nobody made a move to unload the planes until a truck arrived from downhill with another half-dozen people. That was the signal to get to work. The short man then bustled about, jumping aboard each plane to rummage through boxes and consider each one carefully like a bargain-hunter at a flea market. Whenever he reached a decision he pointed and barked directions. We formed lines again and passed equipment from hand to hand.

At some point we had unloaded everything from the planes that this mission was going to take. Then there was a discussion about what we would take from them. While Semanoa and the crews handled that, I walked to the edge of the hill and watched the children splash in the water below. After a while I realized they were working, not playing.

It was rainy season. The last evening's storm had flooded anthills surrounding the Pemón village. The anthills – built by inch-long fire ants – stood as high as four feet and now rose as little islands isolated by standing water that reached up their sloping sides. Slapping away at bites, the children ran from hill to hill picking up the winged ants and stuffing them into plastic containers. Occasionally they couldn't resist so handy a snack – they would pluck off the wings, feet, and head before popping the still-wriggling body in their mouth and crunching away. It must have tasted good – they giggled and jostled each other as they fought to gather as many ants as possible.

"*Bachacos*," said a voice at my side.

It was the L.L. Bean girl. She didn't look at me but watched the children with the kind of resigned patience that an elementary school teacher has at the beginning of the school year. Her outfit was immaculate, her speech precise. Her hair fell down her back with a fineness that even the humidity couldn't disturb.

"Excuse me?"

"*Bachacos*," she repeated. "That's what the fire ants are called. They're a good source of protein."

She sounded like one of my Air Force survival instructors. No doubt she was right but whenever anyone told me something was a good source of protein I heard it as code that the thing didn't taste very good.

"Does it taste like chicken?" I joked.

"No. Blood."

Her tone was casual enough to be unsettling.

"Uh, do they eat ants all the time?"

The supermodel shook her head, still not looking my way.

"No. The Pemón are mostly vegetarians. Their usual diet is casabe bread and tuma. Tuma's a sauce they make with aurusa, peppers, and manioc juice. They boil it all up and eat it for breakfast, lunch, and dinner." There was disgust in her voice as she said this.

"Doesn't sound very exciting," I commented.

The girl gestured downhill. "That's why they like the ants. In rainy season it's something different."

At the foot of the hill one of the children was no longer giggling. A little boy, maybe five years old, ran down an ant mound in tears, both hands clutching his buttocks. Apparently the ants fought back.

I stood looking at the girl who wouldn't look at me. She was so beautiful, so perfect, I couldn't believe I was talking to her. I couldn't believe she was talking to me. I felt an incredible desire to say something to let her know how I felt, to tell her how beautiful she was, to explain that I'd just fallen madly in love with her and would stay in the jungle for the rest of my life if that's what it took just to be near her. My entire future suddenly rested on the next words that would come out of my mouth.

"Do you eat ants?" I said.

She turned, eyes not giving anything away, and opened her mouth to speak. For all I know our lives and the world would have been different because of what she said, but just then someone started the aux power plant on 381. Its high whine burst across the hilltop and interrupted our conversation. Coco yelled to me from the plane.

In the end that was my last chance to speak to her. She rejoined the priests and I never found an excuse to go back to her.

In the end we also never decreased the load of our airplanes since the missionaries had as much stuff to give us as we had to give them. Included in their generosity were some boxes of tile that Coco and I nearly threw our backs out trying to lift onto the ramp. Again it occurred to me that we didn't have any scales. Nobody in Grupo Seis ever weighed anything they put on their planes.

The tile alone must have weighed six or seven hundred pounds but we just stacked it on the ramp as though it didn't affect the gross weight of the plane or its center of gravity at all. When I brought up the subject Sergeant Victoria waved a hand to say he had it covered.

One hundred and fifty miles to the northeast we landed at another strip, this one carved onto a plateau with jungle on three sides and a crumbling approach end that looked down a rocky slope to fast flowing water. A creek flowed through the trees up to the airstrip where it disappeared underground, then reappeared on the far side to launch itself off the plateau's edge like a park fountain. A pair of raptors soared high over the landing area in thermals that rose off the yellow dirt. It wasn't a desolate area but it sure was remote. The map showed a navigable river somewhere nearby but it said something about either the river or the map that we couldn't see it from two thousand feet up.

It was another Catholic mission and this one had genuine priests, two men with black shirts and white collars and a burly third who dressed in khaki but still wore a big cross around his neck. Like the crowd at the first mission, these three all knew Semanoa.

"*Arturo!*" they greeted him. The fellow with the cross gave the major a big hug in welcome. It was like watching an old bear hug a sapling.

"*Don Matteo*," Semanoa replied. "I see the jungle has not yet swallowed you up."

The priest laughed and patted his stomach.

"It tries, but we swallow it first!"

Their "mission" was a village down the hill. A dirt road led through the trees and around the side of the plateau to where the locals lived. It was impossible to say how big the village was but about thirty people showed up in several pickups as we stood there and talked.

The priests stood aside while the planes were unloaded. They hustled the aircrew out of the way and insisted that the locals do all the work.

The villagers emptied the planes. I thought that was it, that we would take off empty to head toward home, but then the pickups returned from taking the cargo to the village. They were full of more stuff – just as at the first mission we were carrying an outbound load, too.

"What are those?" I muttered to César. The villagers carried huge, round objects using blankets as slings. Some of the objects required four people to lug up the angled ramp of the G-222s.

"*Esculturas*," César replied as though it was obvious.

"Sculptures?"

"*Sí.* The villagers carve sculptures in wood and stone. We'll take them back and the churches will sell them."

Many of the sculptures were small, basketball-size, but some were huge. They were faces and heads and animals in jungle settings, many of them attractive in a rustic way. The villagers hefted the stones on board both aircraft and stacked them in a row running down the center of the cabin. The wood carvings we tied up along the walls.

The cabins filled up quickly. It wasn't until they had run out of things to bring from the village that Semanoa clapped his hands.

"Bueno! Gracias a todos!"

He stalked through the cabin of 384, nudging some of the sculptures with his foot, heavy black eyebrows squeezed low over his eyes in an act clearly designed to show the lieutenants that a serious pilot takes care to know what's on his aircraft. He didn't move anything – or lift anything – and exited out the back again with satisfaction that the load was acceptable.

Was he out of his mind?

"Major," I asked him. "How much does it all weigh?"

He frowned at me as though the question was moot. A good pilot, his glance said, knows if the load is acceptable.

Semanoa and I climbed into the seats and started the engines.

"More power," Victoria muttered when Semanoa tried to taxi and the plane refused to budge. The major looked back at his engineer and Victoria shut up.

The G-222 didn't have the General Electric engines of the C-27 or the suped-up transmissions, either, but it was still a Chuck at heart. That meant that if it had to pull itself apart to carry a load then that's what it would do. With enough power from the throttles Semanoa coaxed the plane to break its suction to the mud. We moved up the levee inch by inch and bumped across the grassy area adjacent to the runway. The back blast made everyone on the ground behind us duck and cover, running behind 381 to avoid being peppered with rocks and dirt.

We taxied to the extreme end of the airstrip and turned ninety degrees to face downfield, our tail so close to the trees behind us that someone could have sat on the elevator and plucked leaves from the branches. It was in the turn that the first indication of impending disaster appeared. Just as Semanoa centered the nose gear the whole plane lurched to the right and dropped.

"Mierda!" Victoria cursed and jumped out of his seat.

"What is it?" I asked in alarm.

Semanoa was calm.

"Probably the strut," he replied. He and Victoria had a quick conversation and the engineer went outside to inspect the damage. He came back in and confirmed Semanoa's assessment.

"All the way," Victoria said. "To the stop."

The two of them discussed the situation. Our right strut had collapsed all the way to the mechanical stop, a block of steel that kept the piston from driving down through the wheel itself. Now whenever we moved the weight of the aircraft would be knocking against that block instead of bouncing on a hydro-pneumatic cushion. I looked down the airstrip – the bumpy, rocky, uneven airstrip – and had my doubts that that's what we wanted to do.

Semanoa had no such doubts. He had collapsed struts before. Besides, there was no way to fix the plane at the mission. We could have unloaded all the cargo, of course, to make us lighter and thereby ease the burden on the gear but no one suggested that. Instead Semanoa shrugged.

"*Todo está bien,*" he said.

"We don't need to fix it?" I asked carefully.

He shook his head and pointed down the runway.

"*Recto!*"

Full speed ahead. With a shove on the throttles we started to roll.

The take-off looked odd from the cockpit because we were in a 7-degree right bank. I found myself leaning to the left just to sit up straight. Every bounce and jolt from the strip reverberated through the plane as the right gear pounded against the mechanical stop. Each second I expected the strut to collapse completely and dig itself into the dirt, causing the right wing to dip even more and contact the ground. The stop held, though. Despite an uncomfortably long take-off roll that ended mere yards from the canyon's edge we lifted off and flew out over the water and the trees on the opposite bank. An engine loss just then would have killed us – being a glass-half-empty kind of guy I thought about stuff like that. But nothing of the sort occurred.

We pulled into a right downwind and turned back to fly by the field as Uribe departed in 381.

Uribe's plane was just as heavy as ours. We saw the dust cloud it kicked up as he goosed the engines to get moving. 381 began to move down the airstrip toward the canyon. Victoria and I watched out the right window as it picked up speed along the ribbon of yellow, the heavy green on either side urging it along like a disc launched off a rail.

They were two-thirds of the way down the field and starting to rotate when the ground opened up beneath them. It collapsed beneath the main gear, shearing off the wheels and throwing the plane forward in a belly flop onto the far side of the cistern formed by the flowing stream below. Simultaneously a cloud of dust and smoke billowed up as 381 skidded in the dirt, its nose turning thirty degrees to the right. Had it not been for their momentum the whole plane might have dropped ten feet into the water below.

"*Ay, chuleta!*" Victoria yelled.

"*Qué?!*" Semanoa demanded and banked our plane to see for himself.

381 had a lot of momentum to dissipate. Its engines made the problem worse as for a moment the crew onboard didn't shut them down. The props churned away, dragging the G-222 forward. Uribe must have been along for the ride because when Semanoa instinctively keyed the mike and asked if he needed help the response was quick.

"Not yet. Maybe...when...we...stop."

381 ground to a painful, dusty halt eighty feet short of the canyon.

The villagers ran downfield. 381 sat mournfully in the center of the airstrip, tilted to the left with its engines still running, the props now spinning at idle. As we watched, the crew came to their senses and started shutting things off. The props wound down, going slower and slower but admitting defeat only when the missionaries drew near.

For a while it was quiet in our cockpit. The major reversed his turn and brought the plane around into a left bank. That way he could see better out his window. He could also hide the fact that his mouth hung open in shock. It may not have been the accident per se that threw him off: maybe it was the knowledge that now he was down one more plane in the fleet and that that plane was stuck in the middle of nowhere with no obvious means of recovery. Also, the mission's airstrip was now unusable, a big hole and a stranded aircraft keeping visitors out for the foreseeable future.

"*Bueno,*" he said at last, rolling our plane level and heading us toward the north. "They will have to get home on their own."

It was a long flight back to Maracay.

Someone decided to try using F-16s against the miners. The fighters didn't carry bombs but they could strafe. Theoretically, anyway. Following a report from local officials the government launched two F-16s from Caracas to destroy an illegal barge mining gold in the border region near Bucaramanga. The F-16s went to the area, circled overhead for a while, then dove down to destroy the boat. The problem was they attacked the wrong boat. How they expected to identify the right one from ten thousand feet in a remote region with no ground controllers is unclear. It wasn't like the region was crowded with river traffic but to expect two vessels in an area of several hundred square miles shouldn't have been out of the question, either. Nevertheless, the pilots set up a firing pass and loosed off a chain of 20mm rounds.

Imagine the surprise of the ferry occupants when they saw the fighters rolling in. Imagine their surprise when those same fighters started shooting and tore up a number of trees along the riverbank a hundred yards away. And imagine their extreme surprise when both fighters got target fixation and almost crashed into the river themselves, pulling up wildly at the last second and barely avoiding a smoking hole. Venezuelan pilots never trained for a ground attack role – the glory was in air-to-air, so why bother? This experience confirmed their bias. The F-16s went home empty-handed.

Another G-222 came up faster than any of us expected. 381 was still in pieces sitting on a feeder river to the Arauca and 384 had been carrying the load for the squadron with the expectation that it would be the only flyer for a while. But then the maintainers rolled 380 out of the hanger where it had been hiding for a month.

"She is ready," Master Sergeant Comín promised the commander, wiping his hands on an oil-soaked rag.

"Ready for everything?" Amodio asked.

Comín was tired but confident.

"She will sing like a little bird."

Amodio reached for the phone. Once again he had a fleet.

Caracas wanted the border patrolled. Whenever the G-222s were down for repairs the base at
Maracay launched a Cessna 172 to fill the gap. The
base had three of those. From what I saw of them
parked on the ramp they were in decent shape.

The Cessna pilots didn't want to patrol the border. Their first complaint was that they couldn't
do it from Maracay since it was three hundred
miles away. So they had to forward-deploy. The
base moved the pilots and their planes out to San
Cristobal, the capital of Tachiras province. From
there they flew north and south several hours a
day using the coal town of Casigua as a fuel stop. At
night they slept in the back room of a local police
station.

Their second complaint was of flying a single-
engine plane over remote areas, which is never a
relaxing experience. To patrol the western border
the four Cessna pilots flew over the hinterlands
five times a week. Any place out there was a bad
one to have engine trouble.

Last, to make things worse the smugglers and
miners shot at the planes.

Then one day one of the Cessnas didn't come
back. Ever. It just disappeared. The Maracay planes
didn't have Emergency Locator Transmitters so
there was no radio signal to track. In response we
launched and flew search patterns all over western
Venezuela trying to find the wreckage. Three days

of creeping ladders and expanding squares along the pilot's likely route of flight. Three days of staring out the window trying to see a smoke signal or a mirror flash or a bit of broken wing or even an oil slick on the surface of a river. But the jungle below gave nothing away. Some people guessed the plane's engine quit. Most, angry, figured the miners finally got one. Either way, Grupo 6 had lost one for good.

"I wanted to take you to Ventuari," Semanoa explained one day as we circled a hilltop in the Amazonas region. "But there was a mudslide two months ago. The runway is no longer there."

He banked to the right so that I could get a good look below us. The hill of interest was part of a chain that rose in a forty-mile line of forested pimples across the jungle.

"This isn't Ventuari?" I asked.

"No. This is Yopal."

On the downwind I glimpsed a sliver of brown running across the hill about four-fifths up the side. It slanted upward as though a giant wandering the landscape had swung his machete down against the hill and sliced a divot into the trees and earth.

"Is that the runway?"

"*Sí.*"

"Somebody uses that?"

"*Sí.*"

"For what?"

Semanoa leaned across the cockpit to look past me. In the seat behind us Sergeant Rubin hurried to compute landing speeds.

"I've never asked," he replied.

We flew around the hill to the west and then came back in the direction of our original downwind. There I could get a better look at where Semanoa wanted to land.

"Is that a road?" I asked.

"No. That is the runway."

"Where? Behind the tree?"

"No. Right there. *Allí.*"

I looked where he pointed. Something was missing. At the touchdown point the gash in the forest had plenty of room laterally so there was little danger of falling off the right side of the hill. But it was on an upslope the likes of which I had never seen. And a tree stood where the major pointed.

"Ah, I must be looking at the wrong place, sir," I said. "It looks to me like there is a tree in the way."

Semanoa leaned around me to look. *"Sí. "*

But the major humored me and flew by the landing strip again, in part because he took pride in how difficult the runway was to land on. The strip was maybe eight hundred feet long. It sloped up steep enough that even though the hill fell away on three sides of the strip if you landed on one end there wasn't a chance in hell you could see anything off the far end – you would see nothing but more dirt as you ground your way uphill. The tree at the four hundred foot mark was an immature Santa Maria, a tall, thin widow-maker that sat smack in the way and had absolutely no reason to be there.

"Do we land past the tree?" I inquired.

"No."

"We land in front of it?"

"Sí."

"How? On an angle?"

"No. Recto."

"Um..."

"We will go around it. I will show you."

Semanoa turned and flew back out to a two-mile final. He briefed his landing but kept it short: the substance was that I should just take his word for it and not freak out when we touched down.

"Are there any questions?" he asked as we rolled wings level. Out front the brown soil of the airstrip rose up like a vertical line, bobbing in the wind-screen as we bounced in the heat.

"Just one," I replied, trying to ignore the butter-flies in my stomach. "Why doesn't anyone out here build a runway down low? We're always landing on hillsides. There's a lot of flat jungle out there, you know."

"Yes," said Sergeant Rubin. "But it's all wet. Everything floods. We could never keep a runway open down there."

Then buy a boat, I thought as the strip ahead got closer.

Had we been carrying cargo I would have considered jettisoning it to get light before attempting this approach. As it was we were almost empty so we were as light as we could be. Our only load that day had been half a dozen people we delivered to an Indian village north of Puerto Ayacucho – as a reward they gave us a gallon of homemade moonshine that Rubin claimed was even better than Brazilian *cachaça*. The locals cooked it in great vats and didn't even have anything to put it in when we landed. They finally poured some into an ancient jug that someone told me they had dug up from ruins nearby. The jug had a reed handle and dozens of polished stones inset to the clay. It was classy and smooth to the touch but smelled as old as it looked. Better than *cachaça*? I thought, not knowing what *cachaça* tasted like. I sniffed the bottle and told Rubin I would take his word for it.

"*Basta, basta...*" Semanoa coached himself on short final. He walked a cautious line, trying to keep the nose up so we didn't prang it in but keeping the power back so we didn't accelerate. The G-222 rode the edge of a stall with full flaps. Twice when an updraft caught us the stall warning horn came on, making me reach reflexively for the controls until the major waved me away. He applied power and lowered the nose. The horn stopped.

Three-quarters of a mile. Half a mile. The strip loomed in front of us. We were now too close to abort the approach.

"Basta..."

My left hand hovered near the controls. With my right I locked my shoulder harness.

"Basta..."

The nose tried to fall. Semanoa tickled it up again.

The needle on the VVI leveled off and then moved ever so slightly to the positive. I had never landed while in a *climb*. The hillside rushed toward us. The stall horn sounded again. This time it didn't go out.

"Ya!"

On impact the nose gear hit simultaneously with the mains. Semanoa released the yoke and grabbed the steering grip. He never touched the brakes, nor did he throw the engines into reverse. We landed doing eighty miles an hour and powering uphill like Evil Knievel attacking a ramp.

"Brakes," I called. It was as much a question as an order.

"NO!" Semanoa yelled. *"Recto!"*

In fact we didn't need brakes. We were driving uphill and slowing down enough that we would need power just to get to the top. But before then the tree was still in our way and that's why I wanted to stop. Three seconds after landing we had more than enough speed to crash right through it. We were close enough that I could see how the dirt on the uphill side piled against its trunk. The tree's first branch was a broken one ten feet up, at just the right height to come through the windscreen and skewer my head.

Just when I was about to go for the pedals to keep the Santa Maria from slicing us in two, the major stomped on the right brake. At the same time he twisted the hand grip. Like a taxi avoiding a jaywalker we tipped onto two wheels and lurched to the right. My heart froze. Now we were heading for the edge of the mountain.

"Uno, dos...YA!" Semanoa yelled. He released the right brake and stomped on the left, throwing the grip that way to keep us from plunging over the side. At the same time he shoved the power levers forward with his right hand.

The G-222 tipped the opposite way, taking my nervous system with it. The left wingtip pointed at the Santa Maria tree like an ice dancer spotting her turn. With left wheels skidding in the dirt the right gear spun around the outside of the circle and pointed us back toward the runway. The tail swung out over nothing.

"Rectooooooo!"

Now Semanoa released all the brakes and drove us uphill.

"Ha!"

The Santa Maria fell behind, its leaves fluttering in the blast from our engines.

"Buen trabajo, major!" Rubin shouted in excitement. *"Bien hecho!"*

"Gracias!"

I couldn't breathe.

From there to the end of the strip the challenge was to keep moving. Semanoa kept the power at almost 600 ft-lbs of torque which on the ground back in Panama would have gotten us to rotate speed. At the top of the ridge the strip petered out. He retained our momentum long enough to bring the plane around 180 degrees to the left. Then he chopped the power.

The view in that direction was even scarier. As if I hadn't been terrified enough, when Semanoa applied the brakes for the last time we were now looking down the hill on a slope steep enough that I couldn't sit straight in my seat. Thirty seconds earlier we had attacked the hill from the bottom. Now we poised like a ski jumper at the top of his run, peering down where gravity and momentum would dictate we go.

But we didn't go. Semanoa left the throttles in idle and set the parking brake. He signaled to Rubin, who jumped out and placed chocks in front of all the wheels.

Of all the dumb things I had done since coming to Latin America this was undoubtedly the dumbest. We had almost crashed on a field where we had no business being. We almost flipped off the side of a mountain avoiding a tree that was in the middle of the runway we had no business being on. My heart pounded in my chest. My mouth was dry. My hands shook. To keep Semanoa from noticing I crossed my arms. He looked over and took the action to mean I was unimpressed.

"Bueno," he said, sounding defensive. *"Qué piensas?"*

What do I think? I think you're a Third World buffoon, I wanted to say. I wanted to shout that his landing was the stupidest stunt I had ever seen outside of a silent movie. I wanted to scream that the Venezuelan Air Force was filled with a bunch of Stone Age dumbasses. What do I think?

All of a sudden I knew what I thought. I unbuckled my seat belt to climb out.

Semanoa nodded.

"Yes," he said. "We must get out so you can see the view."

He dropped the power levers into Idle Reverse and then climbed out after me. Had I bothered to consider it that act would also have made my list of stupid things. Here we were stopped on a hill steep enough to inspire vertigo and not only did everyone get off the aircraft – we got off and left the engines running!

When Semanoa caught up with me I was behind the aircraft on the ridge looking north.

"Ah!" he exclaimed. "It is a beautiful view, no? Today you can see for miles. If we could just look around the hill there I bet we could see all the way to the border!"

I didn't answer. I wasn't looking at the view. It took Semanoa a minute to notice the jug in my hand. By that time I'd drunk it down to level with the handle.

"*Teniente...*" he murmured.

The fire in my throat made my eyes water. The booze roared into my gut like roasted air. It hurt but it went a long way toward getting my heart off its treadmill. It would have scorched the butterflies, too, had they not already collapsed from the stress. I hated being scared.

Semanoa wasn't sure what to say or if he should say anything. He twisted the ends of his moustache while I gulped more of what I was sure was a mixture of embalming fluid and nitroglycerine. Whatever this "better than *cachaça*" stuff was, it had the kick of a horse and tasted like formaldehyde sucked from the carcass of a dead bat; I gagged while he stood there and watched.

Finally he cleared his throat.

"I think you are right, Miguel," he said carefully. "We should have a toast."

I gave him the frostiest look I could muster. But after a few more sips I reconsidered. Really, how mad could I be?

I held out the jug.

"You might as well have some before I finish it."

"*Salud,*" he agreed, and smiled.

Twenty minutes later we were back in the cockpit and looking downhill. As yet the moonshine had done nothing to my vision but eerily it made all noise from the engines vanish.

The silence allowed me to focus all my attention on the Santa Maria. It stood directly off our nose, a hundred and thirty yards downhill, a tall, thin, branchy gunslinger. In turn I felt cold. The fire in my gut went out and was replaced by ice. I had just come as close to death as I had ever been in an airplane and now we had to do it all over again. Fine, I thought, the moonshine making me numb. Bring it on.

"Alright, Señor Chuck freaking Yeager," I said to Semanoa. "Now that you got us up this damned hill, how do you propose to get us out of here?"

The major unexpectedly made a grand gesture that the controls were all mine.

"I thought I would leave that up to you, *mi amigo.* Would you like some assistance?"

I looked downhill at the strip and the tree and the sharp turn and the drop-off at the side and

finally at the ragged end of the runway where broken dirt fell away into nothingness. I motioned for
him to release the brakes.

"No," I said as we started to roll. *"Recto!"*

On the 29th of that month Grupo Seis got a formation airborne again. 384 and 380 were both up and
running. Lt Col Amodio directed that both aircraft
would take off early, head down to the Ocaña river
region and fly all day, stopping for gas at Casigua.

Lt Col Amodio never said anything about it
around me but he was clearly under pressure. The
Air Force was turning up the heat on Grupo Seis
and their ability to monitor the frontier.

We took off for Casigua early and flew an hour
and a half to get to the border. We searched rivers there for two more hours before landing at
Casigua to refuel.

By noon we were airborne again, this time
headed north over various feeder rivers of the
Rio Negro. Semanoa's plan was to go as far as
Machiques before turning east back to Maracay. As
we took off there was a call on the radio.

"Turpial Dos, Turpial Dos. Este es Turpial Uno."

"Turpial Uno, buen' día, colonel," Semanoa radi-
oed back.

Turpial Uno was Lt Col Amodio. Just as
Semanoa returned his call we caught sight of the

commander's plane. Five miles to the northeast, it was scud-running below a stratus layer and circum-venting the town. Amodio and Lieutenant Luna – he of the Menjou moustache – were in aircraft 380.

"What is your status?"

"We have just refueled, *commandante.* We're heading north for the Rio Negro."

"Bueno. Continue. We are flying south but will refuel in two hours and then join you."

"Copia."

The region north of Casigua was flat. That allowed us to see rivers from a distance but we still cruised for hours before seeing anything of interest.

The boat was another barge. From the outset something about its operations seemed amiss. First, it was nowhere near any town where barge operations were justified. Second was a pipe at the stern of the boat: shaped like a periscope with a wide mouth, it spewed water back into the river under pressure from a pump amidships. Third... well, third was the guy with the gun who came out as we flew low overhead. He waved at us to get away and lifted the rifle to make his point.

We rolled left to turn and make a second pass. The man gestured again. This time he was joined by two others. Ignoring them, we looked for a name on the vessel. The barge was old and rusted but it did have markings. Unfortunately they were too faded to read even at our low level. Semanoa rolled into a racetrack pattern off the boat's stern.

"We have one," Chavez concluded and the major nodded.

"*Bueno,*" I agreed. "But now what do we do?"

In response to that question in the past Major Semanoa had always sighed. Today he held up a finger to emphasize that he had an answer.

Before he could get to it, however, there was a *CRACK!* across the front windscreen and another behind my head.

"*Qué?..*" said Chavez.

At the sound of a third impact aft of the cockpit Semanoa rolled sharply right and banked away from the river.

"*Mierda!*"

Why we were surprised that the men on the boat actually shot at us, I don't know. After the disappearance of the Cessna everyone in Grupo Seis talked loudly about not getting too close to miners. However, until now none of us had actually been attacked.

"*Motores,*" was the next thing Semanoa said. Satisfied that nothing critical on the plane had been damaged, he then passed me the controls and launched into a tirade of Venezuelan profanity.

"Bueno," I said when he finished. "So now what do we do? *Qué hacemos ahora?"*

The answer was interrupted by a radio call.

"Turpial Dos, Turpial Dos. Turpial Uno."

Semanoa heard the call and his eyes lit up. He raised his finger again.

"You will see!"

380 was fifty miles behind us. Semanoa got on the VHF radio and filled in Amodio about our recent events. Amodio asked a million questions then ordered us to maintain an orbit two miles from the barge so he could pinpoint its position. Semanoa took back the controls and maneuvered us accordingly, although as we watched 380 approach he got distracted and inscribed a smaller and smaller circle until we were no more than a mile from the boat.

Amodio and Luna climbed to a thousand feet above the plain and drove right toward the barge. Only at a quarter-mile out did they bank right and descend. At five hundred feet, still above our altitude, they banked backed to the left and circled the barge at a distance of no more than a thousand feet.

"Van a tirar otra vez," I warned.

Semanoa and Chavez were fixed on the scene. Semanoa nodded.

"Sí, they are going to shoot," he agreed.

380 rolled around the far side of the turn. Only then did I understand what I was looking at.

It wasn't the miners who were going to shoot. It was 380.

The left troop door on Amodio's plane opened. Someone appeared in the door and swung into position a brace-mounted Gatling gun. From the size of the barrels I guessed it to be a 7.62 mini capable of firing up to 4,000 rounds a minute. It was easy to imagine what that meant for an eighty-foot-long boat. As I did, the gunner in the door went hot.

At first we saw nothing to signal the battle was underway. Then puffs of white smoke popped up in 380's wake, coming from the barrels of the spinning gun. But the real result was down below. The only two men visible on deck collapsed immediately, their bodies riddled with hundreds of nine-millimeter rounds. Splinters from the deck shot high in the air in response to the downpour of lead. Then a fire appeared at the bow. Another popped up amidships. Semanoa gave me the controls and I climbed two hundred feet to get a better angle on the scene.

The barge drifted off its course and drove to the right. As the gunner overhead kept firing the roof of the wheelhouse collapsed. Stays on the rear deck disintegrated and the barrels they restrained rolled around deck until they, too, were shot to pieces. Amodio's orders must have been to blast the boat to hell because the gunner in the door didn't let up until the barge drove itself right into the south bank of the river. There it listed to one side, the fires spreading until everything in sight burned. No one got off.

When it was all over Major Semanoa sat back in his seat and breathed deeply. Nobody said anything. He took back the controls and made one radio call to his boss.

"Buen tirar," was all he said. Good shooting.

And that was it. We were low on gas so we turned toward Maracay and led the formation back to base.

I left Venezuela a week later. Charlie Manson flew down in a C-27 with Lt Col Rasmussen to pick me up.

Grupo Seis threw a barbecue in my honor. There was an exchange of mementos between the two squadrons. With Manson translating, Rasmussen presented Lt Col Amodio with our standard squadron gift, a fake machete mounted on a plaque with an inscription that said something about how the two units would always be friends. Amodio returned the favor by giving Rasmussen a real machete.

Amodio had wanted to give me a gift as well but I begged him not to. I knew he didn't have money to waste on presents. Besides, I didn't want to get into a gift-giving contest. When Amodio looked uncomfortable I asked if I could just keep the glazed clay bottle that Semanoa and I had sucked white lightning from on the hilltop in Amazonas. He couldn't understand why I wanted an old jug but, seeing I was sincere, was happy to be generous. *Por supuesto,* he told me, and the jug was mine.

It had taken me days to relate the jug to Walt's list. When I did it was a stroke of inspiration. #18 on the list said 'Warekena pitcher.' I had to look up Warekena at a library in town to learn they were a branch of the Yanomami Indians and that they came from the area around Yopal. Was my jug a Warekena? It was good enough for me. Was it a pitcher? Well, it sure as hell wasn't a flask. And I had never drunk a more powerful boilermaker in my life. Walt had his next piece of treasure.

Amodio made a speech saying how happy they had been to have me there. Lt Col Rasmussen said a few words, too. Then Semanoa asked Rasmussen in a loud voice if I would be at the controls when we flew home later that day.

"Uh, well, maybe," Rasmussen said, confused. "I'm sure we'll get him in the seat for a bit."

Major Semanoa nodded approvingly and then lifted his bottle of beer, the local brew called Polar Pilsner that I had always avoided.

"Then I propose a toast, *señor*," he said. "I would like all of you to raise your glasses and have a drink in honor of Teniente Miguel Bleriot."

All the flyers of Grupo Seis raised their beers. Rasmussen and Manson stuck with their bottled water but tried to be nonchalant about it. Hesitating for just a second, I put my water down and grabbed a Polar, prompting the men to cheer.

"*Al Teniente!*" Semanoa offered.

"*Al Teniente!*" they yelled, and everyone drank.

Then Semanoa set his beer down and leaned close to Rasmussen.

"He is a good pilot, *coronel*," he promised, wiping his mouth with the back of his hand. "But I assure you, he is a *better* pilot when he has a few drinks in him."

4. Myths

FOR A WHILE AFTER we got the first C-27s down to Panama, a battery malfunction in the Emergency Locator Transponders caused those beacons to sound whenever the temperature dropped five or six degrees in humid conditions. Since that happened almost every night, almost every night someone in Base Operations would call down to the Life Support shop in Hangar 2 and ask the late shift there to find the wayward radio and silence it.

Life Support got the call because ELTs were their responsibility. The transmitters were tiny boxes built into airplane tails and parachutes that were designed to activate in the event of a crash or if someone bailed out of a plane. The instant a parachute opened, for example, the radio would start transmitting a panicked, wavering wail over a common frequency that everyone flying was supposed to monitor. The idea was that other pilots would hear the beacon and notify rescuers, who could home in on the signal even if the plane was a wreck or the pilot unconscious. Of course, if a beacon sounded when there was no emergency, it blocked all other transmissions on that frequency. Therefore, when ours starting going off on parked planes in the middle of the night, it was up to the technicians who looked after our safety equipment to find the rogue transmitters and shut them down.

Our night shift Life Support crew consisted of two people: an overweight master sergeant named Cheeves and any random young airman who was unlucky enough to be scheduled with him.

The airman was unlucky because Cheeves was a grump. He should have retired years earlier but hadn't. He stayed because the Personnel system let him, and Personnel let him probably because they had lost track of him sometime back during the Carter administration.

But longevity wasn't doing Cheeves any favors. He was bored and cantankerous and grew lazier and more belligerent with each month he spent in Hangar 2. He grouched over aircrew, over mainte-nance, over his supervisors, and over anyone else who got on his nerves. Yet he stayed on, sheer iner-tia causing him to put down roots.

The roots were almost literal – he moved less as the years went by, using a bad hip as an excuse to boss around the teenagers who worked for him and giving him a reason besides sheer crankiness to send them running whenever he could: for tools, for snacks, or out on errands such as finding which aircraft on the ramp had a short-circuit and was jamming all the radios. He loved to send them out looking for the beacons because he knew the ramp was a spooky place once flying had shut down for the night. The lights were out, the field was quiet, and the warm air off the ocean was heavy enough to weigh on your mind as you felt your way around a bunch of parked planes.

"Get off your ass and find that transmitter!" Cheeves would bark at the airman, some pimply-faced kid who would jump for a flashlight so he could find his way around the stygian ramp. If the kid hesitated or made the mistake of even look-ing like he might talk back – say, to wonder why the master sergeant didn't get off his own fat ass for a change – Cheeves would rip him a new one. He wouldn't even let them use the speedy three-wheeled trikes that the mechanics rode to haul tools around the ramp – he made them hoof it because "they need the exercise."

After the kid was gone, Cheeves would roll his chair back to the long table where he inspected parachute canopies. "Sorry about that, lieuten-ant," he said to me one night when I stopped by after a flight to inquire about some radio manuals. "Normally I would go but with this hip it's a won-der I can even hobble to my car."

The airmen had an unenviable task. There were no set procedures to deal with the beacon situation. When the beacons began to sound that summer (right around midnight, when the ramp was darkest) the techs just went out and wandered around with a flashlight and a homing device. That was bad enough. Worse, the C-27s were parked in Alpha row at the north end of the field, almost a mile away and near the jungle in the blackest area of all. Once the airmen narrowed down our planes as the offenders it was doubly unnerving for some 18-year-old to have to walk over there by himself and figure out which plane had the malfunction. The trees made strange noises, there were animals you couldn't see, and if you had any trouble help was a long way away. Those with active imaginations had a rough time of it.

The first time a beacon shorted out, the airman sent to find it was a youth named Clark. He assumed the problem would be close by, on Ramps 3 and 4 where the Army birds were parked, and didn't think it would be scary to go out there on his own. So he searched for two hours, wandering through the rows of Huey and Blackhawk helicopters, C-12s, Broncos, and C-130s, walking between the tiedown straps, ducking under wings, opening hatches in the nose cone or tail and peering inside.

The hatches creaked. Clark's footsteps echoed. Sometimes mice and birds found their way into interior spaces and leaped out when the panels opened. The flashlight cast shadows that gave the illusion of movement across the ramp. Bats fluttered out of sight. Clark grew nervous. Being alone began to seem like not such a good idea.

He searched faster and did his best to ignore the sense that something was following him around the ramp.

Clark finally found the bad beacon in aircraft #103 but the victory was muted by the experience. He also made the mistake of mentioning his fear to Cheeves when he returned to the hangar – instead of congratulating him, Cheeves chided him for being a wimp.

The next time a beacon went off and Clark had to repeat his trip, things got worse. This time when he got out to Alpha row to find out which C-27 was acting up, he heard tapping and moans and weird skitterings in the grass that were definitely not his imagination. There was a rattle of chains, and movement on the black tarmac just beyond his vision. Something tiny flew through the air and hit him on the back. Clark ran all the way back to the office.

Thus the stories started. Within weeks other Life Support staff reported "experiences." A mysterious shadow was seen on the ramp; there were more noises; someone heard footsteps *on top of the plane.* Fire extinguishers that the techs positioned in one spot outside an aircraft door would be somewhere else when they emerged from the cabin. Once a crew door closed by itself while the tech was inside.

Clark claimed it was a ghost, saying he had heard from someone that an ancient Mayan burial ground was underneath the runway and that victims of cannibalism were now seeking their revenge. Cheeves suggested a poltergeist, and that rumor gained ascendance when mechanics working overnight saw their tool boxes pilfered. Together the rumors morphed until by the end of the summer the accepted story was that a local Indian in the 1940s had been decapitated by a propeller and now wandered headless on the airfield.

Airmen began to refuse to go alone to the C-27 parking area after dark. Cheeves wouldn't join them due to his hip so they demanded that the police or the mechanics or someone from Base Operations accompany them. But the flightline cops said they were too busy. The mechanics – civilian contractors – simply said no. Since Base Ops was required to monitor the emergency frequency on the radio and had a vested interest in getting the frequency cleared, they had to agree – but they regretted it. Some of the most panicked reports later came from lieutenants on the weather shop's night shift.

But the lieutenants weren't the only participants in the growing hysteria. Though flightline police refused to baby-sit the technicians, eventually they did agree to patrol the north ramp more often. Soon after, they began to report sightings of their own. Then flight crew got involved. Nobody ever saw anything definitive but with their imagination prodded to high gear loadmasters and pilots started coming back from sorties with stories. Bird claimed to hear a voice calling to him from the grass, and Luz said that a cold breeze – "like the deadly touch of a phantom!" – followed him around the ramp. Rolo admitted to hearing things and Major Byron of all people noted in his trip report one night that immediately after landing he observed a "stocky apparition gliding unnaturally through the shadows just outside of mini-gun range."

Lowell named the mysterious apparition the Veracruz Wobbly. The weather shop called it Headless Howard. Evan phoned up Art Bell in the States and reported "supernatural military sightings" on his late-night radio show.

I never saw anything but still found myself jumping at little noises whenever we wrapped up a sortie for the night. The one time I tried to put my foot down and ordered the crew to de-brief our flight right there on the apron, they mutinied and said they would meet me in the squadron. Harry didn't help matters when he burst onto the plane as the propellers wound down and blurted, "Come on, guys, get a move on. Headless Howard's on the prowl! You guys have any write-ups, we'll get to them in the morning." Crews began calling in sick when they were scheduled to fly after dark.

It wasn't until November, the height of rainy season, that sanity reappeared. The ghost outed himself.

The airfield managers were prepping for an inspection one night soon after the one a.m. thunderstorm. They had re-positioned light carts and K-loaders at the far end of the field and spread equipment across the dark apron to conduct an inventory when suddenly they heard a crash and a cry of pain. They found MSgt Cheeves lying in a fetal position on Taxiway Mike, the twisted remains of a mechanic's trike lying beside him. He had been racing through the darkness, skidded in a puddle, and crashed into a tow bar. When the ambulance came he claimed that he couldn't remember how he happened to be there but it didn't take long for everyone to put two and two together.

The irony was that after the crash Cheeves' "bad" hip was now truly messed up.

The ghostly events ceased, exorcised as thoroughly as the Life Support shop was later by Cheeves' medical retirement. Evan still called Art Bell from time to time to report "diminished but palpable otherworld energy," but the rest of us resumed our nighttime flights and stopped rushing through shut-down checklists.

Once, months later, a wide, flat shadow moved across the grass just beyond where Vince stood to marshal us in from a late-night flight. Declan and I both saw it from the cockpit. The sight recalled the stories of Headless Howard. The immediate thought of specters from the beyond swallowing our mechanic momentarily blinded us to the signals from his two wands and we almost crashed into the fire extinguisher. Then we turned the landing lights back on and flooded the area in light – to reveal a troop of foraging coatamundis.

For a long while that was the closest we came to an encounter with phantoms.

"So who's this Diegel Doone guy?" I asked Mike Vaneya one day while the Headless Howard stories were still circulating. I stood with him and Charlie Manson at a block party on Declan's street to celebrate Oktoberfest. Declan and his neighbors made their own beer and used the party to show it off.

"Who?"

"Diegel Doone. Skinny Steve and Evan talk about him. So does Walt, although Walt thinks it's a joke. If we're on a low-level Walt likes to plunge into the trees and yell, 'Look for Diegel Doone!' If we're at altitude he says things like, 'I can almost see Diegel Doone from here.' Steve believes it, though. Who is the guy?"

"Some freak creation of Walt's warped, vegan-addled mind?" Mike guessed.

"No, he's just mocking Skinny Steve."

"Okay, then some freak creation of Skinny Steve's warped, anorexic mind?"

"No, Diegel Doone is real," Paul Lappe, a young loadmaster, piped in. "Lieutenant Colmer told me about him. He said Doone was an airline pilot back in the thirties who disappeared in the jungle. Nobody saw him crash, nobody heard a radio call, nothing. He just disappeared. Nobody's even sure where he took off from. Some say Lima, some say Cartagena. He didn't say where he was headed so he could be anywhere. He's, like, the last big mystery down here."

Manson sipped his beer and eyed Paul the way most people regard mimes, reflecting on the wasted talent.

"First of all, Airman Lappe," he replied. "I looked into that Diegel guy a year ago and the story is pure horseshit, an urban legend like cow-tipping and educated liberals, started by some-body who was probably mooching a beer. He never existed. Second, add bullshit to the horse-shit: you're young and impressionable so I'll warn you that Evan Colmer believes in spaceships and crop circles. If you're going to him for the his-tory of aviation you'll end up as informed about flying as Bleriot here is about women. Last, huge piles of cowshit: Steve can fly but his brain is as malnourished as the rest of him. When it comes to anything *but* flying you shouldn't trust a word he says."

"You talking about me?" Rolo asked, walking by.

"No," I said. "Skinny Steve. Him and some guy he calls Diegel Doone."

"Oh, yeah," Rolo nodded. "The missing mail pilot. Took off from Guayaquil one night and was never heard from again."

"You know about him?" I asked.

"Sure. Steve told me. Wasn't he carrying secret messages from Ecuadorian generals about a coup, or something like that?"

Manson wanted to knock Rolo flat but both his hands held bottles, so instead he stepped forward and kicked my roommate in the behind.

"Ow! What was that for?"

"For being an idiot," Manson growled. "You know what the telephone game is? It's where somebody hears a story and then adds onto it before re-telling it to someone else. It's how rumors spread. Hell, it's how religions start. You're doing it now."

"About what?"

"About Diegel Doone," Mike chuckled. "Charlie doesn't believe your story."

"Well, I don't know," Rolo admitted. "Steve's always going on about him so I took his word for it."

"Took who's word for what?" Tommy Goode interrupted, coming down off the lawn. He had his smoking hot girlfriend with him and held a bottle of home brew cooked up by Perry Trapazzano. Trapazzano made beer in his kitchen and flavored it with orchids he collected in the jungle. No batch tasted exactly the same but all had a vanilla hint to them that was smooth and addicting at the same time. I liked the stuff but found it made my teeth tingle and numbed my tongue, so I stuck to drinking only one bottle in any seven-day period. The seven days coincided with most of my local sorties and Walt maintained the beer calmed me down and improved my flying. Our flight surgeon Doc Hinnaneman came to a similar conclusion. For a year he prescribed Trapazzano's brew to patients with food poisoning, thinking it would settle their stomachs, until there was a spate of sleep-walking incidents on base and he learned the orchids were hallucinogenic. At least then I understood why on final approach the runway always seemed to be smiling.

"Skinny Steve's word about Diegel Doone," Rolo explained. "He's a guy missing in the jungle."

"Oh, yeah," Tommy nodded. He turned to his girlfriend. "See, baby, this is a perfect example of what I was telling you about how dangerous my job is. This Doone guy was a world-class pilot, really top-notch, but one day he just ups and vanishes. He had a plane-load of medicine that he was taking to a hospital out in the jungle but he flew into a freak thunderstorm that tore his plane apart. No one ever found the body."

"Medicine?" Manson choked on his own derision. "Hospital in the jungle? Where did that come from? I thought he was carrying secret war messages from the rebels!"

"I hadn't heard that," Tommy said.

"That's Metzger's version of this fairy tale."

"No," Rolo said. "Not rebels. Generals plotting a coup."

"No, it was a hospital," Tommy insisted. "They say a bunch of orphans died when Doone didn't show up."

"Oh, for god's sake," Manson exclaimed. He looked around in frustration for Steve. Not finding him, his gaze fell on Major Farnham so he called over our deputy commander in hopes of a little support from rank and maturity.

"Doone?" Farnham repeated when Charlie explained the situation. "Oh, yes. How about that buffoonery?"

"See?" Manson demanded, glaring at the rest of us. "Buffoonery. You heard it from a field grade officer!"

"Yes," Farnham nodded sagely. "That's what it was. But wouldn't I like to find that plane wreck? You betcha. A cargo hold filled with the Chilean Treasury's gold reserves and this clown of a pilot tries to take it over the Andes on a single-engine. Pure recklessness."

Manson's face dropped.

"You know what I don't understand," Farnham continued, "is if they were acting on secret orders from President Hoover – and I say 'they,' you understand, because Diegel Doone wasn't the name of a person; it was the name of the plane: there were actually seven people on the crew – why didn't they have a larger plane? I mean, a Model 80 was fine for what Boeing offered at the time, but back then Fokker and Fairchild both had better machines with bigger engines – hell, the Fokker had three motors. That would have been helpful once icing caught up with them over Bolivia. To think all those lives could have been saved and – what was it, something like $30 million? – if they had only planned ahead. I still say the Federal Reserve was involved somehow."

Charlie bit his lip so hard it turned white. He turned his back on us and walked away.

"What?" Farnham asked. "What'd I say?"

5. Elves

THE APARTMENT ROLO AND I shared in the Marbella building worked out well for us. It didn't have the spacious luxury or commanding view of our first two rentals but the floor wasn't cracked, the stove didn't burn our food, and the balcony didn't crumble in a breeze. After our first experiences living in Panama these little things mattered.

Another thing that mattered was that we didn't have much furniture. After the flood in our second apartment I had put off buying anything other than a bed. Rolo found a new bed, couch, and TV, but that was it.

Often we would sit on the couch while eating dinner, watching Mexican game shows and commenting on the scantily-clad *mujeres* who pranced across the screen. The TV was the only thing against the wall so while the women were on it absorbed our attention. Once the show cut to commercials, though, we tended to look around the room and notice how spare it was otherwise. Until one night there was something new.

"What's that?" I asked.

Rolo eyed the leather bag against the wall. It looked like the bags we carried our flight pubs in but Rolo's bag was under the coffee table and mine was at the squadron.

"That?"

"Yeah, that bag. Where'd it come from?"

"Your pal Harry dropped it off a few days ago. He said it was for you. Sorry, I forgot to mention it."

"I didn't notice it over the weekend."

"I dumped my laundry there. Must have covered it, sorry."

The bag was black and much worn. From its appearance an airline pilot could have carried it around for decades.

"What's in it?"

"I don't know. He said it was for you."

"You didn't look?"

Rolo considered that, his mouth full of lasagna. "No."

I walked over and opened the bag. It had a flap that folded comfortably over the top and a metal snap to hold it closed. I looked inside, thought for a moment, then closed it and sat back down.

Rolo waited while I went for more lasagna.

"Well? What is it?"

"If you were so curious you should have looked last week."

He chewed his lower lip. "Yeah, I guess so," he said and went back to eating.

A variety show out of Mexico City came on. There were pop stars who sang emotional, forgettable songs and a series of skits that invariably featured women with big breasts and a screechy older man dressed in a clown suit who chased them around. The clown theme never got old in Latin America.

"I give up," he said finally. "What is it?"

"A bunch of money."

"Oh, yeah? How much?"

"I'm guessing about ten thousand dollars."

Anyone else might have yelped in surprise. Rolo did what was for him the equivalent: he put down his plate.

"Really?"

I waved to the bag. He went over and opened it, then tipped it to spill the contents onto the floor. The bills were all tens, wrapped amateurishly with bands of white paper. Rolo sifted through them, counting.

"In the movies these are always twenties," he said. "Or hundreds."

I shrugged. It was Panama.

"What's this for?"

"I don't really want it to get out," I replied.

"I won't tell a soul. Cross my heart and hope to marry a local. You're not into drugs, are you?"

"Almost. Harry needed a pilot a few months ago to fly up to Costa Rica. He wanted someone who could fly in bad weather. When we got there he stole a plane."

"Why?"

"I guess he wanted it. It was abandoned so it wasn't really stealing. Or so he said."

"And now he sold it?"

"Guess so."

Rolo thought about that. "I would have asked for more than ten grand," was all he said.

"I didn't ask for any of it."

"You could have gone to jail if you had been caught. That's worth more than ten grand."

"Twenty. Harry got half."

"Okay, then it's worth more than twenty."

"I don't know. The plane was old."

"Still." He packed the money back into the bag. "What are you going to do with it?"

"I don't know."

"You could buy furniture."

"I guess."

"Come on. You must have something in mind."

"No. Money I don't earn makes me feel funny."

"You earned this."

"No, I didn't. I did a favor for a friend. I didn't know he was going to steal something. And then he paid me for it. That's extra. I'm unclear about the whole thing."

"I think the word you want is ambivalent."

"I'm ambivalent then."

"Well, make up your mind. Having a bag of money sitting around the apartment makes *me* feel funny."

"Funny?"

"Nervous."

"Don't think about it," I suggested.

We watched the opening credits for a new *tele-novela* that was set on a ranch. There were a number of characters who posed on horses...and a guy in a clown suit.

"Okay," he agreed.

After that the bag sat in the corner untouched. From time to time it was covered with laundry. When people came over for dinner we shoved it against the TV stand with our pubs bags and flight gear. In a month we forgot about it altogether.

Mark Jonkris didn't have a bag of money in his apartment but he had every right to be nervous. Someone was out to get him. And that someone was him.

Mark was an aircraft commander in our squadron. He was friendly, bright, and a good pilot. Of medium height with pointy ears that his military haircut couldn't cover, he was the model citizen and officer most of the time, the golden boy who parents love and commanders fawn over.

But every now and then he managed to do something dumb, so dumb it would alter the trajectory of his career. And no one, least of all Mark, ever understood how it happened. He blamed his

"Inner Elf," an alter ego who would pop up randomly to burn whatever bridges Mark had spent months and years building. The expectation of imminent self-destruction explained why Mark usually looked more like a kangaroo rat scanning for owls that a rambunctious junior captain who used to turn the dullest party into a bacchanalia.

Before coming to Panama Mark had been a superstar FAIP, a first-assignment instructor pilot. Before that he had been a model student pilot. And before that he had been the number one graduate at the Citadel with an eye on an Army career.

But at the Citadel he wooed and dumped the commandant's daughter, making his infantry future perilous enough that at the last minute he switched his commission and jumped to the Air Force. As a student pilot he excelled until recklessly rolling his jet in the traffic pattern on his final solo ride. And then as a T-38 evaluator – a serious, popular, professional instructor who everyone loved and who was again on track to get the fighter plane of his choice – he made a phone call.

Specifically, from his Wing StanEval office one day he called down to the squadron to speak to an instructor friend of his. Instead of his friend, the student duty officer answered the phone.

Student Duty Officer was a thankless job. The SDO answered phones, took messages, re-stocked the snack bar, and got yelled at by everyone for anything that was wrong on the schedule. Every student got tasked with a shift and every student hated it because it was an opportunity for people to mess with you.

Without thinking, Mark said, "This is a bomb threat. There's a bomb in the building."

It was a joke. Every SDO was trained to excruciating detail on how to handle these calls – the first step was to grab the lengthy yellow Air Force Form 671 checklist and try to extract from the caller pertinent information like when will the bomb explode, what does it look like, etc. To the extent Mark thought about it at all he figured he would say the bomb was disguised as a Care Bear dressed like Tom Cruise in Top Gun and make the student write down all the silly details like how if you got too close to the bear it would say, "That's right, Ice. I *am* dangerous," and then explode. But this student freaked out. He leaped from the desk before Mark could say anything else and pulled the fire alarm, then ran through the building screaming for everyone to evacuate. Mark was left staring at his phone in horror two blocks away, shouting "No, no, no!" to no avail and wondering how the last five seconds had happened.

Even the wing commander couldn't help him after that incident. He received a Letter of Reprimand, was removed from teaching status, and as usual in these cases was ordered to accept the first assignment available that would get him away from the scene of his crime.

In Panama Mark worked to keep a low profile. He didn't complain when the Group commander refused to make him an instructor in the C-27. He said not a word when he was "loaned" to the wing staff for three months and missed out on much of the early flying in Peru. Mark knew his Inner Elf was waiting: he knew that situations would arise that seemed unfair and that would cry out for an act of desperation but he fought the urge to do anything when they did. At all costs he wanted to avoid bringing attention to himself.

For the most part he succeeded but things still happened. One night downtown he lost his temper over the stealth mariachi band. The band was a floating nuisance that popped up randomly in residential areas of Panama City between two and four a.m. and blared its twenty-man musical strength at whoever was in earshot. On any night, on any street, you could be trying to get some shut-eye when a cacophony of trumpets, guitars, and the singing of fat men in broad hats and chaps would jolt you from your bed. The usual reaction was to roll over and put a pillow over your head but one night Mark's patience snapped. Instead of rolling his eyes he threw open the window of his apartment and emptied the contents of his refrigerator onto the hapless band below. Particularly damaging were the eggs. It seems an egg dropped from nine stories can do a fair amount of damage to a guitar, not to mention the head of the man playing it. As the ambulances pulled away the police launched an investigation.

The Elf took control again in a more complicated situation. Mark dated a Chilean girl, a young idealist who worked for local museums but whose real interest was in raising funds to support impoverished villages on the Peru-Bolivia border on the way to Cochabamba. We liked her because she was from Antofogasta and we hoped that she and Mark would have a child named Antofogasta Cochabamba Jonkris, just for the sound of it. Mark was less committal. Gabriela was earnest and totally devoted to her work but sometimes she was hard to bear. At her best she was a hot Latin Florence Nightingale. At her worst she resembled those annoying people in late night commercials who harp on viewers to "support a child for only 25 cents a day." Mark was in it for the sex but when the investigation into the mariachi beatings turned serious he needed to find a new place to live and fast. When the police closed in and he needed to leave, Gabriela offered to let him move in with her. The Elf said "Yes!"

That was fine on the surface but Gabriela was conservative. Her family was conservative, too, and so was the culture of Panama in general. Sharing quarters meant marriage. Before Mark knew it the Elf had gotten them engaged.

More interesting to us was where Gabriela lived. She had a well-kept but cramped apartment just off Calle 10 in San Felipe, which was the rough, poor *corregimiento* south of El Chorillo. Our base commanders prohibited us from living there, a legacy of the fact that only a year earlier gunships had shot the place to pieces and quite a few people still resented gringos for that. Besides the hard feelings there were also regular fights, killings, riots, prostitution, and drugs in the neighborhood. But Mark and his Elf waffled on the details and didn't report his move. He argued that San Felipe was really only dangerous at night. Even so most of us figured he spent his time there wondering – once again – how he had gotten into that situation and how he would get out.

"I thought, 'Oh, I've done it again,'" Mark confided one night when Rolo and I risked a trip to Gabriela's apartment to visit him.

"Done what?" Rolo asked.

"Done something stupid," Mark said, shaking his head. "I keep getting into these situations where the right answer, the right thing to do, is so obvious but then I don't do it. I do the dumb thing instead."

In this case he wasn't talking about his living quarters. He had just returned from a trip to El Salvador where he had allowed his copilot to participate in a running of the bulls.

"Well, this wasn't your fault. You didn't make him go out on the street."

"No, but I was the aircraft commander. I should have told Little Bud he couldn't do it. He's still dizzy from the concussion."

Rolo laughed and perched with a beer on the windowsill. Outside the open window the street below was quiet. A few late evening workers hurried past the hookers who appeared on the sidewalk. One of the hookers saw Rolo and waved to him to come downstairs. He waved back with a smile and a "*Gracias, no*," and she proceeded to bitch him out in reply. Somewhere over by the water there was a gunshot and then yelling. After a while it petered out.

"That wouldn't have worked with the Chickenhawk," Rolo said. "Little Bud has the short guy complex bad. If you had told him he couldn't run then he would have ridden one of the bulls just to show you he wasn't afraid."

"The point is," said Mark, "that I *didn't* tell him. It doesn't matter if he would have listened to me.

I didn't try. It would have been the right thing but I didn't. It's like I never even try to do the right thing. He's lucky he wasn't killed. When I saw him get thrown against the wall I was sure he was dead."

Rolo giggled at the image.

"You can't always do the right thing, dude," I offered. "Sometimes you just have to do what makes sense at the moment and accept whatever happens later."

"Yeah," said Rolo. "Smart people sometimes do dumb things."

Mark sighed.

I slumped in a sagging futon pushed up against the wall. Mark sat in the only chair in the room, a steeply-angled lawn chair that fronted a coffee table in the center of the floor. The apartment was narrow and sloped toward the street. Whenever anyone went to the kitchen it was an uphill trek.

"Um, this isn't your furniture, is it?" I asked.

Mark stared around him glumly.

"No. My stuff's in storage. It'll be there until I find another place to live."

Rolo nodded. "Will that be before or after the wedding?"

Mark waved for him to be silent. "Shhhhhhh!"

Gabriela wasn't home from her office yet but to judge from Mark's face he feared she might hear Rolo across the city.

"What's the latest on that, anyway?" Rolo insisted. "You really getting married?"

Mark put his head in his hands. "Ohhhhh, I don't know how I get into these things!" he lamented.

"She's cute," I offered.

"Yeah," said Rolo. "As long as you carry a pocket of quarters to give to every homeless kid on the street. Mark, you know that if you marry this tree-hugger you're going to have to move to the Amazon and adopt a village or two. Oh, and you'll have to get about five jobs to finance her work as Saint Gabriela of the Jungle."

"Have you heard her latest?" Mark inquired, peeking out from between his fingers.

"She sold your furniture?" Rolo guessed. "To pay for a printing press that the natives can use to spread the revolutionary word?"

"No." Mark looked around to make sure no one had crept into the room to listen. "Don't tell the commander, but I mentioned to her that I had a trip next weekend to Puerto Maldonado. Now she's all excited and trying to buy a water pump that I can stick on the plane and take down for her."

"A water pump?" I asked. "It's the Amazon, Mark. They have water."

"No, it's not really a water pump. Well, it *is*... it's a pump/generator/filter thing. Really hi-tech.

And the village she supports isn't in the Amazon. It's on the edge of the jungle, east of Maldonado on the Mother of God River."

"On the edge of the jungle. Again, Mark, trust me. They have water there, too. This sounds like a scam."

"No, no. This village is in the middle of nowhere, on some backwater river – literally – and the people there have this sickness Gabriela's group is trying to cure. It has to do with their water."

"They have too much?"

"No, just the opposite. They don't have enough. Not enough good water, anyway. They drink from the river and it's got some bacteria in it that makes everybody have diarrhea and go blind."

Rolo looked at his beer. "Sounds like this stuff."

"I'm serious. They can't drink what's right there so they all rely on one spring somewhere up in the hills, hiking up there every day and hauling it down in jugs. When they run out, they drink the river water and get sick and go blind."

"Sounds kind of self-critiquing," I said.

"Well, I don't know. I've always lived where there was a sink."

"How long have they been doing this?"

"As long as they've lived there. Hundreds of years, probably."

"You would think they would have come up with a way to get around getting sick. Or their bodies would have adapted by now."

"More likely they've adapted to being sick and feeling there way around."

"Well, Gabriela and her friends are trying to help. They can't move the people so they've figured out a way to move the fresh water instead. To get it through the jungle to the village. A pipeline with a small hydro-electric generator attached. That way they get power and water. It just costs a small fortune."

"What's a small fortune?"

"Like, several thousand dollars."

"Several thousand? Oh, man! Don't tell me she talked you into buying it. She really did sell your furniture!"

Mark shook his head.

"No, no. Nothing like that. She's trying to get a couple of local banks to finance it. That's where she is tonight, meeting somebody at the Banco del Istmo."

"So the bank gives her the money, then you carry it down there? And how was she going to get it to the village?"

Mark looked up at the ceiling. "Well, Walt was going to take care of that."

"Walt? What's he got to do with this?"

"He was supposed to be the aircraft commander on this trip. See, he's been puzzling about one of the things on that list of his." From his wallet he pulled a copy of Walt's list. "You know," he said, sitting down again, "the stuff he saw in the dream? One of the things he says an Indian handed to him was the steering wheel from a ship. Ever see one? The big wheel thing with lots of handles sticking out of it?"

"In movies," I replied. "But what's there to puzzle? You can probably buy that from someone here in town."

"No, Walt says he remembers distinctly that the hand holding the wheel came from somewhere in southern Peru. Near the mountains."

Rolo and I looked at the ceiling, trying to picture a map of Peru. On the coast everything was desert. To the east was jungle. In the mountains there was some jungle but mostly it was...mountains.

"Lake Titicaca?" Rolo asked. "Does he mean Bolivia?"

Mark shook his head. "Peru."

"There are lakes there," I remembered. "And rivers. But I don't think they're big enough for steamships, anything the size of what you're talking about. Not that I know boats, though."

"Well, Walt doesn't either. But he says he read about some guy involved in the rubber trade who took a boat through the jungle in anticipation he would find water to float it on. And supposedly that boat is still out there."

"Wasn't there something else on the list from down that way?"

"Yeah, the dirt. The box of dirt he wanted from that clay lick. The locals believe it has some healing properties so that's probably why Walt's dream included it on the list. The lick's not really nearby but Puerto Maldonado's as good a jumping-off place as any to get there. Lowell already picked it up."

"Lowell?" Rolo repeated, surprised. "Lowell doesn't explore."

"I know," Mark agreed.

"So how did he come to change his mind?"

Mark held up his empty hands. "Your guess is as good as his. He was down there two weeks ago with no intention of doing anything but getting drunk and renting hookers. Then he walked by the river and out of nowhere he said he got this feeling to look at the list..."

"I hadn't heard that," Rolo said.

"He's been uncharacteristically humble about it."

"Wait a minute," I remembered. "Those clay licks are way upriver. He must have had to make quite an expedition to get to them. If he was down there long enough to do that, why didn't he get the wheel?"

"Well, he knew the wheel was in the area but by the time he got the dirt I think the magic had worn off. As you said, he's not exactly 'Mr. Enthusiasm' even on his good days. From Puerto Maldonado it took him eight hours to get up to the lick. It's way out in the middle of nowhere, a tiny spot on the river where parrots and other birds gather to munch on salt in the rocks – supposed to be a sight. But along the way he got heatstroke, then he banged up his knee, then he was bitten by a piranha..."

"A piranha?" Rolo exclaimed. "How did he get bitten by only one?"

"He caught it on a fishing pole," Mark explained, "but the thing went ballistic the instant it got in the boat. Then he got sunburned. Then there were bugs. Then he finally got to the licks and dug up the clay but there were thousands of birds over-head and right there with him – you can imagine the mess. By the end of the day he was so miser-able and filthy and mad he was ready to dump the damned stuff back into the river. Searching for a boat wheel was out of the question."

"So now Walt's going to look for it?" I asked, bringing us back to the issue at hand.

"He saw the trip come down from the Group last week. Puerto Maldonado wants to make it big as a jumping-off point for eco-tours and for that they need to attract flights from Lima and Cuzco. Prob-lem is they don't have a fire truck at their airport. Somebody bought one up here or maybe Panama donated it, I don't know. But that's what we have to do: carry a fire truck to Puerto Maldonado. Nation-building and all that, you know? It's an all-day trip so we'll get to spend the night. Maybe two. Walt scheduled himself with me as the copilot."

"But?..." Rolo asked. Mark's tone suggested already the plan was falling apart.

"But...they just tapped Walt for a TDY up to the States for a tactics conference. He tried to get out of it but Rasmussen says he's the man."

"Why do I get the feeling this doesn't bode well for me?" I asked.

Mark gave a wan smile. "Walt said you were the next best man for the job. He wants that wheel."

"Why me?"

"You speak Spanish."

"So?"

"And you do crazy things all the time."

"Yeah, but they don't start out crazy. Usually they make a whole lot more sense than this cockamamie scheme. It's only later that they go downhill."

"Yeah," said my roommate. "He doesn't have an Elf leading him astray. He's just dumb."

"Come on, Mike," Mark pleaded. "If it makes any difference to you, my evil Elf is telling me *not* to do this. I already told Gabriela no but can't get away from the fact that she's trying to help people. That's a good thing, you know?"

"Yeah, but why can't she just buy a pump down in Peru? You know, get the government to finance it or something? And get FedEx or PedroAir or something to deliver it."

Mark stared at me like I had suggested solving a cheese shortage by mining the moon.

"The Peruvian government?" he repeated. "Why would they finance a pump for some dinky village with no political clout? And FedEx doesn't deliver to the jungle. As for PedroAir...that's kind of us, isn't it?"

I finished my beer and let the bottle roll down the floor to the wall. It had been a few weeks since I had worried about dying or being thrown in jail and I didn't miss the stress. How much trouble could I get in for this?

"Walt's gonna owe me."

"Jeez!" Rolo cackled. "That wasn't much of a fight. You folded like a lawn chair."

"Well, it's not technically legal. But it's not like we get anything out of it ourselves. We could do it...maybe..." I wavered.

"Wuss," my roommate muttered. "I don't know why I bother."

"You could go in his place," Mark suggested.

"Right. Sure. Of course I could. In fact, I was just going to volunteer. Oh, wait. You've already mentioned at least two extracurricular activities that are worthy of a court-martial. Besides, there's three of you in the cockpit already – you two and the evil Elf. There's no room for me."

"You could show a little faith," I urged. "Maybe the Elf has lost his edge."

Rolo smiled. "Sure," he said. "And maybe Panas like hard work. Not likely, my friends." He took a last gulp of his beer and stood up. "On that note, I'm out of here. I've got an evil elf of my own and he's telling me to go downstairs and have a word with that ho."

The next week Mark and I landed at Puerto Maldonado in late afternoon. The place wasn't pretty. It was muddy and muggy and no one seemed to have a plan for what the town was supposed to look like. The airport was a good example. It sat four miles from town on swampy ground that had no obvious reason to recommend itself for the landing of airplanes. A kudzu fallow flanked one side while on the other was a marsh filled with upland rice. The runway itself was dry but a section of the paved area had settled into the muck and already begun to separate from the rest.

At about the thousand-foot-down point when landing to the north a crevasse opened up in the center of the strip. The locals knew of the fissure, of course, but even before the issue of getting money to fix it there was the problem of figuring out who could make the decision to do so. Apparently no one could because all arriving planes either hit the crack, landed left of it and rolled through the dirt, or landed past it and stood on their brakes to stop before hitting the swamp. The skill of arriving pilots varied as evidenced by a handful of aircraft carcasses lying in the mud around the field, slowly sinking into oblivion. Harry would have had a field day collecting parts.

"Have you been here before?" Mark asked after we off-loaded the fire truck.

"No."

"It looks like Iquitos."

His observation came from the fact that the airfield was eerily quiet, surrounded by jungle, and had a handful of *motocarros* (motorcycle taxis) parked outside the one-story terminal building. By that logic every airport in the Amazon Basin looked like Iquitos.

We took two taxis into town. The road was dirt and the damage every pothole did to the motorcycle was more than the driver would make up from our fare.

A town of ten thousand people, Puerto Maldonado had only one hotel. The reason for that was that hardly anyone ever visited. There was one road to Cuzco and it was in such bad shape that it was described by any who traveled it as *the* worst road in all of Peru, which said a lot. What visitors did arrive usually came by boat.

Puerto Maldonado was a port, after all, and sat at the junction of the Tambopata and Madre de Dios rivers. We found rooms in the hotel, which was at the north end of town on Billinghurst Street which ran along the bluff above the river. Below the bluff were high reeds and long-rooted trees that choked the soggy ground leading to the river's shore. Running through them was a wooden pier where boats tied up to accept and deliver cargo.

"Nice," I said as we rolled to a stop. "*Muy bonita.*"

The hotel wasn't nice at all. It was three stories of loose clapboard topped by tin plates. When the driver stopped he had to park two feet from the wooden sidewalk due to the gulley worn by rainwater that poured off the roof.

"*Sí!*" he replied with enthusiasm. "There will be more soon. *Puerto Maldonado es muy importante. Vamos a ser grande!*" He held out his arms to show just how big the town would soon be.

"Really?" our loadmaster replied. Junior Flats was skeptical. After the driver had gone he confided, "They can build as many hotels as they want. This place is still a hole."

Our cynicism aside, the driver's optimism was evident everywhere in town. There was a frontier atmosphere to the place, an excitement that came from thinking anything was possible. Mark called it a boom town waiting to happen. Somebody must have thought so: we had brought them a fire truck, after all, presumably to help build an infrastructure that could deal with all the new people someone expected to come to town. Or, conversely, to deal with the inevitable fiery crash that would result when nobody fixed the runway.

There were soldiers on the streets. It was common to see two or three walking along with their rifles dangling almost to the dirt. They were there because of the proximity of the border more than any threat from rebels. Still, when we went out looking for the office of Gabriela's aid organization their presence made me feel guilty. I was here to find a boat wheel. Any sign of local authority reminded me I probably wasn't supposed to have it.

We walked to the south end of town but didn't find the office we were looking for. A woman selling boiled *plátanos* told us she thought the office had closed. A rainstorm came through, dripping onto her stove and making a sizzle that rose with steam from the bananas.

"Hey, look at that!" Mark grabbed my arm and pointed. "That street is named 'Fitzcarrald'!"

"So?"

"So, Fitzcarraldo is the name of the guy who had the boat."

"What boat?"

"The boat with the wheel. The one you're looking for. He was a rubber baron or something. Didn't you see the movie?"

"No."

"Well, you should have."

"Wait, there's a movie about this boat? Is that where Walt got this crazy idea?"

"No, I already asked him that. He'd never heard of it."

In the marketplace we drank hot chocolate and asked among the locals for information on Gabriela's village. The problem was that the village didn't have a name. It was an Indian community near the Las Pampas nature reserve about halfway to the border with Bolivia. That was only 20 miles as the condor flies but it was an hour and a half by boat, an eternity in a land where most people never left town.

"We're not having any luck," Junior commented. "You should have brought your girlfriend with you," he told Mark.

Mark shook his head and thought for a minute.

"Ask them about the boat," he suggested to me.

I asked the boy who sold us the hot chocolate if he knew anything about a crazy rubber baron and a big boat. He in turn asked some grown-ups nearby who immediately nodded and smiled.

"Fitzcarraldo?" Mark prompted.

The locals giggled and said yes. They pointed downriver and then vied to tell us what they knew. The most animated was a twenty-something man with a nervous smile and black hair combed flat in a style that hadn't been popular in the U.S. since Watergate. Fitzcarraldo's boat is only an hour away, he assured us. Near the cacao plantation along the river.

Then an older man stepped into the conversation. He had been hanging on the sidelines smoking a pipe but now he said something in a language I didn't understand. Whatever it was provoked a mild argument.

"What's that about?" Mark asked.

"It is not Fitzcarraldo's boat," the old man explained, speaking in Spanish now.

"What do you mean? There really was a Fitzcarraldo, wasn't there?"

He smiled patiently. "Fitzcarraldo was real. The boat is real. But it is not Fitzcarraldo's boat. Moisés just wants to take your money."

The man gestured in a friendly way to the guy with the black hair, who smiled, not denying any of it.

Junior handed me a crude tourist brochure that he had picked up at the hotel. He pointed to a tag in red letters on the bottom that offered a trip to Fitzcarraldo's boat for only six dollars. I showed it to the old man.

He shook his head in irritation.

"Of course. The boatmen want to make money, too, so they say what visitors want to hear. If they say it's just a broken-down boat, who will want to go?"

"Is it a paddle wheel? Does it look like Fitzcarraldo's boat?"

That was tough to translate. I didn't know how to say 'paddle wheel' in Spanish and the old man hadn't seen the movie. We went through a few minutes of interpretive dance.

"Oh, no!" the man laughed. "It's just an old fishing boat!"

That wasn't what we expected. Mark, Junior, and I discussed our options and debated whether to try to see the boat anyway. I asked where it was again and the crowd of people pointed.

"Downriver?" Mark repeated.

"Something wrong?"

"That's not what Walt said. He said it was close to the mountains. That's upriver."

The mountains were a long way away. I commented as much.

"I know but this still doesn't feel right. It's too pat."

We had come three thousand miles to a rainy town in the Amazon and the boat was another twenty miles away down a snake-infested river. His definition of 'pat' eluded me.

"*Qué buscan Uds?*" the old man asked.

I answered that we were actually looking for two things. The desire to find the wheel aroused a little sympathy but it seemed the crowd offered that only because they respected that Walt had had a vision in the first place, not because they wanted to help him achieve it. However, when I explained about Gabriela's generator the crowd looked at us in a new light. Ahh, so we were here to give, not just to take!

"If you are here to help the village," the older man said with enthusiasm, "then we can help you."

He held another conversation with the crowd in their local language. Eventually Moisés announced that he knew someone who could help us. He left the marketplace and promised to be back in half an hour.

While he was gone an old woman sidled up to me and whispered in my ear.

"There's another boat?" I confronted the old man.

"Qué?"

"Another boat," I repeated. "There's one down-river but there's one upriver, too. Is that right?"

He wavered, clearly less enthusiastic about the upriver option.

"There is a boat," he acknowledged. "But it is farther."

Mumbling in the crowd suggested that wasn't the only problem.

"There are bandits, too," he finally admitted. "You should go downriver."

"But which one is the Fitzcarraldo boat?" Mark pressed. "Which is the big one?"

Half a dozen hands came up in the crowd, pointing toward the mountains. The old man, however, rushed to reassure us.

"You don't need to go that way," he promised. "It is dangerous. Go to the boat downriver."

"But why would we go to that way if it isn't what we want?"

The old man shrugged. "It's easier to get to."

True to his word, Moisés returned thirty minutes later with Eudes. Eudes worked at the pier, Moisés explained, and took people downriver all the time. He didn't know Gabriela but was pretty sure he knew which Indian community we were interested in.

Eudes didn't confirm everything Moisés said. In fact, he didn't confirm anything because he didn't talk. He was thin, dressed in shorts despite the evening chill, and wore a white cloth hat that covered his head like half an eggshell. He had a round nose and the tendency to stare open-mouthed into the distance when people talked to him, especially women. When the old woman said something to him he turned away.

"Something wrong?" I asked.

Moisés shook his head.

"Women make him angry," he explained.

"Tell him to join the club. But does he have a boat? Can he take us to the village to deliver the pump?"

Moisés looked at Eudes who nodded.

"Yes," said Moisés.

"Can we also stop and see the 'Fitzcarraldo' boat?"

Moisés got another nod from Eudes.

"Yes."

"Well," I said to Mark. "That seems to be settled."

"We going to need a translator?" he asked, nodding to Eudes.

I shrugged but Moisés understood Mark's concern.

"Do not worry," he promised. "Eudes is a good boatman. He just does not like to talk."

"And he doesn't like women."

"Yes, he does not like women. But mostly he does not like to talk."

"That's okay."

"And he does not like people to talk to him too much. And you will not like it, either."

"Why? What does he do?"

Moisés sucked in his breath and raised his eyebrows, picturing the scene. Then he exhaled.

"Just don't talk too much," he repeated.

"How much is too much?"

"Oh," he laughed. "He is fine for you today."

So half our problem was solved. That was better than nothing. Now the issue became one of timing.

The next morning we flew to Lima and picked up the water tank for the fire truck. We were back in Puerto Maldonado by two o'clock and on Eudes' boat by two-thirty.

The trip down the Mother of God River was beautiful and quiet. Ten minutes out of Puerto Maldonado we saw no one but the occasional fisherman in a reed canoe.

Eudes' boat was sturdy. Ugly but sturdy. It was a pontoon boat with no railings, an aluminum floor, and a torn yellow canopy to block the rain. It was as aesthetically pleasing as a box car. There was nothing on it but some boxes of engine oil, an old Coleman cooler where Eudes kept fish he caught, and the mount for the outboard motor.

The motor pushed us into the current with a modest *whirrrr* and then marked time as we drifted along. We stacked Gabriela's generator and its accessories in the middle of the boat. With no waves and little acceleration there was no need even to tie them down. Then with nothing else to do we sat and watched the shoreline pass, the dark water doing what it always did in this part of the world, rising into the trees so it was never clear where the river stopped and the jungle began.

"How long?" Mark asked our boatman. "How long to the village?"

Eudes didn't look at him but he did reply. *"Una hora."* It was the first thing we had heard him say.

"You know, something just occurred to me," Mark said a moment later. "What are we supposed to do with this stuff once we get there?"

"What do you mean?"

"Well, do we just throw it on the beach and say, 'Here you go?' I don't know who's going to be there."

"Didn't Gabriela give you any contacts?"

"Um, not really."

"Did you ask for any?"

"Look, I was doing her a favor. I thought we would bring the pump to town and that was it."

"She didn't tell you anything?"

"Yeah, she told me there was an office for her aid group, Proyecto de Ayuda. There isn't. And some guy named Alfredo. He isn't, either. That guy at the market told me there might be someone named Hector out here. Obviously things have changed since the last time she was down here."

"When was that?"

"Several months ago, I think."

"But Hector works for the same agency?"

"No, a different one, I think. I got the impression there's competition between his group and Gabriela's. Who knows why – it's not like there's a shortage of poor people down here."

"So they don't even work together?"

Mark shrugged.

"The market dude said they work together all the time. They just don't get along. It's a funds thing."

Junior spat and kicked a june bug that flew out of the trees and landed on the floor of the boat. The bug skidded across the aluminum and plopped into the river behind us. Something ate it before it could sink.

"You know," he said. "There seem to be a lot of things about this adventure that you don't know. For officers you guys don't do a lot of planning ahead."

"Hey," I pointed out. "I was a last-minute add-on to this little trip so don't blame me."

"Well, I don't like boats so this village better not be too far."

"You could have stayed in town," Mark reminded him.

"And never see you guys again? Not likely. I'm coming along so I can bring back at least one of you to fly me home."

An hour out from Puerto Maldonado Eudes pointed the boat upstream into a tributary. At its mouth a tall chicle tree fallen from the bank lay over the water. The current pushed it parallel to the shore and now it pointed the way for us, accompanied by a trio of giant otters that basked on its sun-bleached bark.

"*Paucarmanu está aquí,*" he announced, but then pointed farther down the Madre de Dios. "*La barca está allá.*"

Mark's Spanish was pretty good. "Paucarmanu. I guess our village has a name."

"Yes, but the boat's over there."

"One thing at a time."

Paucarmanu was two miles up the tributary. How Gabriela found this place was beyond me. The tributary was half the size of the Madre de Dios and had bends tight enough that when we rounded them overhanging trees scraped against the boat. The water was deep. Near the shore were roots that stretched yards from their owners and posed a hazard Eudes was careful to avoid. Cecropia and rainforest palms abounded, standing in and out of the water and making it hard to know where the shore lay. Butterflies flew everywhere while macaws and parakeets clustered on branches overhanging the water.

We rounded another bend and saw the river widen. On the far bank was a collection of huts. Several cayucas sat on the beach near them, half in and half out of the water.

At first glance Paucarmanu encouraged the doubts we shared earlier: primitive to the point of any modern technology being useless. Fortunately, we were naive. As Eudes guided his boat onto the sandbar a half-dozen people who looked like they could have just walked off the streets of Puerto Maldonado trotted down a staircase carved into the hill.

"Hola!" one of them called and waved to us.

He turned out to be Hector. He was a native of Lima who worked for a different non-profit group than Gabriela but who lived sometimes in Paucarmanu because he hated staying in Puerto Maldonado.

"It's boring," he explained. "And every building has those tin roofs. When it rains I can't sleep from the noise." He marveled over the generator. "*Increíble!* Where? How? And how did you get it here?"

We told him about Gabriela's efforts in Panama. At her name Hector glowered, jealous.

"I could have gotten one in Lima," he insisted.

Hector gave us a quick tour of the village. He spent most of the time explaining how his aid organization was superior to Gabriela's even if she had found a way to buy a pump. When he offered to take us farther up the hill to show where the hydroelectric project was underway we declined. The guy was too interested in his own empire for our tastes. Besides, we had only two hours of daylight and still had to get to Fitzcarraldo's boat.

"This boat had better be close. It'll be dark in a while," Junior said as we cast off from the village.

"Our driver says it's close."

"Yeah, but farther down the river."

"Junior, you could have stayed in town."

"Oh, no."

"Then quit complaining."

"Who's complaining?"

"You are."

"I'm not complaining. And may I point out that this part of the trip at least made sense. Going to this boat sure doesn't. They'll test us for drugs when we get back, this is so stupid."

"What do you mean?"

"I mean, the good captain here is set: now that he's delivered his woman's generator to the village he's gonna get laid for the next six months easy. She's going to be real grateful. A little charity in return, if you know what I mean. You, sir, on the other hand, aren't getting anything out of finding this boat. Am I right?"

"Not really..."

"Well," said Mark. "Walt will be happy."

"Ah, yes," Junior agreed. "But I think we can all agree that the gratitude of the squadron scheduler isn't the same as the gratitude of a woman. In other words, you won't be getting laid if you find this boat hook, will you?"

"Wheel. It's a boat wheel."

"Whatever. No sex for you, is there?"

"No."

"In that case, may I suggest that we just forget about it and head straight back to town to find some hookers?"

"No!" Mark and I said in unison.

The otters were gone when we emerged from the tributary. Eudes pointed the boat downstream.

"*Cuánto tiempo?*"

"Diez minutos."

It was more than ten minutes away. We passed the cacao plantation or so Eudes said – the only sign of it was a wooden dock jutting into the river. Half a mile beyond it was another feeder stream. Eudes steered his boat into the mouth of the stream and immediately had to yank the motor out of the water as the river shallowed. The bottom scraped against sand.

"Allá," he pointed.

I looked around. There was nothing in sight but the stream and an adjacent bluff. The bluff was a full boat length away. We had come to with the current against a deadfall of two trees. Climbing over them was the only way to cover the twenty feet to land.

"Where?"

Eudes indicated that there was a path.

"A path? To the boat?"

Eudes nodded and pointed again. It was hard to understand a man who so loathed to talk. So far, however, Moisés' promise held good: Eudes didn't freak out on us. Finally we dragged out of him that the stream used to go farther; the boat we were looking for was up another few hundred yards but to get there we had to cut over land.

"Oh, no-no-no," Junior protested. "I saw this in Apocalypse Now. Never get off the boat, you guys."

"It's just up the way a little," Mark argued, though he, too, looked at the trees with considerable doubt.

"Not a chance. I'll wait here."

"What about making sure we're okay so you can fly home?"

"I'll make sure you're okay from right here. If you get eaten by a jaguar, yell for help."

"And what'll you do?"

"I'll go back to town and find a hooker."

Mark and I looked at the shore.

"So how do we get there? Climb the tree?"

The fallen trees were old enough to be bare of leaves but they still had sharp branches. Mark took a second look over the side.

"Maybe we can wade there."

But as he started to climb overboard Eudes grabbed his arm.

"*Arena movediza*," he said, pointing at the current.

"What's that?"

Eudes pointed at the current again and made a sucking sound.

"Quicksand?"

Eudes nodded and smiled. He seemed to like his role of bearer of bad news.

Mark shook his head.

"Walt can come get his own wheel," he said. "I'll wait here with Junior."

"Oh, come on."

"Mike, you want to walk on a thin tree trunk over quicksand just to get a moldy old boat wheel?"

"I thought you said this wasn't even the right boat."

"Then it's even dumber. You're going to walk on a thin tree trunk over quicksand to get the wrong boat wheel. And we could get lost in there."

He had a point. I turned back to Eudes.

"*Muéstrenos el sendero, por favor.*"

Eudes pointed at his boat. I told him Junior would stay and watch it for him. He wavered. I told him we would go to the steamboat and come right back. He wavered some more. I offered to pay him five dollars. He swung himself over the side and onto the nearest tree limb. With no shoes on, in fifteen seconds he was across the tree trunk and standing on the shore.

"Looks like we have a guide," I said, and followed him.

Mark wavered, watching me maneuver between the branches, then decided he couldn't let me go without him. He jumped onto the tree and caught up with me just as I reached shore.

"Your evil elf couldn't resist," I snickered.

"My evil elf wanted to stay on the boat."

"Hey!" Junior called. "You guys can't leave me here alone!"

Eudes mumbled something behind me.

"What'd he say?"

"He said you're not alone. There are crocodiles in the river so don't go to sleep."

On the river sunlight made the current sparkle. In the jungle it threw only scattered rays above our heads. As soon as we left the bluff the light dimmed. Foliage closed around us.

"These things have spikes!" Mark whispered as he stepped cautiously around plants, trying to keep up with Eudes. "Ow! You can't even see some of these things."

"Don't touch," I recommended. "And don't fall down."

"This is a scary place," he said. "I don't understand how anyone can live here."

"Nobody does live here," I pointed out.

"There's probably some odd stuff in here. Stuff that science doesn't know about yet."

"The stuff science does know about is odd enough," I told him.

We squished our way up the trail. I wished I'd worn shoes sturdier than sneakers.

The path often vanished to my untrained eye but Eudes followed it as though walking in a park. After ten minutes he stopped and stepped aside. He gestured forward.

"What?" Mark asked. "What is it?"

It was the boat. The stream at whose mouth Eudes' boat was parked ran this far into the trees and then cut left, crossing our path. At this spot it was no more than a trickle at the bottom of a wide ravine. Trees grew up where once flowed water deep enough to carry a forty-foot boat. We knew that because in front of us now, squatting almost level in the near side of the ravine, was a forty-foot boat.

It was metal or it had been, at least. Now it was rusted from bow to stern. Most of the hull was hidden in underbrush but the midsection was accessible. The wheelhouse was encased in vines cast down from the trees above.

"It looks like it's being swallowed," breathed Mark.

"It is," I said. "I wonder how long it's been here?"

I posed the question to Eudes who shrugged and signaled with his hands – maybe sixty years.

"Sixty years? I'm amazed we can see it at all."

At spots around the boat someone in the past had chopped away trees and bushes to gain a handhold on the deck railings. Though the vessel had sunk into the mud, the deck still rose six feet above the ground, high enough that one had to be prudent about clambering over the side. At the stern a wooden ladder had long since disintegrated, leaving only rusted stanchions and a base plate abeam the tiller. Someone had leaned a long metal fence post back there to facilitate climbing. Midships was a wooden plank for the same purpose.

"What do you think?" Mark whispered.

"I think there's absolutely nothing of value left on this boat," I told him. "And I think that if I were a deadly venomous snake looking for a place to live, this is where I would hide out. You'd better be careful climbing up there."

"Me? Why me?"

"Why not you? This was your idea."

"No, the pump was my idea. This is Walt's idea. You're Walt's stand-in."

Eudes stood at the top of the trail, bored.

"Well, I'm not going up there alone," I vowed.

Mark looked at the rusted hull from several angles. The boat's design was unimaginative: blocky and wide with a shallow draft. The closer you stood to the hull the more you had to look straight up.

"We should have brought gloves," was all he said.

In the end we went for the midsection. He made a cradle with his hands and hoisted me high enough that I could see what I was climbing into before launching myself over the side. Then when I was aboard I leaned over and pulled him up. Stuck in the mud and pinned by roots, the boat didn't even creak.

The deck was intact but nowhere in sight. It lay somewhere beneath a loamy layer of dead plants and dirt. All vertical structures on the planking had long since collapsed, the exceptions being two knee-high sponsons toward the aft end that may have once held fuel.

"Be careful," I advised. "This deck might be rotted."

"Oh, it's definitely rotted," Mark agreed. "Look at that."

He pointed to a hole toward the back of the boat. It was three feet across and pitch black inside.

"Is that a hole or a hatch?"

"I don't know. Let me see."

"You see. I'm going up front. If there's a wheel we're taking it and getting out of here."

I maneuvered with care to the wheelhouse. The vegetation on the deck had been there so long it was no longer just fallen leaves. It was its own top-soil. Plants grew out of it as high as my waist and the ground layer was spongy.

My trip was short. There were two steps going up to the wheelhouse but I could see before climbing them that it would be in vain. Part of a wall had col-lapsed, revealing everything inside. Revealing noth-ing inside, that is. Even the instruments were long since ripped from the panel. If there ever had been a wheel it was nothing like what all of us treasure hunters imagined: the hole where it belonged was too small. This boat came with something akin to a cockpit yoke and no more. We had wasted a trip.

"We can go," I relayed to Mark back at the stern. "There's no wheel here."

He was in an uncomfortable crouch behind the hole in the deck, doing what we called the "Thunderbird squat" in honor of the Air Force performance team who thought it looked cool. The position was necessary due to the angle of the hole and to the vines that spread like power cables across the deck. Mark peered past them into the hold.

"Nothing? Nothing at all?"

"*Nada.* What's down there?"

He maneuvered sideways and crouched lower.

"I can't...tell. Something. There's a lot of stuff in the way."

"There's probably a giant fricking python down there. I wouldn't be too curious."

"Yeah, yeah."

"Dude, I'm telling you..."

"No, Mike. Something's catching the light."

Keeping back from the hole I worked my way around an old boom stand that still clutched a coil of steel cable. From the other side I saw into the hole but not well. The light was fading fast. All I could make out was that the plant life below was at least as dense as the stuff on deck.

"We should have brought a flashlight," Mark lamented. "There's something down there."

"Moldy plants," I told him. "Let's get out of here before the mosquitoes come out."

"Just a minute."

He leaned behind him and grabbed the fence post.

"What are you doing?"

The post was thin but heavy enough that he needed both hands to maneuver it. Balancing on two tangles of creeper vines he angled it through the hatch.

"There's something shiny, I'm telling you. I'm not going down there but let's see if I can hook it and bring it up. See, it's just off to the left..."

He was right. Now that I was at his angle I could see something glisten in the darkness. Every now and then it shimmered in the light that still made its way through the trees, an ecru tint that bounced in the shadows below. It was a fascinating illusion that enticed me despite my suspicions. Several seconds went by before I made the connection.

"Mark, that's a web!"

"It's what?"

"It's webbing, you idiot. Put that down!"

He dropped the fence post like it was hot but it was too late. We had already knocked on the wrong door. Just as the post *squished* into the muddy deck, the scariest creature I'd ever seen in my life flew out of the hatch and landed on the sponson next to Mark.

"*Guauugggh!*" Mark yelled.

He jumped away so fast that he would have landed on me had I not jumped faster. Forgetting about the deck giving way, I spun around the boom stand and jumped for the railing where we had climbed aboard, launching myself into space and rolling onto the ground below. I came up covered in mud but was off and running before Mark cleared the deck, stopping only when Eudes grabbed my arm.

"*Qué pasó?!*" he exclaimed.

I couldn't form words but suddenly I didn't have to. The monster tarantula leaped across the deck to the mass of steel cable. It poised there as though for another jump, it's hairy legs stretching out to all sides. The thing was the size of a Frisbee.

"*Allí!*"

Mark popped up alongside us and looked back. "Oh, my god!" was all he could say. "Oh, my god!"

Eudes took several steps back to increase our already thirty-foot spacing.

The spider jumped from the cable to the boom, a move which nearly gave me another heart attack. It sat there on an old piece of red paint, waving two legs.

"What the hell?" I said. "What is it? *Qué es?*"

"*Comedor de pollo,*" Eudes said.

"A chicken eater?" I said. "What's a chicken eater?"

"The largest spider in the world," Eudes explained, suddenly loquacious though he never took his eyes off the tarantula. "In Venezuela they say they have a bird eater, but this one is bigger."

I hoped to hell there was nothing bigger. This spider was easily a foot across from leg to leg. Chicken, hell. It could have taken down a mule.

"Don't worry," said Eudes. "It's not poisonous."

"It doesn't have to be, you fool," Mark hissed. "Those fangs will cut your head off!"

He sounded in pain and I looked at him. His left hand was covered in blood.

"Dude! What did you do?"

"Oh, man..."

He'd caught it on the boom while jumping over the side. Something ripped his hand open from the meaty part of the palm straight up to his little finger. So much blood streamed out that his pant leg was wet. I realized what the tarantula was sitting on wasn't paint.

Mark pushed the flaps of skin together and tried to hold them there. I peeled off my shirt and tore it into three strips. With Eudes' help we lashed them around Mark's hand and wrist. By the third wrapping all the fabric below was soaked. Mark's face turned pale.

I looked to Eudes to tell him that we needed to get back to his boat but Eudes was staring up at the spider. Around the boom a score or more of smaller tarantulas suddenly appeared. They crawled over the railing and started down the side of the boat. Eudes spun on his heel.

"Vamanos!" he called.

Only when we were in the middle of the river motoring upstream did I know we had gotten away.

Mark of course got in trouble upon returning to Panama. The flight doc grounded him and referred him to a physical therapist. Lt Col Rasmussen had no choice but to give him some kind of administrative punishment for being stupid and injuring himself on duty. I received a Letter of Counseling, too, but it was the kind the colonel promised to keep in his desk for six months and shred later if I stayed out of trouble. The "counsel" he gave me was that I seemed to hang around with a lot of people who did dumb and dangerous things.

"You need to assert yourself more, Mike. You're one of the few guys here who really has everything together. You've got a good head on your shoulders but there are times when you just don't use it."

But the colonel was wrong. I didn't have anything together. Worse, I had a feeling I would keep hanging around the wrong people.

Junior was wrong, too. Despite Mark's accident, no one ever tested us for illegal drugs.

But Junior was right about one thing: Mark became a hero to Gabriela for taking the pump to her village. She shagged him silly during his recovery and then went down to Puerto Maldonado soon afterward to survey the new installation herself.

It was because I was in trouble that I missed out on the next trip south.

Gabriela swooned over Mark's sacrifice. Besides sex, she decided to make it up to him by getting our ship's wheel for us. Mark was the first to hear about it because soon after her disappearance Hector called him from Peru. Mark immediately called Walt, who phoned Rolo, who called me.

"She was what?" I shouted into the phone. "Rolo, I'm in Honduras and the connection isn't the best, but that's the craziest thing I've ever heard in my life. Say it again."

"Kidnapped by monkeys," he repeated. "I guess she went upriver to wherever this boat was and these giant apes grabbed her and took her into the jungle."

It was late and I had worked all day. As punishment for my poor judgment, Rasmussen had sent me to Soto Cano Air Base for a month to work with the Army. He knew I hated ground-pounding so part of my penance was to sit at at an empty airfield in the Honduran desert and think about my sins.

All that thinking must have confused me because all of a sudden my roommate was speaking Greek.

"Rolo, hang up. I'm calling Walt."

I caught Walt at home and got the story straight. Then I called my roommate back.

"*Guer*rillas, Rolo! *Guer*rillas, not *gor*illas. Rebels!"

"Oh," he said. "Okay, that makes more sense."

Nobody knew who kidnapped Gabriela. Hector received a note from her two days after she went upriver. She said she was okay and had found the ship's wheel but that armed men had kidnapped her and wanted $25,000 for her release. If they didn't get it within the week they threatened to kill her.

Mark went crazy from worry. He called the U.S. Embassy in Panama. He called the Peruvian Embassy and the ambassador from Chile. He called Quarry Heights and the wing commander and Vince. He bought a commercial ticket to Lima with the intention of going to Puerto Maldonado on his own but then couldn't get a visa. His hand became infected and he needed daily treatment at the hospital but still he wanted to go south. He talked about stealing a C-27.

Rolo updated me on all the events through daily phone calls from Panama that as often as not were wildly inaccurate.

"Someone said it's a group of about a thousand guys, maybe a whole new rebel group."

"Who said that?"

"I don't know. I just heard it over lunch."

"Rolo, people get kidnapped all the time in these countries. It doesn't have to be a major military operation."

"Yeah, but we don't know that it wasn't."

"Well, stop guessing. You'll just make the situation worse by spreading rumors. She was kidnapped and somebody wants a ransom. That much you know so go with it."

"We're trying. It's just that we can't get anybody to help on this."

"Why can't all those soldiers down there do something?" I asked. "When we were there we couldn't swing an iguana without hitting a couple of them on patrol."

"I don't know," he replied, the connection scratchier than ever since we were talking via a military line from Honduras to Howard Air Base and then through a phone patch to our apartment downtown. "Mark said they weren't there anymore. Pulled out for some reason. And you know that town has no cops."

"But what about the embassy?" I insisted.

"Which one?" Rolo snorted. "Get this: she's a Chilean citizen traveling on a Panamanian passport and working in Peru on a tourist visa. A *tourist* visa, not a guest worker visa. Everybody says she's not their problem. And I guess somebody in Lima told Mark they don't believe she's even been kidnapped."

"What do you mean?"

"They think she might have run off with someone."

"But her fiancé is in Panama."

"Exactly. The Peruvians think she went to Puerto Maldonado to get away from him."

"They obviously don't know Gabriela. It's more likely that Mark would have paid a rebel group to kidnap her."

"Yeah, well," Rolo sighed. "They don't believe she's been kidnapped at all."

"When are they going to believe it?" I asked. "When they pluck her body from the Tambopata?"

"Hey, don't say that, dude."

"Well, I don't know what kidnappers are like down there. And let's say it *is* rebels. If they're Sendero they might have killed her already. Who else is down there? It wouldn't be Tupac Amaru – they like flakes like her but they never leave the cities. Maybe this is some private operation – you know, target of opportunity and all that."

Rolo chewed over that for a while.

"Well," he said. "Mark's getting desperate. Everybody's trying to think of something."

"Like what? A mercenary operation? That's out of our league. Did someone talk to Vince?"

"Yeah, we did. He's up in Costa Rica getting revenge on someone there but Harry sent him a message. He can't help. If it were Colombia he could help but Peru's out of his neighborhood."

"So, what then?"

Rolo sighed. "I don't know but Walt's working something. We're counting on him."

Walt was working something but it aborted quickly. He tried to pursue a lead through Harry, who had bought a stolen airplane from a Chinese businessman in Colón, who had received the plane as collateral from a drug dealer in Caracas who had flown the plane up from Bolivia with the connivance of corrupt Peruvian air traffic controllers at a military base in Tacna. Talk about a long shot. In Walt's fevered imagination this connection could lead to influence over a band of jungle thugs in the Andean foothills. Fortunately, Harry raised the b-s flag early.

"Whoa, whoa, whoa!" my Costa Rica partner in crime called out, shaking his head and crossing his arms. "Step back from La-La land, gentlemen. There's a much easier, much faster, and much-more-likely-to-succeed way to handle this."

Walt and Mark stood in the hangar where Harry had all the parts of a C-130 pressurization control laid out in no order whatsoever on a greasy drop cloth. They begged to know what that way was.

"You're looking at this from the wrong angle," Harry lectured. "You're looking at this as a crime."

"It IS a crime!" Mark shouted. "They kidnapped my girlfriend!"

"It's not a crime at all. It's a business venture."

"So what are you saying?"

Harry spread his palms as though the answer was obvious.

"Pay them."

"I don't have $25,000," I told Rolo over the phone.

"Neither does anybody else," he said. "And the guys who do – like Flutie – can't get it quickly. Not in cash, anyway, and I've never heard of kidnappers who take checks. Vince has it but he won't be back until Saturday. Walt's got a plane laid on for tomorrow."

"What do you mean, 'laid on?'"

"There was a Guard C-130 heading to Chiclayo but Walt got the guys at the Group to change the loads so a C-27 could go instead. Then he found out there was another 'nation-building' load sitting on the ground in Lima that Faucett airlines was supposed to take to Puerto Maldonado. He called the station manager in Lima, that guy Georgie who looks like Benny Hill, and got him to make up some story for the AOC why a Chuck had to deliver it instead. So this is a rush job but under the circumstances you can see why everybody's going along with it."

"Who's flying the plane?"

"Well, Mark wants to go, of course, but the Pinheads have duct-taped him to a gurney in their house. They know if he goes down there we'll be out one pilot and probably have an Andean war on our hands. Besides, his hand's still infected. He messed it up so bad he may not fly again."

"So it's Walt then?"

"Of course. He asked Charlie Manson to be his copilot but Charlie...well, you know. He never liked Gabriela in the first place and besides he hates being shot at."

"So it's you?"

"Can't, I'm DNIF. Threw out my back scrubbing the toilet."

"Who is it, then?"

"Well, Walt wanted somebody big, tough, and mean."

"We don't have anyone like that."

"I know. So instead he's decided to go with meek and polite in the hopes that'll keep the bad guys calm. He's taking Evan."

"Evan? Our narcoleptic conspiracy theorist? The only kidnappings he's familiar with are the alien kind. Besides, at the first sign of trouble he'll fall asleep."

"I know. But he volunteered. He speaks Spanish and he's hoping if he saves Gabriela she'll hook him up."

"Tell him not to count on it. Couldn't Walt find somebody bigger? Evan's no taller than he is."

"I know, they're both leprechauns. Maybe Walt's thinking there'll be safety in numbers."

"How's that?"

"Jem's going, too."

"Another short guy. Why's he going? He's got a girlfriend."

"Dixie? She's not his girlfriend. They just hang out because she likes his Jeep. He's not going for the women, though. He's going to keep an eye on Evan. You know those two are joined at the hip – they fly together, drink together; they even share the same hookers. Besides, if anything happens to Evan, Jem will have to move out of their apartment because he can't afford it on his own."

"Does Rasmussen know?"

"Are you kidding?" my roommate said. "You can't involve a commander in stuff like this. As a person he might be all for it but as a commander he's got that long leash of responsibility around his neck. He would quash it in an instant."

I could see this all going very bad very quickly. For just a moment I was glad I was stuck in Honduras.

"Anyway, we need cash. I called to know if I can offer Walt your bag o' money."

It took a few seconds to remember what Rolo was talking about.

"Oh, the one by the TV? Sure, go ahead. It's not enough, though."

"Walt's hoping they can bargain."

"Take Harry along. He's good at that."

Walt didn't take Harry. Harry was too good at negotiating and that's why Walt didn't want him. Walt feared that even in a hostage situation Harry might smell a business opportunity and make promises or offer stock options that would just confuse the issue. Instead Walt convinced another mechanic to go with him, our reclusive de-briefer who went by the name of Johnny Luca.

Johnny was another bit player in the strange cast of characters who were drawn by gravity to contract jobs in Panama. He wasn't strange like Vince in that he enjoyed killing people, or like Harry in that he talked to himself, or like Tyrel the hydraulics specialist who insisted that even his supervisors call him 'Doctor' because, after all, hydraulic fluid is the lifeblood of an airplane. Johnny just had a split personality that came and went like rainy-season showers.

One personality was quiet and studious, perfect for a man who spent most of his time not actually working on planes but in debriefing crews after their flights and then tracking the histories of malfunctions in order to spot trends in mechanical discrepancies. Johnny was very good at that. Discussion was important to him. At times like that – most of the time, in fact – Johnny was thoughtful, polite, and a pleasure to be around.

The other personality wasn't such a pleasure. It was loud and frenetic. Obnoxious, like the overly-friendly, fast-talking salesman who won't leave you alone. When that personality took over you couldn't shut Johnny up.

Fortunately, this second personality appeared only rarely, usually when Johnny was nervous or in a situation he didn't understand. The only time I heard of it happening was when we redeployed from Honduras after an exercise and the plane Johnny was on flew through a thunderstorm. Jamie Tunkelman said Johnny leaped to his feet in the cabin and started preaching with the fervor of a born-again Christian. Except he wasn't preaching religion: he was shouting at the top of his lungs the science of meteorology and the physics of thunderstorms. *"WHEN HOT AIR RISES IT TAKES MOISTURE WITH IT!"* he screamed, stomping through the cabin and scaring the hell out of everyone on board. *"AS LONG AS THE MOISTURE SURROUNDING THE BUBBLE OF HOT AIR IS WARMER THAN AMBIENT CONDITIONS, THE AIR CONTINUES TO RISE! EVENTUALLY THE THERMAL CANNOT RISE ANYMORE AND A CATASTROPHIC COLLAPSE BEGINS!..."* The visual was a nervous breakdown but the aural was a college lecture. Jamie had to sit on him when Johnny tried to carry his presentation to the cockpit.

But such outbursts were rare. As long as Johnny stayed calm the boor stayed away. And anyway, it wasn't the talkative personality that Walt wanted. He wanted the "good" one.

The "good" one was around most of the time. That's when Johnny was calm and studious. Intensely studious. He read voraciously. He researched things to minute detail if they piqued his interest. That explained his knowledge of thunderstorms – and volcanoes, and the national park system, and the Reformation and cubist art and string theory. He learned Manx that way. There wasn't a drop of Irish blood in his body but after a bout of dengue fever in Panama he'd become obsessed with infectious diseases. Dengue led him to malaria and malaria led him to cholera. The history of cholera told him about a nasty outbreak on the Isle of Man in the 1800s, which told him about the Isle of Man and then led him to fall in love with an Irish Florence Nightingale named Nellie Brennan who had been dead for 150 years. Johnny *loved* Nellie Brennan, truly loved her, to the point that he needed to prove himself to his long-deceased amour by learning her native language.

It was that kind of obsessive-compulsive behavior that Walt was counting on. Besides Manx,

Johnny's specialties were astronomy, botany, ancient Greece, large-animal veterinary science, and shipbuilding. He was the only person who could engage Big Bud in a lucid discussion of naval architecture and come out on top of the conversation. Big Bud thought Johnny was a genius. The rest of us thought he was strange. Walt thought he was very convenient.

"He'll know if the boat wheel's real," Walt explained to me over the phone before he took off for Peru. Johnny didn't like to travel but it was no surprise Walt had talked him into it.

"Walt," I reminded him from the comfort of my nearly empty Honduran hooch, which was located in a two-acre plot of other empty hooches, which was located on a two hundred-acre airfield that was completely devoid of both aircraft and anything interesting to do, "you're not going there for the wheel. You're going there to get back Mark's girl-friend before she gets killed."

"Yeah, we're going for her, too," he agreed. "Hector's got it all worked out where we'll just pick her up in town. But she's got my wheel. I need Johnny to verify it's what I'm looking for."

"It's a boat wheel, Walt. It's a boat wheel from the middle of the jungle. How can it not be what you're looking for?"

"Now Mike, don't be upset because you didn't get it yourself."

"I'm not upset. And I tried."

"You did," he conceded. "But you could have tried harder. You went to the wrong boat."

"But we didn't know that! Besides, you should be grateful. By going to the wrong boat we eliminated it as a source of the wheel so Gabriela could go back and go to the right one."

"And get kidnapped."

"Are you blaming me for her getting kidnapped?"

"Not at all. I'm just saying that you went to the wrong one so she went to the right one and got kidnapped. In any event, she has the wheel and it might be what I want."

"Of course it's what you want."

"Not of course. It could be fake. How do I know it's from a paddlewheel steamer of the late 1800's? I don't know anything about paddlewheel steamers. Do you? Remember the problem I had with the fishhooks T.J. brought me from Brazil? They were supposed to be bone, made from the tusks of a tapir. They were plastic."

"T.J. didn't know that. They looked the same."

"Exactly my point. But the fact is he brought back plastic fishhooks. How am I supposed to square that with the old pilot in my dream?"

"Well, Walt, you have to expect a certain amount of latitude..."

"And the lotus fiber mat that Kurt swore was genuine? He stole it from a church in Suriname on that flood relief trip? It turned out to be made from horse hair. Horse hair, Mike! They don't even have horses in Suriname! Not enough to be trimming them for mats, anyway. There has to be some quality assurance on this collection or we might as well call it off. And I can't call it off. I would never get to sleep again."

That much was true. The treasure hunt had taken over Walt's life. Out of a list of 26 items, over the course of a year we had collected only 14. He had begun to despair of finding the rest.

They took off on a Tuesday morning and by nightfall were dismounting their trikes on a rain-soaked Billinghurst Street.

On Wednesday Johnny Luca went missing. After enduring a fitful night due to rain on the tin roof, the crew woke up and he was gone. So Walt set the others on the hunt for Hector while he went after Johnny. He found the wayward crew chief two hours later, down by the river collecting water lilies. Evan and Jem didn't find Hector but they did find a friendly hooker. She knew someone who could take Hector a message. She also had her own motor scooter that they used to run around town. In doing so they learned that the rebels weren't there.

On Wednesday night Hector came in from Paucarmanu. He told them the kidnappers had changed their plans: Walt and company would have to go upriver to meet them. But don't worry, he promised. The "rebels" were really a bunch of nice guys and there would be no danger. He told them where he thought they could find Gabriela and that he had arranged a boat.

Would he be going along? Walt asked. Hector chuckled at the question. Not a chance.

It rained again Wednesday night. No one got any sleep. Then on Thursday morning there was a problem. Everyone on the crew was accounted for but when they went down to the river, the boatman Hector promised refused to go upriver.

"Why not?" Walt asked.

"He says he's afraid," Hector said with a shrug.

"Of what?"

"Of the rebels, of course."

"But you said the rebels weren't bad," Walt reminded him. "You said they aren't even rebels, they're just a bunch of poor guys who took Gabriela because they thought your group would pay to get her back."

"Well, yes," Hector apologized. "But there have been rumors..."

"What kind of rumors, son?" Jem demanded, suspicious.

"Rumors that they are worse than I said," Hector apologized, holding out his hands to indicate what could he do? Deciding the answer was not much, he left the crew to their own devices.

The boys discussed their options. Walt doubted the rumors (and wanted his wheel) so he wanted to go. Evan believed the rumors were true but wanted to go anyway because he wanted Gabriela to find him a girlfriend. Jem stated his belief that Hector "lies like a no-legged dog." He thought they should just wait in town and tell the kidnappers to come get the money on their own. Johnny picked through his water lilies and smiled.

Eventually they decided to go but then needed to find a new boatman. Searching the riverfront Evan stumbled on Eudes sleeping on his houseboat. Having nothing to do that day and knowing nothing of Gabriela or rebels he agreed to take them upriver.

"How much do we have to pay him?" Walt inquired.

Evan shrugged. "Don't know. The guy doesn't talk. I just said 'upriver?' and he nodded."

"Then that's all we need to tell him," Walt decided.

They were about to set off when Walt realized they didn't have the money. Rolo had given the satchel to Evan who locked it in the hell-hole on the C-27 with the rest of their flight gear. Evan had left it there thinking that a locked airplane was safer than the hotel. A wise move but now a time-consuming one. Walt fidgeted as Jem and his hooker raced out to the airport to retrieve the cash. They got back just before ten, Jem leaping triumphantly on board as Eudes cast off. He was splattered in mud and breathing hard.

"Got it!" he exclaimed, holding up the bag. He winked at Evan. "Sorry we took so long. We took an extra ten minutes on the plane."

"For what?"

"She wanted to join the mile-high club."

"But you were on the ground."

"I know, but she said it might be the only time in her life she got on a plane."

"Ten minutes?" Evan repeated, checking his watch. "How the hell did you get back so fast?"

Jem cackled happily. "I told her to hurry. Man, that girl can ride. She drives that bike good, too!"

At last ready to go, the crew then discovered they had one more issue. Johnny Luca, the expert on shipbuilding, the man who could lecture Big Bud on naval design, didn't like water. He could swim but just didn't like being on water. The sensation of being on a boat, even a flat-bottomed barge like Eudes', made him ill.

Walt was beginning to despair that nothing would go right for him. The day was progressing and they needed to move. He had already stayed one night too many in Puerto Maldonado and it would be hard to convince the AOC to give him another.

But in the end he talked Johnny into going. Johnny finally hopped aboard and said he was alright. He just asked Eudes to stay close to the shore.

Where the rebels hung out was closer than Gabriela's village. Walt described later how only ten miles up the Tambopata they were already close enough to the mountains that rocky bluffs appeared on both sides of the river. Following Walt's guidance, Eudes hove to against a sandbar where the river made an oxbow. It was the sharpest turn for miles and also one where a jagged stalagmite of granite jutted from the river near the opposite shore. The river shallowed and rippled over rocks in a loose approximation of rapids, creating a hiss unlike any downstream. The sound echoed off the bluffs and masked sounds of the jungle. Despite the current, the crew tied up to a treefall on the beach and waited.

By early afternoon nothing had happened. The sun overhead cooked the riverbank, forcing the guys to remain in the shelter of the boat's torn yellow tarp. Evan slept. Eudes fished. Johnny sat on the edge of the boat, his feet hanging overboard so they could touch the sand. He wanted to go ashore but Eudes gave his standard warning about quicksand. Johnny suffered but despite the rocking of the boat, touching the shore kept him happy. Walt grew more impatient with each passing hour.

Shortly after one o'clock there was a shout from the opposite bank.

Six men appeared. One waved a rifle and yelled 'Hello!' over and over. Another led Gabriela.

Gabriela wasn't bound in any way. She looked, Walt said later, tired and dirty but healthy, as though she had spent a week camping and not brought enough supplies.

"Where's the wheel?" he asked the others on Eudes' boat. "I don't see a wheel."

"I don't see a wheel, either," Evan noted. "But I do see a guy with a gun."

"Yeah, what's up with that?" Walt asked. "Hector didn't say anything about guns."

"They're rebels," Jem reminded him.

"They're not rebels," Walt replied. "They're locals. Backwoods types. Peruvian hillbillies."

"Hillbillies? My kind of folk!" Jem exclaimed. "And I ain't worried about no cracker with a gun."

He unwrapped a blanket he'd laid next to the bag of money. Inside was one of the AR-15s from the plane.

"Hey, why did you bring that?" Walt demanded. "I told you no guns. We don't want to spook these guys."

"Well, hell. They don't look spooked to me," Jem pointed out. "And I knew they would bring guns so I thought, as long as I had to go back for the money I might as well grab a little protection."

"I don't think guns are a good idea," Johnny threw in.

"What? The hermit speaks? You don't like water, now you don't like guns, either?"

Johnny's eyes were as wide as the river. The trip wasn't turning out to be something he enjoyed.

"No, I don't like guns."

"Too late," Jem shrugged.

"Keep it out of sight," Walt insisted. "And if you have to shoot anything, don't start until after we get the wheel."

The rebels appeared to have had a plan right up until getting to the river. However, the place they chose to exchange Gabriela was almost a hundred yards across. They pulled a canoe out of the trees and then seemed unsure what to do with it.

"They going to send her across?" Evan asked. He looked at Eudes, the boatman being their source of all knowledge aquatic. Eudes stared back.

Unsure what to do, the rebels decided to give their problem to somebody else. They shouted instructions across the river.

Walt and the others strained to hear.

"What'd they say?" Walt asked Evan, their only Spanish speaker.

Evan listened closely and then shouted *"Qué?"* across the water a few times. The rebels shouted some more.

"Well?" Walt demanded.

"In a minute," Evan replied, holding up his hand.

The shouting went back and forth. The rapids made it hard to hear and Evan kept asking them to repeat themselves. After a while the rebels grew hoarse.

"I'm waiting," Walt pressed.

"In a minute."

"You had a minute. What are they saying?"

"It's complicated."

"How complicated can it be?"

Evan looked apologetic.

"I don't know."

"What do you mean you don't know? What have they been saying?"

"I can't make it out."

"None of it?"

"They're saying something about the river," Evan offered meekly.

"Well, no kidding, Sherlock. I could have told you that. You told me you spoke Spanish."

"I do. All the time. With my maid."

"Well, how is your maid's Spanish different from their Spanish?" Walt wanted to know.

Jem giggled. "Because they're not telling him to get naked," he explained.

Walt threw up his hands. "You mean to tell me the only Spanish you know has to do with screwing your housekeeper?"

"No!" Evan argued, then added, "Well, maybe. Conversation with her always seems to move that way."

Walt looked around his crew and then turned on Eudes.

"You! Eudes! What are they saying?"

Eudes was caught off-guard, like the kid in class who knew the answer to the last question but not this one. He shrugged and concentrated instead on his fishing line.

Walt surveyed his crew with disgust.

"I don't believe this. What good are any of you? I've got one guy who's a deaf mute, one who's seasick, one who thinks he's back home squirrel-hunting, and one who can't say anything in Spanish outside of calling Merry Maids and ordering a hooker. I'm on a boat with the Four Stooges."

"I don't see you ponying up any *español*," Evan observed.

"I'm the strategist here," Walt countered. "I build the plan and expect my crew of hand-picked specialists to carry it out."

"Well, son, seems to me you picked the wrong specialists," Jem said, sitting down next to the bag of money.

"You're telling me."

Walt put his hands on his hips and stared at the river. One of the rebels, impatient, shouted something across the water.

"Shut up!" Walt yelled back.

Jem cradled the satchel in his lap.

"You know, I didn't ask for this," Walt mused. "I was minding my own business, sleeping in my own bed. By all rights I should have been dreaming about having sex with my wife. No, by all rights I should have been *having* sex with my wife. But nooo, instead I dream about an old guy who tells me to wander through the biggest flea market in the Western Hemisphere and pick up bargains that even the owners don't want anymore. Why couldn't he have just asked for an Elvis-shaped clock or something?"

The impatient rebel grabbed the rifle from his comrade. Standing over the canoe he fired a shot into the air to get Walt's attention. He failed. Everyone on Eudes' boat jumped to their feet except Walt, who continued to stare into the water.

"An Elvis clock I could get easy," he mused. "A stupid boat wheel from some Peruvian Mark Twain, though..."

"Oh," Johnny Luca fretted. "They're shooting."

"So what?" was Walt's reaction.

Eudes mumbled to himself and started untying the anchor until Evan stopped him.

Jem went to the side of the boat with his carbine.

"Hey, son!" he yelled. "Don't be gettin' smug over there! We have guns, too!"

He pulled the trigger and didn't notice the switch was on Auto. Instead of sending a single round skyward he fired a burst that ripped through the boat canopy. Everyone ducked. Johnny Luca almost fell off the boat.

"I'm not really in the military, guys," he announced, speaking at a fast clip and in a loud voice like a guide gathering tourists to cross a street. "I know I work around guns but studies consistently show that situations where guns are present almost inevitably involve them being used and usually it's in a case where they wouldn't have needed to be used if people had just bothered to sit down first and rationally discuss the underlying cause of the disagreement that caused them to be there in the first place. I highly recommend..."

Everyone ignored him.

"Whoa, Jem!" Evan grabbed his roommate's arm. "Don't be escalating things."

"Sorry, son. I meant to fire only once."

The rebels scattered on their side of the river. They took cover in the trees, momentarily leaving Gabriela the only one out in the open. Walt stared across the water for a minute and then chuckled.

"What's so funny, son?"

Walt pointed at Gabriela. "Her! We're standing here yelling in broken Spanish."

"So?"

"So she speaks English and she's standing right there."

"Oh."

Suddenly having a way to communicate, all three of them began yelling across the river until Walt slapped the others down.

"Gabriela!" he yelled.

"Yes?" she called back.

"Are you alright?"

She looked around at the rebels hiding in the brush but ultimately decided she was.

"Do you have the boat wheel?" Walt shouted.

"Son, that's not..."

"Shh!"

"Yes!" she yelled.

"Great! She has the wheel!" Walt rubbed his hands together. "Now, how do we get them over here?"

"Ask them," Evan urged.

"We have the money!" Walt yelled. "Tell them to send you over in the canoe and we'll send the money back!"

On the far side of the water Gabriela turned and had a conversation with the jungle. After a while there was movement in the brush. A hand waved anxiously at her. She turned back toward Walt.

"They said for you to throw your gun into the river!" she called over.

"We can't!" Walt replied. "It's not ours."

"But they want it in the river!"

"No, they don't! Tell them if we do that the whole U.S. military will come down here to look for the damned thing!"

One of the rebels shouted something across the water.

"He says they'll kill me if you don't!" Gabriela yelled.

Something in her voice suggested even she thought she was being melodramatic. Walt thought so, too. Johnny Luca didn't and started complaining to Jem in a low voice that the situation was rapidly becoming "fraught with uncertainty" and they should go back to Puerto Maldonado and get help. Jem was more interested in the cross-river dialogue and shunted Johnny off to Evan, who directed him in turn to Eudes, who was stuck in the corner of the boat with his fishing line and had nowhere to go to get away. Johnny sat down and began to describe to Eudes how a similar breakdown in communication had contributed to disastrous results from the Melian Dialogue during the Peloponnesian War.

"No, he won't!" Walt assured Gabriela. "If he does we'll just get mad and he won't get his money."

Gabriela stared back with a look that even a hundred yards away they could decipher as "is that the best you can do?" But she relayed the message anyway.

"They want to know if you brought the money?" she called. "All of it?"

Jem hugged the satchel and thrust a hand inside for a reassuring feel of the pile of cash.

"Absolutely!" Walt yelled with the conscience of a car dealer. "Tell him it's enough to buy something better than that .30-.30 he's got!"

The feel wasn't enough for Jem so he popped the lid open to gaze on Harry's money. Then he snapped the satchel closed again and held it tight to his chest.

"You know you have to give that up," Evan reminded him.

Jem nodded enthusiastically.

"Oh, yeah," he said.

"No keeping any for yourself," Evan scolded.

"Wouldn't think of it, son. It's all theirs."

On the far shore the rebels emerged from hiding. They held an animated discussion and then got together to push the canoe into the water. Following instructions Gabriela got into it and sat down. Then she got out and one of the rebels took her place. Then he got out and the boat sat empty while they conversed some more. Finally Gabriela *and* the rebel got in but then they just sat there. Through all the variations the crew tried to figure out the ramifications of each change.

"How's this going to work?" Jem demanded.

Evan pointed across the river and then at his own boat and then back again as he did the math.

"She comes over, we give her the money, she goes back, then comes back here...No: he comes over, we give him the money...No, that won't work. Ah, there! They send an empty boat, then...No, that's a non-starter. Okay, both of them now? They both come over, we give him the money, he goes back. Okay, that we can do."

"What about the wheel?" Walt wanted to know. He shouted as much across the river.

Gabriela could be seen pointing into the jungle, obviously trying to explain to the bemused rebels that the wheel was just as important as she was. The rebel with the rifle disappeared into the trees and returned carrying a gigantic spoked wheel that could have come off the bridge of the Titanic. Walt was ecstatic. He hopped up and down in his excitement. The rebel could see him from across the way and tried to hold the wheel up for viewing but in doing so he dropped his rifle. The gun landed butt first on a rock and fired again.

The bullet sailed across the river and splintered one of the poles holding the tarp on Eudes' boat. That corner flopped down and smacked Eudes on the head. He shrieked. No one was hit but the rebel's companions all scattered back to the trees anyway, fearful that Jem would return the favor. Jem didn't. The rebel with the wheel set it down quickly so he could wave 'Sorry! Sorry!' with both hands. That calmed Walt and his crew but not Eudes. It didn't calm Johnny, either, who now clutched Eudes with both hands and expounded on the science of ballistics and the development of modern firearms. Eudes began to shake.

"Send them both across!" Walt yelled.

The canoe wasn't big enough for two people and the wheel. The boys watched with concern while the rebels tried to make everything fit. The problem was that the wheel was too heavy to stand up inside the canoe and if you lay it down the unlucky person underneath it had to lie almost flat. That precluded a crew of two. It also meant that whoever carried the wheel couldn't paddle. After several attempts Gabriela became angry – the boys could hear her lecturing her captors. She got out of the canoe and the chagrined rebel was left by himself.

"We're going to be here all day," Walt sighed, looking at his watch.

But then someone on the opposite shore had an idea. The rebels went back into the jungle and returned with two coils of rope.

"Now what?" Evan asked.

The rebel in the canoe started paddling. He didn't have either the wheel or Gabriela but he dragged one of the ropes behind him.

"Cover him, Jem," Evan urged.

Walt waved Jem to keep his seat.

"He doesn't even have a gun," he pointed out.

Jem agreed. "I'll keep an eye on the money," he offered instead.

The rebel finally crossed the rapids and nudged his boat against Eudes'. Evan grabbed the prow of the canoe to keep the man alongside.

"*Hola,*" said Walt.

The man wasn't interested in conversation. Since no one on board except the silent Eudes could understand him anyway, that wasn't a problem for Walt.

"So how are we going to do this?" Evan asked.

The rebel wanted to see the money but despite Walt's prompting Jem would only hold up the bag and smile.

"You get the money when we get the girl, son," he insisted.

The rebel didn't protest. He was impressed by how big the bag was. Envisioning it full of U.S. dollars was enough for him.

With elaborate sign language and a lot of "*sí, sí*" all around, the two sides discussed various ways to accomplish the exchange. Walt did most of the talking. He proposed a host of possible trades, growing increasingly frustrated as one after another was shot down and several times telling the rebel to 'get a life.' Jem wasn't fond of any plan that involved giving the rebels the money before the last possible moment.

"You're being pretty selfish with that bag, dude," Evan frowned, growing impatient.

"You don't know the half of it," Jem replied.

Finally, a solution materialized when the rebel figured out that the wheel was just as important to Walt as Gabriela was. With that information, he paddled back to the opposite shore (assisted this time by his friends pulling on the rope) and put Gabriela in the canoe. Then Walt and Evan pulled her across with the rope the rebel had left with them. She climbed aboard the houseboat clearly annoyed.

"Your rescue plan has them confused," she complained. "Me, too."

"What plan?" Walt replied.

But at the last minute they did have a plan. Seeing the empty canoe and realizing they now had access to both lengths of rope, Jem jumped up and whispered in Walt's ear.

"They won't give you the wheel unless they have the money," Gabriela interrupted.

"How do you know?"

"Because they said so. You can talk all you want but they won't give it to you. I'm not sure they'll give it to you even if you pay them."

"That's not right."

"Of course, it's not right! You are naive. They were thinking of kidnapping you, too, until they saw that you had guns."

Jem wagged an I-told-you-so finger at each of his companions.

"Wait a minute," Evan insisted. "We came all the way up here to get both of you. They have to give us the wheel."

Gabriela looked ready to slap him.

"They don't have to give you anything! And that wheel...why is that so important? You talk like it is human. I am more important than a wheel from a boat."

"That depends on whether you get him a date," Jem informed her.

"What?"

"Never mind."

"Maybe I don't want a date now," Evan huffed. "You haven't even thanked us yet."

"*Cómo?*"

Walt held up his hands for silence. Everyone complied except for Eudes who whimpered at the back of the boat while Johnny explained to him why a fish's short attention span made it not mind being caught.

"They'll negotiate, won't they?" Walt asked. "They already have."

"Not about the wheel."

"I'll go talk to them."

Gabriela shook her head.

"They won't listen to you. That man didn't like you."

"Why not?"

"You're not friendly. His exact words were, *'El hace el tonto.'* Which means he thinks you're crazy."

"Cool!"

"No, it's not cool," Gabriela chastised him. "People here are superstitious."

"Oh, come on."

"*Qué quiere decir,* 'come on?' If they think you are crazy they won't have anything to do with you!"

"Okay, okay. I won't act crazy. I'll just go talk to them."

"No!"

"Why not?"

"Because *tu haces el tonto.*"

Walt started to protest but hesitated. His eyes narrowed.

"They want friendly?" he asked.

"*Sí.*"

He chuckled. "Okay, they'll get friendly."

Into the empty canoe went a reluctant Johnny Luca.

"No, no, no, no, no, no, no, no, no," our debriefer chanted even as Walt guided him into the rocking canoe. He looked as nervous as Eudes was relieved.

"Johnny, it's simple," Walt assured him. "I know you don't like water but you don't even have to paddle. Not until you get the wheel anyway. You just go and make sure the wheel is what we want. If it is, you put it on board with you and push off from the shore. We'll meet you halfway."

"What if it isn't what you want?" Johnny asked, not liking the situation at all. He sat sideways in the canoe so he could maintain one foot touching the nearest pontoon.

"Well, you should probably pretend it is," Walt admitted.

"But what about the money?" Johnny insisted. "They want the money."

"Tell them to take the other rope," Walt explained, pointing to the one on the prow of the canoe. "We'll tie the other end to the money. When you push off they can start pulling the money across to their side."

"That is your plan?" Gabriela gasped in disbelief.

Jem grabbed Eudes' old Coleman cooler and tipped it over, dumping two river eels onto the floor of the boat. Eudes howled but Evan rushed to console him, grabbing the eels and slipping them into his backpack.

Into the cooler Jem crammed the entire pubs bag. He stamped the top down with his foot and with a roll of speed tape wrapped it tighter than a boxer's hand.

"There!" he beamed. "This baby'll float better than that canoe!"

Now Johnny looked ready to cry.

Walt hailed the rebels. They hauled on the rope and began to pull Johnny to the opposite shore. He rode backwards, sitting in the middle with his hands clutching the sides of the boat, his face that of a man going to certain doom. We needed only a one-eyed punter to complete his misery.

"How do you know they won't just keep him?" Gabriela demanded. "They might just take him as another hostage."

Walt crossed his arms and watched Johnny go.

"Trust me," he said evenly. "They won't keep him. It would be The Ransom of Red Chief all over again."

From their side of the river the crew watched as Johnny approached the opposite shore. He stepped out of the canoe in shallow water and stood on the rocks as the rebels gathered round.

Their reaction when they realized he didn't have the money was just as Gabriela predicted. They freaked, yelling across the river and waving their rifle in Johnny's direction to indicate they viewed him as their new hostage.

Then Jem got their attention by holding up the cooler, tied by one handle to the rope the rebels had at hand. He set it down in the water where it bobbed contentedly alongside Eudes' boat. For a moment the two groups looked at each other across the water. Then the rebels got the clue.

Two men hurried into the water to untie the other end of the rope from the canoe. Like kids at a tug-of-war they yanked as hard as they could at the rope, pulling the cooler away from the house-boat and out into the river.

Their progress was slow. The cooler drifted in the current, swinging wide downstream and making them work. Still, the men hauled away happily. One must have said something along the lines of keeping Johnny because at the same time the rest of the band pulled our debriefer out of the shallows and nudged him along the shore at the barrel of the rifle.

"Oh, that's not good," Jem groaned.

"Just wait," Walt counseled. "Eudes, get the motor running."

Eudes was at the end of his own rope, figuratively speaking. He'd been shot at, yelled at, and almost lost his eels. His boat was damaged. There was a woman on board. It was hot and he was tired. Someone had yapped into his ear for over an hour. Now his cooler was on its way to strangers. Even with Johnny gone, he sat by the motor mumbling to himself.

"Eudes, let's go!"

"*Aaauurgghah!*" was the shouted reply, catching everyone off-guard. But Eudes wrapped up his fishing gear and started the motor.

On the far shore things didn't look good for Johnny. The money was on its way to the rebels and still they showed no sign of letting him go.

In fact, one of the rebels grabbed a third piece of rope and made ready to tie him up.

Then he got a reprieve. Before the cooler traveled twenty yards from the pontoon boat it caught between two rocks.

The two men on the rope pulled harder. They shouted in frustration. The rebels still on shore shouted, too, running along the treeline and giving directions to the two in the water. Those two splashed upstream until the water became too deep, trying to get a better angle on the rocks. The man wanting to tie up Johnny ran into the shallows to help the other two and stepped into a hole, momentarily disappearing beneath the surface. The shouting got worse. Johnny was pushed back and forth as everyone bickered over how best to get the cooler free.

"Hang on! Hang on!" Evan yelled to them as Eudes pushed away from the sandbar. "We'll get it free!" Gabriela translated for him but it did little to dampen the rebels' panic.

Eudes maneuvered his boat out into the rapids. There under frantic direction from everyone on the boat he steered them close enough to the cooler to knock it free of the rocks. The rebels rejoiced. They returned to pulling on the rope and threatening Johnny.

It was as they maneuvered to the middle of the river that the crew heard a new sound above the hissing of the water. It was loud, wailing, and plain-tive. At the same time it was cajoling. It howled like wind and rode on the air like the call of a coyote. The boys heard it and looked around in confusion. Eudes heard it and went into hysterics.

It was Johnny.

You couldn't blame his own evil elf for finally taking over. Eudes might have thought he was having a bad day but his was nothing compared to Johnny's. Here it was only two o'clock and our resident hermit had already been scared, confused, seasick, kidnapped, and prodded with the barrel of a gun. He'd crossed half a continent, spent two sleepless nights in a hot, leaky hotel room, been dumped in a canoe, and was now being yelled at. He'd had enough.

The warehouse of words that strained under the day's pressures suddenly burst wide open – he launched into a full-throated babble. In Manx.

From the water Walt and crew saw the rebels stop and stare. Even the two men pulling the money paused in their efforts.

Johnny waved his arms. He stomped his feet. He shouted, he laughed, he cried, he joked, he thrust his hands before him and then bowed to underscore a sarcastic aside. He lectured them, pointing with one hand and then the other. He rambled in a brogue that would have made Nellie Brennan proud. He looked down at the ground, he looked up at the sky, he gestured at the jungle and the river and each of the men in turn. He even put his arms around two of the rebels to bring them closer to his monologue.

Who knows what he said – the rebels didn't have a clue. When Johnny hopped onto a tree stump and danced a jig they could be forgiven for thinking Walt had sent them a madman. They pushed Johnny away and tried to discuss the situation amongst themselves. Johnny joined their huddle with a desperate yell, not wanting to be left out. The rebels dashed left along the shore to get clear – Johnny followed them. They dashed back toward the canoe and he followed them there. The lead rebel jumped into the water and yelled across the water to Walt, who stood on the pontoon boat with his arms crossed, indifferent.

Eudes guided his boat to the middle of the river, turning it into the rapids to maintain position. When he saw Johnny freak out he stared, thought for a while, and then reversed course, going with the current to get as far away as possible.

"Hey, where are we going?" Evan asked. "Eudes, turn around."

Eudes ignored him.

"Eudes!" Walt ordered. "Go back. We have to get Johnny!"

Eudes looked away from them, downriver, and shouted something in a language they didn't understand but that clearly meant there was no way in hell the lunatic who'd lectured him on attention-deficient fish was getting back on his boat. He'd had enough.

Jem scrambled up from the floor and tried to turn the tiller. Eudes fought with him, screaming. Evan went to help. Eudes smacked him. Evan replied by tackling the boatman's legs. The three of them fell to the floor in a pile.

"Get his hands, Jem!"

"The boy's as slippery as one of them eels...*you* get his hands, Evan!"

Walt stepped over them as they struggled. He took position at the motor and turned the boat back to the middle of the river.

Gabriela watched the scene with her hands on her hips.

"I am going to tell Mark all about this," she vowed. "I cannot believe he sent you to rescue me. You don't know anything about rescue!"

Walt shrugged. "You ought to see us fly."

When Eudes tried to sail away the movement panicked the rebels. It looked to them as though the Americans were leaving and abandoning Johnny to them. They realized they had traded an attractive girl for a crazy man and even money wouldn't compensate them for that. They pushed Johnny back into the canoe.

"They've almost got the money," Walt observed.

That the rebels did. As they pushed Johnny out of the weeds and back into the river, the two men pulling on the cooler announced success. The others ran to join them. The Coleman floated in chest-deep water but together the six men pounced on it and fought with each other to drag it ashore.

While they were thus distracted Johnny came to his senses. He stopped pontificating in the language of his love and looked around. For a moment he was alone. Just him, the canoe...and the wheel from the paddle boat only ten feet away.

Carefully he climbed out of the canoe and waded to the shore. The wheel lay where the rebel with the rifle had dropped it. Johnny pulled it through the grass and into the water. Getting back into the boat was more difficult – he gave up trying to heft the wheel aboard with him and instead dragged it along outside, using it to push himself out of the shallows and into the current proper. There the water gave the wheel buoyancy and allowed him to hang onto it with one hand.

Walt watched as Johnny drifted faster with the current. He maneuvered Eudes' houseboat to meet him.

The rebels got the cooler to shore and tore at the tape. They saw Johnny drift away but did nothing to stop him, not realizing he had the wheel.

"Evan! Evan! Help me over here!" Walt called.

He turned the houseboat sideways to the current so that Johnny's canoe drifted into them, clunking against a pontoon.

"Grab him! Gabriela, hold his hand! Evan, help me with the wheel."

They got the wheel on board and then Johnny, too. Johnny was so happy, so flush with adrenalin, that he immediately started talking – in English this time – telling everyone what he had just done even though they had all watched him do it.

"I got it!" he exulted. "I got it!"

"You did get it. Good job, Johnny!"

Walt bent over the wheel and ran his hands over the wood.

"I got it! Did you see me? I took it right under their noses. You were right, Walt. It's a good wheel! It's brilliant. It's real. It's real! At least one hundred years old. Look at the grain on these handles..."

Evan sat on Eudes to hold him down but the fight soon went out of the boatman. With everyone back on board Jem slid over to the tiller and turned the boat downstream, aiming toward the closest bend that would get them out of sight of the rebels.

As he did that the rebels looked up and realized that Johnny had taken the wheel. They were still fighting with the miles of tape Jem wrapped around the cooler but they took a moment to yell their anger.

"You've got your money!" Walt shouted back. "What are you complaining about?"

"Maybe we should go tell them why the wheel's so important," Evan suggested.

"I don't think so, son," Jem replied. He revved the motor as high as it would go to hurry them downstream. Eudes, calm again, frowned so Jem made a motion for the boatman to take his place. Eudes sulked, then changed his mind and did as Jem suggested. He took the tiller and sat down with his back to everyone else. That way he could watch the river pass and look forward to the moment when he got back to Puerto Maldonado and got rid of his nightmarish passengers.

"Well, they've got their money now so they should be happy. It would be good for relations, you know, to tell them what this was all about."

Jem patted his roommate on the shoulder.

"An 'A' for kindness, son," he said. "But an 'F' for judgment. Those boys ain't so happy. Look."

He pointed back toward the rebels who were just about to disappear from view. They ripped away all the tape and threw off the cooler top. The flight bag came out. So did its contents.

"Where did you get all that money?" Gabriela asked. "It's a fortune, you know."

The rebels scrambled for their rifle.

"Ah think we should hurry," Jem urged. He crouched down behind Walt, who looked at him in confusion.

"What's the problem?" he asked. "Did you keep some?"

Evan smacked his roommate, angry.

"Jem, I told you to give them everything!"

"I did!"

"You didn't. Look, they're mad as hell."

"I'm telling you, I gave them the whole bag. I didn't keep a thing."

"Then why are they...hey, everybody get down!" Evan cried.

But before the rebels could shoot Eudes' boat motored around the bend. The rebels were lost from sight. They no longer even had their canoe to give chase since it rode the current a hundred yards behind the houseboat.

Everyone looked at Jem who shuffled his feet. Walt was the first to catch on.

"What was in the bag?" he demanded.

"We were, um, in a hurry," he said. "She said it was the only time she would be on a plane..."

"What was in the bag?" Walt repeated, tapping his foot.

Jem looked at the floor. "I grabbed the wrong one."

"What do you mean, the wrong one?"

He pointed back up the river and looked sheepishly at Gabriela.

"I don't suppose they'll have any use for approach plates?"

6. The State of the Union

CLUBS IN PANAMA CITY were loud, dark, and filled with smoke. When I added my incomplete knowledge of Spanish to the mix it often made for embarrassing misunderstandings talking to local ladies. I once answered a girl's question about how I liked Panama by saying yes, I was excited to be there – except I used the wrong verb and unintentionally implied that I was getting turned on just talking to her. Which was true but still a conversation-killer.

Talking to women at all was difficult. Panama had distinct social classes: a large lower class which existed well below the poverty level; a tiny upper class derived from the dozen or so families who controlled most of the money in the country; and a small but growing middle class made up in part of immigrants escaping conflict in countries like Colombia and Nicaragua. To make a huge and unfair generalization, the girls of the lower class were ugly. The girls in the upper class were beautiful. And the girls in between were a hit-or-miss mix. All spoke different levels and styles of Spanish; trying to interpret any of them above the cascade of salsa in clubs was a challenge.

The Pinheads and guys who hid out on base most of the time frequented The Pit or the Strac Club when they wanted to hook up. The Pit was the NCO club on Howard. The Strac Club was a dive bar outside the back gate of Fort Clayton. Both were bars filled with poor local girls willing to sleep with you in exchange for dinner. Though it was hard to choose which was sleazier the Strac Club probably had the edge.

I went to the Strac Club once but it was such a bad experience I never returned. I got drunk too quickly. My last clear thought was to stagger out to the parking lot and pass out in the bed of Lowell's pick-up truck, thus ensuring I would get a ride home. The next morning I woke up – still in the truck – in a driveway in Balboa and realized I'd climbed into the wrong vehicle.

Josh wouldn't step inside the Strac Club if you paid him. He loathed the place, preferring instead the hipper, more financially independent crowds at downtown clubs like Pavo Real, Patatús, and Dreams. The place he really wanted to get into – but couldn't – was the Union Club, the exclusive preserve of the Panamanian aristocracy, pure-bloods who were either descended from old Spanish families or who had enough money to pretend they were. They called themselves *ladinos* but everyone else called them *rabiblancos*, "white-tails." It wasn't an affectionate term. The *rabiblancos* prided themselves on their lighter skin, their money, and their closed society.

Protected by armed guards and heavy gates, the Union Club sat on a low hill near Punta Paitilla. On Friday and Saturday nights its curving drive-way hosted a parade of shiny SUVs that drove slowly through the gates, the better for its pam-pered occupants to be seen by the hoi polloi. The only way Josh – or anyone else not from the right circles – could get into the complex was as hired help. Lucky for him, however, it's lonely at the top. Sometimes young women of the upper-crust tired of their inbred relatives and descended the heights to party at Josh's favorite haunts. That's where he preyed on them. Often he talked me into coming along as his wingman.

"Just be nice," he advised. "They love Americans."

"Who says?"

"Oh, come on. We're white, we have money, and we're more sophisticated than their local layabout boyfriends. I never have trouble meeting them. Why else would they talk to me if they weren't interested?"

Because they're bored rich girls who are slum-ming, I thought, but didn't say for fear of burst-ing Josh's bubble. Josh was like most of us, not ugly but not handsome, either. Very average. His strongest suit in terms of getting women was his persistence.

"Have you ever gotten one to invite you to the Union Club?"

Josh shook his head in disappointment. "Not yet. But I'm working on it."

"Why do you want to go there anyway?"

"What do you mean, why?"

"I mean, why? What's so special about it?"

"It's the Union Club."

"So?"

"So it's the most exclusive club in the city. In the country."

"And?"

Josh peered at me aghast, like a neighbor who suddenly realizes what the Mormon missionary at the door has been saying.

"Are you nuts? *And* nothing. Exclusive is enough."

I mulled over my next question and then decided to ask it anyway.

"Jem says you won't get in because you're Jewish."

He scoffed. "No, if I don't get in it's because I'm not that good-looking and not well-connected. Being Jewish has nothing to do with it. I know for a fact that a good third of the Union Club hails from the tribe, my friend. Who do you think holds on to most of the money in this country?"

One night we went to a place called Mango's that had just opened on Calle Uruguay. It was a few blocks from my apartment and close enough to the bay that when the tide went out the smell of sewage and ocean bottom permeated your clothes. Mango's was new. In Panama that meant it was trendy and cool. Everyone who wanted to be seen went there. During the late afternoon the children of privilege hung out on the sidewalk patio flashing designer clothes, talking on cell phones, and glancing at passing cars to see if it was anyone they should know. There was a lull period from about 7 to 9pm but after that the evening crowd arrived. Josh and I got there one night as the crowd was picking up.

"There's a girl called Eva I've been working on," Josh said over the blaring rhythms of Jon Secada. He tried to scan over the crowd.

"How so?"

"Her dad's a banker at Banco del Istmo. Boatloads of money."

"Is he a member of the Union Club?"

"No. He's not a *rabiblanco* but half of them are in hock to him so he's just as good. I want her to invite me home sometime."

"Your mercenary instincts are inspiring."

"Hey, she's easy on the eyes, too, don't get me wrong. But if you want to swim with the big fish you've got to get into their waters, you know what I mean?"

"I like the waters I'm in. Don't hook me up with her sister unless she's the down-to-earth, raised on a farm, not afraid to get her hands dirty type. And hot, too."

Josh continued scanning. "Not likely. These chicks don't do farms. They might *own* a few but the chance they've ever been on one themselves is slim. And getting dirty?" He chuckled.

Mango's was narrow with a dance floor deep in the back of the building. The place was dark and crowded with only the illusion of space offered by mirrors facing each other from every wall. People clustered, starting at the bar and spreading out among the tables. The flash of leather was every-where, not the glossy leather of bikers but the muted suede of people who jetted to Bogota for the weekend. Heavy perfume and cologne competed with a cloud of cigarette smoke that hung feet thick at the ceiling. Some people wore designer jeans but most had dressed up. The women were prone to glittery dresses. A formality prevailed in Panama even among the young.

"*Hola,*" said a voice at my side.

I turned and saw a girl in her early twenties. She was five-feet-six in two-inch heels and would have been slender if not for ample breasts that instead threw her squarely into the voluptuous category. She wore a short jacket over a glossy blouse that was deliberately designed to lack buttons above a certain latitude. She turned away from a circle of friends to greet me. Now she stood with a half-smile and lifted eyebrow.

"*Hola*," I replied.

She was gorgeous and her breasts had a gravitational pull. Way too hot for me, I knew. I wasn't handsome and I wasn't rich.

"That's a nice jacket," I said in Spanish.

Her eyes rolled to the right, a practiced gesture that let her look bored with minimal effort. She started to say something and then chose instead to glance at the cigarette in her hand, which she held between two fingers like Marlene Dietrich prompting a cue. She wanted a light.

"Are you waiting for a bus?" I tried again, flashing a big smile, "or posing for an advertisement?"

She started to say 'neither' and then, realizing I was making fun of her, looked around for someone else to ask. No one was convenient. The moment it took to realize that gave her time to recover.

"I was hoping," she said lightly, "that you had a light for my cigarette."

"I do," I said. "But I don't like cigarettes. They make you unhealthy and then they kill you, so I think only ugly people should smoke them. You are not ugly, therefore you shouldn't smoke them and therefore I won't offer you a light. Besides, I think you're much more attractive just standing there holding it as a prop. It's classy."

The eyebrow dropped, then rose again.

"You're American."

"What makes you say that?"

"You're rude."

"I'm not the one smoking," I pointed out.

"Well, apparently neither am I." With practiced skill she flicked the cigarette off her middle finger. It sailed ten feet through the air and hit a Lorenzo Lamas wannabe on his carefully unshaven cheek. He turned, ready to defend his honor, but she blew him a kiss and mouthed, *"Lo siento!"* He then switched emotions on a dime, feigning pain and trying to be suave and flirtatious through the crowd, but she cut him off without a second glance.

"Where were we?" she asked.

"You were saying something about being rude."

"Ah, yes. You're American."

"Un norteamericano, a tu servicio."

One of her company handed a drink over her shoulder and she took it. It was a Blue Curaçao, perhaps chosen because it matched her blouse. The blouse I worked hard not to stare at.

"I've never liked how you call yourselves *norteamericanos*," she declared. "You're not the only ones in North America, you know."

"We don't call ourselves *norteamericanos*," I replied. "We call ourselves 'Americans.' *Norteamericanos* is your language."

"Yes, but you see? You call yourselves 'Americans.' You're not the only ones in the Americas."

She had a point but I shrugged.

"I don't make the rules, *chica*, I just follow them. Besides, what else could we call ourselves. *Estados Unidadistas?*"

She gave me the lifted-eyebrow look again.

"*Yanquis*," she suggested, thinking it an insult.

"Yankees is good," I agreed. "We like 'Yankees.' It's one of our best baseball teams."

Lacking her cigarette, she plucked the straw from her glass and toyed with it instead, annoyed that I refused to be insulted.

"Are you in the military?" she asked. From her tone I could tell she was hoping I would say yes, since that would give her another reason to dislike me.

"Kind of. I'm in the Air Force."

"The Air Force is military."

"Our Army wouldn't agree with you. The Navy might."

"You're still in the military."

"You say that like it's a bad thing."

This time she didn't feign her surprise.

"*Claro que sí!* Of course it is."

"Why?"

She paused. "It just is. You invade people."

"We invade countries," I corrected her. "But not that many."

"You invaded Panama," she said, pointing her straw at my chest.

"No, we were already here. We just kicked out your president because he was a dictator who sold drugs."

"You're about to invade Iraq."

"Because Iraq invaded Kuwait and Kuwait is our ally."

"You want the oil."

I shrugged. "We all want something. *Mira, chica,* I'm not here to argue foreign policy. Believe me, my life is easier if we don't invade anybody. That way I get to stay home, fly during the day, and go to clubs at night."

"You fly?" she asked. *"Eres piloto?"*

"A tu servicio."

She rolled the straw around her lips.

"Isn't that dangerous?"

Her tone was breathless, just sarcastic enough to let me know that she wanted me to say yes so she could laugh at my narcissism.

"Not at all," I said. "Flying isn't dangerous. Crashing is dangerous, but not flying."

"But airplanes are dangerous," she insisted.

"Well, there's a reason they call the airport the 'terminal,' after all. But we have a perfect record in aviation: we've never left anyone up there."

She pounced anyway.

"You're a pilot," she repeated.

"*Sí.*"

"Then that is why you have a big ego."

She turned her back on me. Our conversation was over.

"*Mucho gusto,*" I said and turned to find Josh.

"Well, you do have a big ego," he agreed when I found him, toward the back of the club explaining to the waitress that he wanted a new *cuba libre* because the lime in the one she brought him wasn't fresh.

"I do?"

"Of course you do. You're a pilot, therefore you have a big ego. A pilot without ego is like a turtle without a shell."

"Okay, but I'm a pilot because I have a big ego, not vice-versa. She's dwelling on a stereotype that in my case isn't true."

"Whatever," he said. "Why do all these people have cell phones?"

"Because the phone companies here have no infrastructure," I reminded him. "And it takes six months to get a land line hooked up in your house."

"Okay, but it's loud in here. You can hardly hear the person next to you much less talk on a phone but there they all are shouting into them. And they look stupid walking around with the thing pressed to their head."

"It's a fashion thing."

"For the Third World, maybe. Cell phones will never catch on in the States."

"Why would they?" I agreed. "We have good land lines."

"Thank god. Anyway, I don't see Eva."

"Well, let's have a drink and wait."

I ordered a beer but Josh was impatient. He hated being in a club without a woman at his side.

"Let's go," he said. "This place sucks. Maybe there's more action at Sahara."

"There's plenty of action here. Besides, I just ordered a beer."

"Well, let's go before it gets here so you don't have to pay for it."

He tried to make for the exit along the bar but the crowd was unyielding. We were forced to deviate to the far side of the room and make our way through the tables. There, by pure luck, we ran smack into Eva and one of her friends. Her face lit up at seeing Josh. She motioned for us to join them.

Eva was short and pencil-thin with long black hair. She had pale skin that suggested fragile health but a bright smile that insisted just the opposite. She laughed quickly and frequently touched or pushed against whomever she was talking to.

Her friend was gorgeous, a twenty-something named Estrella who was the calm counterpoint to Eva's exuberance. She also had black hair and wore a sleeveless blouse with a plunging neckline that stayed in place from the heroic effort of a sole strand of fabric connecting the two sides. Besides the décolletage, something about her poise caught my attention – she wore a ring.

After introductions, Josh noticed the ring, too.

"Eva, I can't believe this," he exclaimed. "I'm here with my friend Mike who desperately, *desperately* needs a woman, and you bring a friend who's married?"

I wanted to make the point that I wasn't in fact desperate but it was too late.

"*Ay, pobrecito!*" the two women cried, grabbing my hands to comfort me. The table behind them turned at their outburst. I saw my large-breasted acquaintance from earlier look our way.

"Thanks, Josh."

"Miguel, I'm so sorry, *pero mi amiga ya se casó!*"

"And my best wishes to you, *señorita*," I said to Estrella. "Whoever you have chosen is truly a lucky man."

"Thank you, Mike! You're so sweet."

Tell that to the girl who calls me a *yanqui*, I thought.

"Josh, I have not seen you in sooo long," Eva complained. "Where have you been?"

"Working. I've been working a lot. I haven't had time to go out to the clubs."

He'd been working on other girlfriends, I'm sure he meant to say. Josh saw the Air Force as an hourly position rather than a salaried one: he gave the taxpayers his eight hours and then ran for the door. To Josh, time was money and money was women. Therefore, time was women. With the social life he led he couldn't afford to linger in the office.

"You shouldn't work so hard, *querido*," Eva purred.

"Well, Mike here has been on vacation for a while so I had to fill in for him several days."

The two girls looked at me in reproach.

"Miguel, you should not have Josh do all your work. You'll make him exhausted."

I'll make him exhausted by kicking his ass, I thought, but Josh flashed me a pleading look that I should go along.

"I needed a vacation," I explained instead.

"But Josh has no time to rest himself. He cannot do the work of two people."

"He barely does the work of one," I agreed.

"Are you back doing your own job now?"

"Uh, I don't know. Josh, am I back at my job now?"

"So, Eva," Josh dragged the conversation back to himself. "How's your father?"

Josh huddled with Eva, steering the conversation toward a liaison at the Union Club. Eventually he took her over to the bar. That left me and Estrella on our own.

"*Bueno*, Miguel. Now I know so much about you. You are difficult and you are desperate. Why, Miguel, are you desperate? *Tu eres guapo, inteligente, y tu hablas español.*"

"I'm picky," I offered. "I'm looking for the perfect woman."

Estrella tilted her head back and said, "Ha! She does not exist! We all have our imperfections."

"Even you? I don't believe it."

"Believe it. Even I have my flaws!"

As though to prove it she pulled out a cigarette. I immediately proffered my lighter – she was married, after all. As she inhaled I saw over her shoulder the girl in the blue blouse. My erstwhile companion glared at me. I smiled back.

"Is she a friend of yours?" Estrella asked, glancing back at the girl.

"No, I just met her." I explained the conversation we'd had. "I think she likes me but doesn't know how to express her feelings."

Estrella blew a column of smoke upwards out of the side of her mouth and glanced back again.

"Really."

"Well, okay. Maybe she doesn't like me."

Estrella studied the girl a moment.

"No, es probable que tu la confundas."

"I...confuse *her*?"

Estrella smiled.

"Claro que sí."

"How?"

She sighed gently, accepting her role as educator of the ignorant.

"She is pretty – she knows that. In particular, she has *bienes* – assets – that draw men's attention." She looked down toward her own chest and I nodded quickly that I understood. "She knows that, too. You, apparently, did not fall under her spell. Why you didn't is something she does not know. I assume it is because you are, as you say, difficult. And now here you are sitting at a table laughing with me, another pretty girl. That makes her confused *and* jealous."

Estrella flicked her hair and posed dramatically to show that she was aware of her own hubris.

"Not just another pretty girl," I corrected her quickly. "A far, far prettier girl."

"Well, yes, of course," she giggled. "But you see what I mean."

"So she is jealous."

"*Claro. Celosa.* And it is easy to make her more jealous."

Estrella reached across the table and put her hand on my arm. She smiled sweetly, her fingers playing with my sleeve. The girl in the blue blouse looked our way and stiffened in her seat.

"People want what other people have," Estrella explained, squeezing my bicep. "Women especially. If you have no one here, she will never notice you.

But if I am here, obviously there must be some-thing about you. You must be someone to notice." She moved her hand up to my shoulder.

"You're evil," I said. "*Mala.*"

"*Sí!* I'm a woman."

"But she is pretty. Why should she want what you have?"

"Everybody wants something, Miguel."

"But me?"

"You are handsome."

"I'm okay," I corrected her.

"You are okay enough," she insisted.

"For her?"

"*Ya te lo dije.* I just told you. People want what other people have. She is a woman. If someone else has you, that puts you over the top! Her whole family is that way."

"You know her?"

"*Claro.*"

"How?"

"It is a small country, Miguel."

"What's her name?"

"María Luisa Estébanez. Her family is from Davíd."

Estrella named Panama's third-largest city as though it was the sticks.

"Are you friends?"

Estrella was amused at the question. "*No.*"

"*Por qué, no?*"

A long drag on the cigarette.

"We move in different circles."

"I don't understand."

"No soy rabiblanca."

Ah. Estrella was wealthy but María Luisa Esté-banez was wealthy *and* in the right family.

"She's aristocracy?"

"*Rabiblanca*," Estrella corrected.

"Is that good?"

Estrella studied the glow of her cigarette. Eventually she shrugged. Kennedys are amusing to have around, her look said, but not everyone wants to be one.

"Then how do you know her?"

"Clubs. Parties. Everybody knows everybody."

"If she's from Davíd what is she doing here?"

"They are *from* Davíd but they have a house here. They have business everywhere."

"What type of business?"

"*Cerveza.*"

I waited. "*Cerveza*? That's it?"

Estrella blew a column of smoke downward onto the table where it rolled like wingtip vortices across the surface. She pursed her lips when she exhaled. It gave her a cynical look that she appeared to like.

"That's not enough?"

"I don't know. Is beer big business here?"

"Beer is big business everywhere, Miguel."

I suddenly felt embarrassed that, as a guy, I had to be told the importance of beer. Something else clicked in my mind.

"Her family produces beer?"

"A lot of beer."

"Where is the family's house?"

"In Paitilla, It is very big."

"By the Gran Morrison?"

"*Sí*. You can't miss it."

"I think I've seen it. In fact, I almost moved into her garage once."

"*Cómo?*"

"Nothing. They must have a lot of money."

"Now you are interested?"

"Mostly I'm interested that you seem to know so much about her. Or rather, that the community of people with money here is so small that everybody knows everybody."

Estrella put out the cigarette and lifted her glass of wine. She was really pretty, a china doll, so attractive it was hard not to look at her. But when all was said and done she was a spoiled little rich girl and she knew it. That came across not in anything she said but in the gestures she made as we talked. She was bored. She was no more than 23 years old, she was gorgeous, nothing had ever been expected of her and as a result she had never really done anything, and now she was married. The simple acts of lighting a cigarette or drinking wine or smiling said, 'This is what I do.' The times she forgot about being bored were when I teased her or made jokes or was the blunt American asking about the girl with big boobs. Estrella enjoyed talking to me because I was different and I was no threat – not to her, certainly, because she was married but probably not to the single women, either, since no one in her circles would consider a relationship with a gringo anyway. She was bored and for a while I pushed that boredom away. Maybe Josh's strategy was on the mark after all.

"Ya te lo dije," she explained. "It is a small country."

"Well, sure, but still... I don't know everyone in Chicago," I pointed out.

Her eyes lit up and we both knew she wanted to say 'Because you don't travel in the right circles,' but didn't. We shared another laugh.

"It's hard not to know her family. There are only two *cervecerias* in Panamá, Nacional and Baru. Her family owns Baru."

"So her family has money," I repeated.

"Well, Nacional is an older company and bigger. But yes, it is safe to say her family has money."

I looked carefully past Estrella's shoulder. María Luisa and her friends prepared to go. She made a point of ignoring me but every few minutes couldn't help checking up on my progress with Estrella. This was a new one for me. For once the tables were turned.

Estrella squeezed my hand.

"So, now that you know she has both beer and money you must be interested in her, yes?"

"Beer and money are good," I agreed. "And she's a *rabiblanca*."

"*Sí.*"

"And she has...*bienes*."

Estrella exploded in laughter, attracting attention again. This time María Luisa didn't hide her displeasure. I took my companion's hands and grinned conspiratorially.

"You are evil, lady. I'm evil, too."

Estrella leaned forward, happy to hear it.

"*Por qué?*"

"Because I have an idea. *Una idea por una intriga.* A plot."

She giggled excitedly.

"*Cómo?* You are plotting over María Luisa? Can I help? Please let me help!"

"Perhaps," I said with a smile. "Since you know so much, would you happen to know if she is a member of the Union Club?"

The next morning at the squadron Josh wanted to kill me.

"I don't get this," he fumed. "I don't get this at all. I spend months trying to get an invitation to dinner up there and in one night you saunter into a bar and have it all wrapped up. That's wrong."

"It isn't wrong at all. You should be grateful."

"I should be but that's not the point. What did you say to her?"

"I hardly said anything. I was playing hard to get."

"Hard to get? You? Women walk away when you do that, they don't try harder. You must have said something. You must have a special line you've been keeping from me."

"No, really. I just ignored her until she came up to me."

"But why would she come up to you?"

"Because I had a secret weapon that she couldn't resist."

"Ah-ha! I knew it! You do have a line."

"No. Even better. I had Estrella."

"Say again?"

"Estrella. She's gorgeous, right?"

"She's alright," Josh sniffed.

"Alright? She's a twenty-seven on a scale of one to ten. She's got a beautiful face and a body that grown men cry themselves to sleep over. What do you mean she's 'alright?'"

"I didn't like her nose."

I reached across the ops desk and slapped him on the side of the head.

"If you saw the Taj Mahal you would complain about the gutters. You don't like her nose? Then stare at her breasts, you idiot! She could have been missing a nose and I wouldn't have noticed."

"Yeah, well. That business you pulled at the end of the night was dangerous. You were lucky you were in a corner and no one was paying attention."

"What do you mean?"

"Come on, I saw you kiss her. You locked on like you were trying to see what she had for dinner."

"That's disgusting. And you won't believe this but she kissed me. I wasn't expecting it."

"Yeah, right."

"She's married. Why would I kiss her?"

"She's gorgeous. You said so yourself."

"True, but the reason she kissed me was because she was helping me to make María Luisa jealous. I told you, it was a surprise. An awesome surprise, holy cow! But it worked. You have to give her that. She knew what she was doing."

"Yeah, except that she's married. She of all people ought to know that she doesn't need to have word get around that she's making out with guys in clubs – American guys, especially."

"You're right. Sorry. I hope it was dark enough. You said no one noticed?"

"No one except me. And the other chick. What's her name again?"

"María Luisa."

"How did you get María Luisa to invite you to the Union Club?"

"*Because* of Estrella," I repeated.

"How exactly?"

"I don't know. She was watching us the whole time. Estrella kept saying that women want what they can't have so she flirted with me to make María Luisa jealous. The kiss must have put her over the top because once Estrella walked away María Luisa comes up and hands me her phone number – written in lipstick on a napkin, by the way. I thought that was a nice touch. Says she's going to a party on Saturday and wants me to meet her there. At the Union Club."

Josh slapped himself on the forehead.

"Incredible. And what did you say?"

"I told her no."

He vaulted over the desk and grabbed me by my flight suit.

"You WHAT? You did WHAT?? Are you out of your mind?"

I pushed him away. "Hey, I know what I'm doing!"

"You don't have a clue what you're doing! You were supposed to say, 'Yes, hell yes, I'll come to your party *and* I'll bring my good friend Josh.' You weren't supposed to say, 'No, sorry, but that's the night I re-arrange my sock drawer...'" He collapsed into a chair.

Walt came into the office and plopped himself behind the scheduling desk. He saw Josh holding his head.

"The market down?" he asked.

"Worse," Josh answered, his voice muffled behind his hands. "Mike just passed up a golden opportunity I've been working on for months."

Walt nodded. "That sounds like Mike. His golden opportunities don't have much in common with the rest of us. That's why I like him. We'll both be passed-over majors together."

"Josh, relax. We're still going Saturday night."

He looked up in alarm, afraid he might have heard me wrong.

"What?"

"You and I are going to the party."

"I thought you told her no."

"I told her no, I wasn't going to meet her there. I didn't tell her no, I wouldn't go to the party."

"Huh?"

"I told her if she wanted me to accompany her to a party then it was going to be a real date. I would pick her up at her place and *take* her to the party."

Josh was so happy his eyes welled with tears.

"Mike Bleriot, you wonderful, brilliant, Neanderthal gentleman, you!" Then he thought for a moment and frowned. "Wait a minute. You're not brilliant. You're a dumbass. If she goes to the Union Club she's got tons of money. Are you going to show up at whatever mansion she lives in driving your beat-up Jimmy?"

"That car smells like urine," Walt agreed. "Probably not a good idea."

"It doesn't smell like urine."

Walt nodded. "Yes, it does. You need to stop pissing there."

"I don't piss in my truck!"

"Somebody does."

"You can't pick her up in that truck," Josh warned.

"It does *not* smell like urine. And look, you're not letting me finish. I told her if she wanted to go out with me I would pick her up and take her to the party. She seemed to like that. But then we started talking about the party and she said there would be drinking and we would probably both have a good time...the upshot is she didn't want me to have to drive home after I'd been drinking."

"Ohhhh," said Josh. "That's so sweet."

"Did you tell her you drive drunk all the time?" Walt asked.

"No, I didn't. And I don't. I don't drink and drive and I don't piss in my truck. And don't be saying things like that. Driving drunk isn't as fashionable in the Air Force as it once was."

"Mystic Pete says you drive better when you've had a few."

"Mystic Pete spends so much time in front of a judge himself it's a wonder he has time to worry about my driving."

"He says you did some demolition derby with your truck where you banged up a bunch of locals' cars."

"Now wait just a minute! He's thinking of that time I backed into a Mercedes. That was as much his fault as mine."

"Forget about that!" Josh demanded. "How are you getting to the party if you're not driving your piece of junk?"

"She has a driver. She's picking me up."

"Us," he reminded. "She's picking us up."

"Well, that's the other part of the story..."

Josh threw up his hands. "You're killing me here, Bleriot! You just said I was going to the party!"

"You are."

"And how's that supposed to happen if I'm not going with you?"

"Well, what's she supposed to do? Take both of us? She doesn't even know you."

"Yeah, but I'm with you!"

"So? She's going to take two guys to a party? One of whom she's never even met?"

"But...but..." he stammered.

"Look, you're still going," I insisted.

"How?"

"She's got a friend."

Walt leaned back in his chair and propped his feet on his desk.

"This is why I hang out with you guys," he remarked. "I can live vicariously through your single life. Hey, when you're done you'll need to go back to the beginning to let me know what I missed."

The ops desk was long. It stretched a good twelve feet from the door to the far side of the scheduling board. Now Josh worked his way along it like a burglar on a ledge, getting nearer to me and watching my face closely to see if he was about to fall into a trap.

"A friend," he repeated. "Was she there last night?"

"Yes."

"Uh-huh." He moved closer and folded his arms. "And she wants to go to this party with me?"

"She said she did."

"How could she say that if she doesn't know me?"

"I pointed you out to her."

"Uh-huh."

He watched my eyes for any sign of deception, the kind that usually shows up right before a guy says, 'Hey, pull my finger.'

"If you pointed me out to her," he inquired, picking his way carefully through the logic, "why didn't you just introduce us?"

"Hmm, let me think about that, Josh. Could it be because you were WITH ANOTHER WOMAN?!"

Josh had been working Eva hard all night. He just now remembered that.

"Oh, yeah. I forgot."

"You really should trust me more."

"Hmmm. What does she look like?"

"Does it matter?"

"Yeah," said Walt. "Does it matter? You're single."

Josh looked at Walt as if noticing him for the first time. Walt might as well have suggested we slather ourselves with chocolate and dance around the hangar.

"What does that mean, it doesn't matter what she looks like? I'm single so I'll date anybody?"

Walt nodded. He had been married since he was 22. "Of course. Isn't that what single guys do? Who cares what she looks like?"

Josh leaned over the ops desk and poked Walt to make sure he was real.

"What college did you go to?" he asked carefully.

"The Air Force Academy," Walt replied. "Why?"

"*Ahhhhhhh*," said Josh, reassured. "Now I understand." He turned back to me. "So what does she look like?"

"Well, now, Josh," I began. "Remember what your goal is here. You want to get into the Union Club, right?"

"The Union Club?" Walt interrupted again. "What's that?"

"It's a club," I explained. "Very exclusive. Very rich. Very hard to get into."

"Then why do you want to go there?"

I gestured to Josh. "Ask him."

"Well?" Walt asked Josh. "Why do you want to go there?"

Josh grabbed his head in both hands.

"Would you go away?" he begged Walt. "I'm trying to find out some very important information here – from someone who is suspiciously reluctant to share."

"But I just want to know what club could be so interesting that you're having a nervous breakdown trying to get into it."

Josh stomped behind the scheduling desk. He pushed Walt aside and found a two-week old copy of La Prensa stashed next to the computer. Opening it, he pointed to an article about one of the Miss Panama contest after-parties held at the Union Club. Accompanying it was a picture of the beauty contestants posing in the lobby of the mansion.

"There! That's what it is. It's exclusive, it's loaded with money, and everybody who's anybody goes there. They don't let just anybody in the door. That's why I want to go. Now, leave us alone."

He turned back to me.

"She's ugly, isn't she?"

"Josh, don't be superficial. Remember, beauty is only skin-deep."

"Uh-huh, and ugly goes right to the bone, I know. How bad? Her face? Moles, scars, a weird sideways-pointing nose?"

"No..."

"Her body? Is she fat? No breasts? Oh! She's not one of those girls who you hug and her stomach touches you before her boobs do, is she? I don't know if I can go out with something like that. I mean, I'd have to pretend to be interested in her but if we're talking Jabba the Hut..."

"Well, maybe she's a little on the chunky side..."

"Is she tall or short?"

"Short. Pretty short."

"What color hair?"

"Kind of a steel color."

"Steel color? *Gray hair?* How old is she?"

"Oh, she's not old. I think she's just had a lot of stress in her life."

"Good god! Short, fat, and gray hair?"

"But she's your ticket to the Union Club."

Josh threw up his hands. He turned back to the desk, thinking. Whenever he thought hard the bald spot in his curly hair turned from pale to pink. It did that now as he calculated with the intensity of a Cray computer just how much it was worth to him to go on this date. As mentioned, Josh was like most of us guys. No matter how bad we look we want our women to be flawless. His desire to crack the upper crust now required a huge compromise of his principles.

"What's her name?"

"Renata."

"Renata," he repeated, trying to imagine how hideous a woman named Renata could be. "I don't know, Mike. I just don't know. Give me your honest assessment. How bad is she?"

"She could make an onion cry."

"Really?"

"She fell out of the ugly tree, Josh. Fell and hit every branch on the way down."

"No!"

"Afraid so."

"*Auugghhh*!" he cried, pounding the desk. "Why me?! Why? Why can't it ever be easy?"

He did that for a while. Beyond his fist rising up and down I saw Walt staring in my direction.

"What?" I asked.

He pointed to the newspaper.

"This...this is the Union Club?"

I looked at the picture. Fourteen contestants in evening gowns flanked a small table behind which was a stocky man holding up some certificate that was impossible to read. The floor they stood on was parquet. Lighting came from chandeliers. Behind them on the wall was a shield with a blue-and-yellow crest. At the top of the shield was the profile bust of a knight in armor. Below the knight were a handful of stars and the words *Club Union*.

"Uh, I've never been there but going by the sign I'd say yes."

Walt never took his eyes off me. He tapped his finger on the page.

"Mike, it's the coat of arms!"

"What coat of arms?"

"*The* coat of arms! From my dream. That's it!"

His finger rested on the picture, pointing to the shield. The crest had a diagonal slash and designs in all four corners. A Latin inscription around the edge read *Ad Coetum Geniti Sumus.*

"You're kidding, right?"

"It's as clear as day," Walt whispered. "Blue, yellow, the slash across the middle. Oh, my god. It's all real."

"Relax, dude. You probably just saw it somewhere and your brain remembered. The human brain is a strange thing." I watched Josh grab his hair with both hands and pound his forehead on the desk. "Sometimes a very strange thing."

"No," Walt vowed. "I've never seen it before. This is it. I have to get that crest."

"What crest? The one on the wall?"

"I don't care which one. I just have to get one from the Union Club."

"Well, they're in the phone book," I suggested. "I'm sure for the right amount of money they'll hook you up."

Josh stopped pounding his head and looked up. He exhaled a long sigh.

"Alright," he said. "I'll do it."

"You'll go with Renata?"
"I'll go. If that's my only way in."
I clapped him on the shoulder.
"Godspeed, John Glenn."

I didn't have a tuxedo. The only formal wear I owned was the Air Force mess dress, a tuxedo-like outfit that made me look like the maître-d' at the Ritz. I couldn't wear it to the Union Club partly because it would be bad form to show up in military garb and partly because within minutes of walking through the door someone would tell me to fetch them a drink. So I looked around for a tuxedo to rent.

There were shops in town that sold men's formal wear but the concept of renting an outfit wasn't well-known in Panama. The proprietors of the first three places I visited gave me condescending smiles and suggested I seek elsewhere for *un alquilo*. The fourth place, a luxury store near the Mezzanotte that had an in-house tailor, had a pleasant owner with a soft handshake and thoughtful face. He agreed to rent me a suit but then named a price so high I wondered later if he was just having fun at my expense.

So I did what I always did when I had an insurmountable problem. I called Billie.

"What do you need a tuxedo for?" she asked.

"A party."

"Where? Can I come?"

Her first question was understandable – how many occasions did an American in Panama have for a non-military formal affair? The second question was pure woman. If there was an opportunity to dress up, she wanted in.

"Um, no. I have a date already."

"Oh."

Though it was eighty-five degrees outside the phone line between my office and hers congealed in ice.

"Look, it's something Josh set up. He wants to get into the Union Club. To do it he has to date this one girl and the only way he can do that is if he finds a date for her friend. I'm just doing him a favor."

"Who is she?"

"Just some girl from downtown."

"Ah-ha."

Another long pause. Billie ran hot and cold as far as our love life was concerned. She dated me when she felt like it but mostly didn't so her possessiveness was both amusing and frustrating. I had a feeling she wanted to see me regularly but any number of factors in her female psyche – an ugly breakup with her previous boyfriend, doubts about getting serious with a pilot, the desire to keep a good friendship going, her lawyer friend

Emma's ambivalence toward me – so far kept it from happening.

"And you don't know her?"

"Not really. Do you know where I can get a tuxedo?"

"What does she look like?"

"Panamanian. Nothing special. Do you know where I can get a tuxedo?"

"Is she pretty?"

"Billie, I need a tuxedo."

"People in hell need ice water, Mike! Even if I knew where to get one, why would I lend it to you? You'd probably just take it and hop into bed with this bimbo and mess it all up."

"Oh, I don't think you need to worry about that. It's been so long since I've had sex that I've probably forgotten how."

"Anything she can do I can do better."

"Prove it."

"Bring back a clean tuxedo and maybe I will."

"Ah-ha! So you know where to get one."

"I'll call you back."

Of course she did. Asking Billie to find clothes was like asking a lemming to find a cliff. On Wednesday she called and told me to come by her office. There I found a garment bag draped across her desk.

"Wow, that was fast. Where'd you get it?"

"Does it matter?"

"No. So long as nobody died in it."

"It belonged to Emma's ex-husband."

"Ah, so someone did die in it. How many bullet holes are there?"

"Be nice. They've been divorced for a while. I don't know why she keeps it."

"Target practice?"

"I said be nice."

"How do you know it fits?"

"She said he was about your height and weight. Before she carved out a pound of flesh, anyway."

"It looks in good shape."

"It is. Her husband was a Zonie from an old family down here. I'm sure he wore good quality."

"Well, now it's wasted on me."

"You need to return it in one piece," she lectured.

"I promise. If she rips off my clothes I'll tell her to be gentle."

Billie's jaw locked into place like a tank finding its position at Kursk. She came around her desk to stand directly in front of me. Though she was only as tall as my shoulders, a weird warping of physics momentarily shrank me down so she could stare level into my eyes. She pushed a finger into my chest.

"If you know what's good for you, lieutenant," she warned, not a hint of humor in her voice, "you won't do anything stupid."

"That was stupid," Josh whispered.

We were standing at the front entrance of the Union Club. I had just promised a girl I didn't know that I would see her home safely at the end of the evening.

"Sorry," I apologized. "She's so pretty. I thought it was the right thing to say."

"You've already got a date," he reminded me. "And she has one, too. Don't promise anything to other women. Not if you want to come out of this alive."

We hadn't yet entered the Mecca of Josh's society ambition and already I had made a faux pas. The whole evening was throwing me off balance. The tuxes, the chauffeurs, the limos, the jewelry, the exquisite lighting on the grounds of the Union Club – it was like prom night with adults. I hadn't felt comfortable at my prom and I didn't feel comfortable now.

It began right when we met María Luisa at her house. The moment she saw me in my tuxedo she feigned shock.

"*Buenas noches, guapo*," she exuded when I emerged from her chauffeur's SUV. "You look luscious enough to eat."

Her tone matched the teasing in her eyes. Nothing changed with this girl. From word one she was trying to put me on the defensive.

I didn't know how to say "Curb your appetite" in Spanish so settled for reminding her that dinner awaited us at the party.

"*Bueno,*" she shrugged but squeezed my hand and whispered, "*Then perhaps we will save dessert for later...*"

Good lord.

"And this must be your friend..."

The plan had been for María Luisa and Renata to pick up Josh and me at the Torres Bahia Vista. But when the stretch Montero pulled up to our door the driver was alone. He explained nothing so it was up to us to reason out the change in plans. Josh's analysis proved to be accurate: in Panama a woman doesn't pick up the man. She certainly doesn't wait on him, even if he's driving around in her car. Exactly the opposite takes place.

So it did. The chauffeur drove us across Avenida Balboa and onto Punta Paitilla, then to the east side of the point where it touched El Cangrejo. There we entered a small, select neighborhood dominated by a hill of black rock and shade trees.

On our left were posh homes with walls and security gates. On our right was the hill, a giant cupcake of land that loomed over the neighborhood like an Arizona butte. Its sides were sheer rock out of which grew trees sixty feet high. At the top was a wrought iron fence. Inside the fence were more trees, lush knolls, and enough flat land to build a rugby pitch. Or a mansion.

The chauffeur circumvented a quarter of the hill and turned in to the main driveway. There the gate was opened for us by two security guards.

"I should ask them how they like my house," I commented as we drove by the barracks inside the gate.

"What are you talking about?" Josh asked.

"Those quarters," I pointed. "Rolo and I almost moved in there. Last year when we were looking for a new place."

"Sure you did."

"We did. We were promised a kegger every Friday."

"Whatever," Josh sniffed. He was nervous now that his big date was at hand.

"Fine, don't believe me. We turned them down on the details. But if I had known then that María Luisa and her boobs were just up the hill I might have reconsidered."

The house was beautiful, a stone hacienda that sprawled left and right from a center section two stories high. María Luisa met us and then disappeared inside to retrieve her friend. A maid escorted us to a lobby to wait.

"Nice place," Josh whispered, adjusting his tie in the gilded six-foot-square mirror that hung by the door. He studied the room, eyeing the Queen Anne table, the marble floor, and the oriental vase before the mirror as though mentally appraising whether he could afford anything within a checkbook's throw of his borrowed suit.

"I don't know," I demurred. "There's a lot of glass. A lot of windows."

"So?"

"A lot of windows means a lot of windows to wash."

Josh gave me his usual look, the one that said he wondered why he hung out with me.

"People who live in houses like this don't wash their own windows," he lectured.

"Good point."

"Where did you get your tuxedo?" he asked, fiddling with his tie again.

"From Billie. She got it from a friend. Why?"

"It's nice. It fits you perfectly. Better than mine – I got this from Major Harmon. The pants are fine but the jacket's too big. It's huge. He's got the physique of a lollipop. I'm swimming in this thing. Two people could wear it."

"You look fine."

"Easy for you to say."

"Dude, it's a suit."

"I look like Batman," he complained.

"Batman doesn't wear a tuxedo."

"No, but he has a cape. I'll probably trip on it going into the club."

"Why are you so nervous?" I demanded. "It's just a date."

"Just a date?!" he hissed. "It's the Union Club!" He stopped short and peered at my collar. "What's that?"

"What's what?"

He pointed to my lapel.

"That."

"Oh, a pin of some sort. It was on the tux when Emma gave it to Billie so I left it there."

The pin was small and high on the lapel. It had a pineapple plant engraved on its face. I didn't know what it was for but left it in place since the suit was Emma's. She disliked me already – the last thing I needed was to lose one of her husband's ornaments.

"You look like a sorority girl with a pledge pin," he warned. "Take it off."

"It's just a pin."

"Whatever. It looks silly."

María Luisa swept back into the room accompanied by her friend. That moment for me was worth all the pain associated with the evening.

Renata was gorgeous. Stunning and in an expensive way. In our luxurious surroundings she glided into the room like a hovercraft slipping into a regatta. She was also tall. With heels she stood five-ten, just a hair shorter than Josh and tall enough that when she air-kissed him he swooned and almost fell over. She had a pale, oval face and jet-black hair that swept around her neck to fall over her left shoulder like a fine shawl. The hair reached down to her chest and stopped where her dress began, a splash of vertical white slivers high on the blouse sliding out from the ends of the hair like sparkles. Her look was haughty but not unfriendly. When I introduced Josh she smiled and thanked him for agreeing to be her companion that evening – a step that put her way ahead of my date who so far had only toyed with me like a six-foot pile of catnip.

"*Eres...eres hermosa!*" Josh stuttered.

Renata smiled a polite thank-you, accompanying the words with a nod that signaled his information about her beauty wasn't new.

"It's just that..." he continued, and then wisely decided not to relate how I had described her as a warthog.

We returned to the car. The Montero's interior resembled that of a London cab: Josh and I sat facing the girls with enough spacing that we could have set up a card table between. I had the Herculean task of ignoring how María Luisa's breasts jiggled each time the SUV bounced over Panama City's rutted streets.

"*Pues*, Matteo," Renata began the conversation. "María Luisa tells me you are a pilot. *Es verdad?*"

"*Sí,*" Josh said proudly. He was still in awe of his date but struggled hard to overcome the shock. Given a chance to talk about himself helped. Like all pilots he was good at that.

"Would you take me flying sometime?" she purred.

The look on Josh's face suggested he would commandeer Air Force One if that was the only

way to get Renata airborne. He assured her he
would. That led them into a conversation of the
places they would go. It wasn't long before they
forgot María Luisa and I were there.

"Pues, Miguel," my date said, reaching over with
her toe to nudge my leg. "Why don't you offer to
take me flying?"

In contrast to Josh I wasn't nervous at all. The
luxury of the evening was throwing me off but
not María Luisa. She was using me like a compact
mirror and I knew it. If I got anywhere with her it
would be because she wanted me to, not because I
did anything to deserve it. Knowing that obviated
the need to suck up.

"The only way I would take you on a plane,
señorita," I said, "is folded up in a suitcase."

She stiffened in her seat. *"Cómo?"*

Then she saw the smug look on my face and
realized that getting under her skin was exactly
what I hoped to do.

"Americanos," she muttered.

Our drive to the Union Club took a while. María
Luisa lived in Punta Paitilla and the Union Club
was in Punta Paitilla but after a while I looked out
the window and saw we were on Calle 50, a mile
away and only a block from the club Pavo Real.

"Adónde vamos?" I asked.

"Al Club Union."

"But it's only two blocks from where you live."

Maria Luisa sighed. "We don't go *directly* there."

Josh, smiling like a Cheshire cat, flung his arm over the seat as though stretching and flicked me hard on the neck.

"Claro," he oozed. "Of course we don't go *directly* there."

We drove around for half an hour. The route appeared random but it was anything but. First we cruised by Pavo. Its covered entrance on a residential street was quiet and lacked a patio but enough people stood in line waiting to enter the club that some had to notice the Estébanez Montero roll by. Then it was off to Sahara, and Dreams, and of course Mango's where we made a trip up the street and then circled the block to do it again. A few people at the outdoor tables looked up as we cruised by. One even pointed, which I'm sure made the chauffeur's efforts worthwhile for Maria Luisa and Renata. Bacchus was next, then Blue, then Zanzibar, and finally The Wine Bar. When we finally arrived at the Union Club I felt like I had been to all those places and was ready to turn in for the night.

At the top of the club driveway we rolled to a stop short of the porte-cochère that fronted the entrance. I reached for the door handle but María Luisa gave me a horrified look as though I had tossed her a cat.

I sat back.

Lesson #1: don't get out of the car where nobody will watch you do it. Wait for the red-carpet treatment.

The red carpet treatment involved getting under the porte-cochère where two representatives of the club opened the car doors for us. The point of getting out *at* the entrance instead of before it was the crowd of other arrivals who stood around watching everyone else arrive. Also, to the right of the Club doors was a large picture window where guests stood inside and watched to see who got out of which car, what they were wearing, who they were with, and so on.

"We're on display," Josh muttered.

"See anybody you know?" I whispered back.

"Yeah, right."

It was as we moved up to the door that I made my next mistake. A tall girl from the car ahead of us stumbled in her three-inch heels. She tottered and almost fell. I caught her before she passed the point of no return and got her back on her feet.

"Ay, lo siento!" she apologized. "These shoes are new."

"No problem," I said.

She noticed I wasn't a regular and gave me a once-over, curious. The novelty must have appealed to her for her next words came with the same playfulness that María Luisa used like an accent.

"I can't change them now," she said and looked me straight in the eye. "You may have to help me all the way home tonight."

"I'll be happy to do that," I replied without thinking.

Josh slapped me when the girl turned away. Lesson #2.

We stayed under the awning for ten minutes. When it began to rain the crowd huddled closer but showed no hurry to move up the steps. People trickled inside at the same rate that newcomers arrived so the assemblage didn't shrink. There was an unspoken rule about lingering where everyone could see you: for this social set, true humiliation would be going to a party and having no one notice you were there.

María Luisa left my side and bounced around the crowd blowing air kisses. Renata bounced less and kept Josh with her, introducing him to the people they encountered. I stayed where I was left in the center of the steps and tried to look like I knew what I was doing.

The original Union Club began as a compromise. That wasn't the one we were currently in. The original was over in Casco Viejo, on the other side of the bay in the *corregimiento* of San Felipe, not far from where Mike Jonkris hid from the authorities with his

Chilean girlfriend. That building was now deserted, a crumbling relic of early 20th-century architecture surrounded by tenements and cheap bars.

The El Casco Union Club came into being because from the day Americans arrived to build the Canal there was a colonial nature to their relationship with the locals. From the moment work began on the canal in 1903 there were Americans and there were Panamanians and rarely did the two groups mix. In a way there were two Panamas with parallel establishments: Americans had the Hotel Tivoli while the Panamanians had the Hotel Central; Americans had the Zone while Panamanians had the city; Americans considered local women to be of ill-repute and local women (at least, the *rabiblancas*) in turn considered American men barbarians.

That changed a little in 1923 when the wife of the Canal Governor and the wife of the Panamanian president met. They became friends and determined to punch a hole in the wall between their two groups. They did so by founding the Union Club.

On Calle Primera in the Casco Viejo area of the city – at the time a fashionable location – the club became an oasis of social mixing. Military engineers met with government appointees. Canal managers mingled with the city's upper crust. American officers plied the local ladies with food and drink.

As chinks in walls go, it was a success and one that endured. For decades the club was a haven of cordiality. Leaders from both societies knew that no matter how fractious their diplomacy might be through official channels, there were few problems that couldn't be resolved informally behind the walls of the Club Union in the company of fine wine, fine cigars, and fellow movers and shakers.

Thus the Club worked because people made it work. And the people who made it work best were those at the top. Throughout its heyday the club's officers and unofficial cheerleaders were a coterie of Zonie families and Panamanian aristocracy. They made up the *Carta Bella*, a private list of those who had the stability, the influence, and the money to hold the club together and keep relations in the city calm.

That Union Club lasted until the 1960s. Then changing attitudes and turbulent politics brought it onto hard times. The power of the Zone decreased; the interests of the aristocracy turned more toward wealth. The increasing nationalism and materialism of younger generations caused problems that were harder and harder to fix in smoke-filled rooms. By the time of the '64 riots no one turned to the club for guidance. Older members stopped trying. The club fell into disrepair. Members drifted away.

That was the original Union Club. The current Union Club, the modern stucco building we now attended in Punta Paitilla, came years later, founded by and for *rabiblancos*, the wealth-seekers who had no public-service ambitions. The new club never had social mixing as its goal, at least not any which involved non-*rabiblancos*. Though the Club's motto as advertised by its crest was still *Ad Coetum Geniti Sumus* (rough translation: "We are born to be together") that was never intended to include anyone not a member of one of the twenty-three families who controlled the key industries and business on the isthmus.

"Quieres entrar, mi amor?" María Luisa asked, returning to my side.

I hesitated. "You sure you want me in there?"

"Claro," she said. She slipped her arm under mine.

"Why? This is your club."

"Sí."

"Your *exclusive* club," I reminded her. "I'm not exclusive. Why bring me here?"

"Why not?"

"But why me in particular?"

She looked at the doors. For the first time I saw her face turn thoughtful and believed she was on the verge of confirming Josh's conviction that it was lonely at the top.

"My other date canceled," she said simply.

So there. If our date weren't so improbable already I would have felt insulted. As it was, I couldn't help but be amused. There were no illusions here.

"Well, then," I told her. "I am here for you."

"You are such a gentleman."

We went up the steps. People looked our way and I realized everyone knew María Luisa and she in turn knew them. The circles here were small indeed.

Someone held the door for us and we entered the Union Club.

The lobby of the Club had a drawing-room quality to it, albeit one decorated in a Spanish renaissance theme. The walls were white. The ceiling beams were exposed. A red carpet covered the middle of the floor and stretched over ceramic tile meant to resemble flagstone blocks. Against the walls were high-backed wooden chairs and ornate secretaries carved from cherry; above them were mirrors with gilded frames. Here and there were brooding prints of Goya masterpieces. The Spanish colonial look was de rigueur among the wealthy in Panama, as though everyone worried that at any moment the Spanish ambassador might knock at their door and inquire about dinner.

A guitarist sat in a corner and picked softly through a Villa-Lobos suite. The room sparkled from chandeliers. One modernist exception was a short track light that illuminated the club shield facing the entrance.

"Where did that coat of arms come from?" I asked my date. She glanced at the shield on the wall as though noticing it for the first time.

"Who knows?"

"Do you think I could get one somewhere?" I asked.

"Why would you want that?" she asked, her tone disinterested.

"A friend collects them," I lied.

"Tell your friend to get a life."

A waiter floated by holding a tray of drinks. She plucked two glasses and handed one to me. It looked like a Harvey Wallbanger in a champagne flute.

"What is it?" I asked.

"Taste it."

I tasted it.

"*Sí?*"

"*No,*" I replied. Whatever it was, it was a chick's drink. I kept the glass so as not to be rude but prevailed on the waiter to bring me a beer.

We moved away from the door and were instantly confronted by a couple returning from the bar. The fellow had slick hair and a gaunt build and the kind of intense bored expression that can only be acquired through effort. I was relieved to be holding two drinks as it gave me an excuse not to shake his hand – not that he offered his. Instead he appraised me without acknowledgement, too cool for school. His two-inch-taller companion ignored me.

"Hola, chiquita," she oozed to María Luisa. "Where is Danielo?"

María Luisa shot her a look that would have frozen my beer.

"I wouldn't know," she replied between clenched teeth. "Perhaps there's a mirror somewhere he chose to keep company."

"But it is so sad to see you alone," the vixen purred.

I cleared my throat to say something but María Luisa didn't let me.

"Oh," she smiled. "Alone is nice. You should try it." Her eyes flickered to Slick Hair. "Really, you should try it."

"Who's Danielo?" I asked when we moved away.

"Who do you think?"

"Your boyfriend?"

"My ex-boyfriend."

"Is he here? Is that why you brought me, so he could get jealous and we could fight?"

"Would you fight for me?" she giggled.

"No."

"Then it is good Danielo is not here. He may arrive later but I expect he is too busy with his new *novia*. As he apparently has been for some time."

"Oh, I'm sorry."

"Do not be. I hope they are very happy."

She bit the words off as though they were her ex-boyfriend's fingers.

We met more of her set as we moved along the social gauntlet. One couple after another approached, made shallow conversation, and moved on. None was pleased to see me but it didn't seem personal: they simply wanted to be seen, to know who I was, and then after determining that I wasn't anyone important, to ignore me. María Luisa enjoyed disappointing them. She was spoiled and angry and wanted to tell them all that they and their stupid club meant nothing to her. I was the tool she used to do that.

The only club members who took an interest in me were older – grandparent types who I guessed were being polite. But Maria Luisa pushed us on whenever we ran into them. She wanted to offend, not get into a conversation about my family or where I went to school.

Josh didn't do any better. Normally he was social only when there was an opportunity to hook up so now that he already had the hottest girl in the room at his side it was a curious thing to see him mingle just to be friendly. He wasn't good at it. He was too real to disguise the fact that he had no interest in the various bimbos and their boyfriends. They didn't like him, either. Even the older crowd gave him short shrift.

"This sucks," he proclaimed in the men's room. "They won't talk to me."

"Not at all?"

"No."

The room was decorated in dazzling gold wallpaper that made the mirror over the sink the safest place to look. Josh studied his reflection with a critical eye. "It's this suit," he concluded.

"What does your suit have to do with it?"

"They know this tux is borrowed."

"Um, how?"

"How? Come on, this jacket belongs to a circus strongman."

"So what?"

"So they can see right through me. If I don't even have a jacket that fits then obviously I'm not wealthy or connected. They'll never invite me back."

"They didn't invite you tonight."

"You know what I mean."

"Well," I said, combing my hair, "my success rate isn't much better. 90% of these folks hate me. Only 10% think I'm okay but they're the old ones."

"Ten percent is better than none," Josh sniffed. "And don't dismiss old people. They have money – and some have hot granddaughters."

A man came into the room and paused when he saw me and Josh. For the briefest of seconds he considered the social consequences of using the restroom at the same time as a couple of Americans and apparently decided it wasn't worth the risk. With a clearing of the throat that suggested he had changed his mind, he returned to the hall.

"They won't even piss with us," Josh lamented.

"The ultimate put-down," I agreed.

He studied himself in the mirror again.

"Trade jackets with me," he said suddenly.

"I beg your pardon?"

"Trade jackets. Come on."

"Why?"

"Because you work out. You're bigger than I am. This jacket won't look as bad on you."

"It also won't look as good as the one I have on now. Forget it."

"Come on, Mike. Please! I look like a goof here!"

"So I should look like a goof instead?"

"You won't. Not as much."

"No."

"Come on. You're not trying to join this place. What do you care?"

"I care about looking good. No."

"Please? I'll get you Estrella's phone number..."

"Josh..."

"Just try it on." He whipped off his jacket and shoved it in my face. "See how it looks. See how it looks!"

I argued but took the coat.

"See, it's not nearly as big on you. You look good."

"It's still big," I complained, having to squint into the mirror because of the yellow blaze around us. The jacket did look less voluminous on me but that didn't mean it fit. Whereas Josh had had the look of an orphan who shopped at the thrift store, I now had the look of a younger brother test-driving his first suit.

"But not nearly," he insisted. "Not like on me. You're huge, dude!"

"Josh..."

"No, really. You've got a big chest and arms – you fill that out more than me."

"Alright, cut it out. Anyone hears you they'll think we're gay."

"I'm just saying you look better in that than I do. Let's trade, okay? Please?"

"Why can't...?"

"Please...?"

"Oh, for god's sake," I sighed. "Keep the jacket, already."

Victorious, he slipped on Emma's jacket and then twisted and turned before the mirror to study its fit.

"Oh, much better," he beamed. "Much, much better."

Dinner was a frosty affair. The main dining room was set with long tables and tall chairs that could have come from a turn-of-the-century Boston tea room. The tablecloths were damask and had the club seal embossed in their center. A podium stood in a corner where the president of the club gave a short and boring welcome speech.

I was seated at the same table as Josh but at the opposite end. That was good because it meant we weren't totally isolated but it was bad because with Renata at his side and María Luisa next to me we were hard put to be social with anyone except those directly across from us. In my case that meant four people in their fifties – stern men and their heavily made-up wives – who made no effort to hide the insult they felt over being seated near an American. Josh was in the same boat. At first it seemed that none of them would ever warm to either of us.

Some time after the shrimp ceviche, however, the couples at Josh's end changed their attitude toward him. All of a sudden they couldn't get enough of my now comfortably-attired friend. It was as though they suddenly noticed that he carried himself like the filthy rich landowner he yearned to be. In return Josh chatted eagerly in Spanish as they asked him about his time in Panama, his family, where he'd gone to school, and what businesses he liked. He mentioned the Air Force only briefly, glossing over it as though it was an internship that really only indulged his penchant for banking and finance – which wasn't far from the truth. He enjoyed the attention, hoping it meant he was on the fast track to joining the club himself. Renata enjoyed it, too, perhaps wondering how she had happened to come with the light of the party.

No one asked about my career. I didn't get so much as an *hola* from the couples at my end of the table. Instead they slid their chairs closer to the crowd around Josh. That sat well with María Luisa who was happy to dissociate herself from the clique.

With no one to talk to I spent my time studying the architecture of the room. It had a high ceiling and chandeliers and carved wood beams. Despite the fact that the interior decorations hadn't been updated since the sixties, the place looked the way a formal dining room should.

There were photographs on the walls of Panama City throughout the decades. Nobody else gave them a second thought but as soon as dinner was over and we were able to move about I went from one to the next to see if I could spot familiar landmarks.

"What are you doing?" Josh hissed, hurrying up behind me.

"Looking at these pictures. Look, here's Calle Cincuenta in the early '40s."

"*Oooo*, Calle Cincuenta," he mimicked, glancing around the room. "Who cares? Look, the ice is cracking. We need to mingle, make contacts. You have to come with me."

"Why? They don't like us."

"They like *me*," he corrected.

"Yeah, what's up with that? All those old guys talking to you all of a sudden. What are you telling them?"

"Nothing. Just small talk. They asked about my family and stuff. Kept wanting to know if I had relatives down here. It's like we were playing Six Degrees of Separation. They don't believe I'm from Connecticut. I really impressed them when I told them my family was here in the Sixties."

"Your family was here then? I didn't know that."

"Well, sort of. My parents took a cruise that went through the Canal."

"That's not exactly being here," I pointed out.

"Yeah, but they don't have to know that. I just said they were here and these old guys got all excited."

"Well, nobody's talking to me so I'm just going to be a fly on the wall," I told him. "I got here, I'm in, that's enough."

"It's not enough!" he barked. "I want to fit in. We need to milk this conversation so they invite me back. You're a good talker – come with me."

"Nope, I've got other fish to fry. I have to figure out how to get a coat of arms."

"A what?"

I nodded toward the front door. He followed my gaze.

"A coat of...the thing Walt wants? Aw, you're kidding, right? That big thing?"

"Yeah."

He laughed but then got angry.

"Forget it, Mike! Don't even think about it. I swear, you cause a scene here, Bleriot, and I'll see to it that Giverson gives you a check ride every day for the next three years. You understand? Don't ruin my night!"

Renata walked by then to collect him so he smiled, patted me on the back, and moved off with her. I looked around but María Luisa was chatting on the other side of the room. She needed to be seen with a man from time to time but wasn't averse to ditching me when it was convenient. So I stayed with the pictures.

Before our party, Walt came to the club several times to try to buy the coat of arms. He never got past the front gate. He did manage to get somebody from the club on the phone and explain why the shield was important to him but that only made things worse. They hung up on him once he described his dream. After that he scaled down his ambition, asking for anything smaller they would give him, but by then it was too late: Panamanians are as sensitive to value as anyone else – once you say you want something they immediately deem it more attractive themselves. So I was his Plan B.

"I'm not stealing anything, Walt," I told him.

"Why not?"

"Because I'm not, that's why. They may be Panas but I'll be a guest. That girl invited me and I'm not going to do anything to embarrass her."

That was easier said than done. The tall girl who I helped at the entrance appeared out of the crowd twice while I inspected the pictures. Once was a drive-by: she slid her hand across my shoulder and mouthed *hola* as she glided past with her date. Apparently he didn't notice so she came by again to blather in a breathless voice about me being her knight in shining armor. He did see that and hurried over to collect her, glaring at me as they moved off. I knew she was playing a game but she was so gorgeous that part of me wanted to encourage her. To avoid my own impulses I moved away from the wall and struck up a conversation with the first person I met.

That happened to be a thin man in an expensive suit. He was in his forties, distinguished, and looked around constantly to ensure no one came too close. Whenever anyone did he moved as needed to maintain a comfortable two feet of personal space. He had gold cufflinks inset with the club logo, a gold tie clasp, and his watch was a Patek Philippe.

"*Soy consultor,*" he said.

I didn't ask him what he did but he was anxious to tell me. He was also anxious to let me know that his suit was tailor-made and that the dinner we had just eaten was "pedestrian" to his tastes. "*Pedestre,*" he repeated, fondling his cufflinks.

"Really?" I replied. "What kind of consultant?"

It turned out he wasn't a consultant at all. He was an intermediary for companies that did business in the *zona libre* of Colón. The *zona libre* was a clearinghouse, a free trade zone where merchants could meet and make deals regarding commodities arriving and departing from the port. What my sartorially self-satisfied companion did to make his money was take advantage of the corruption and bureaucracy involved in all the transactions that took place every day in the zone.

"You see," he explained, rubbing his finger along the rim of his glass, "many people want to work in Colón but in order to do business there one needs to be incorporated."

"So you're a lawyer," I concluded.

He chuckled. "Hardly."

What he did was provide desirous traders with the paperwork they needed to start their business. In essence, he sold them an off-the-shelf corporation to preclude the need to form one on their own. All for the paltry sum of fifty thousand dollars. Once in hand the businessman could buy and sell whatever he wished.

"Fifty thousand dollars?" I repeated.

"Well, of course," he observed, "merchants can always establish their own corporations. They can come to the city and talk to the relevant offices themselves." He put down his glass and pretended to count on his fingers. "Commerce, Registration, Permits, License of the State, License of the Zone, back to Commerce... There are many offices. Sometimes the process can take weeks, months, *years*. One must talk to the right people and, you know, the right people are not always available. Even when they are, you may have to...encourage them to sign your permit." He smiled. "The more efficient way to do business is to come to me."

"Very convenient," I observed.

"*Sí,*" he agreed, pleased with himself. "But that is not all. When someone wishes to *un*-incorporate, to sell their license, they cannot just do it themselves. Oh, no, no. no. They cannot just sell to whomever they wish. For that they must get approval, too."

"So you can help them in that event, too?"

The fellow touched his nose, pleased that I'd marked his genius.

"Life in Panama seems to depend on knowing the right people," I remarked.

The man moved left as a couple passed too near his personal space. He surveyed the woman's back and twirled his cufflinks, never picking up on my sarcasm.

"*Sí,*" he smiled.

I moved on. Josh and Renata found me under the porte-cochère where I had gone for fresh air.

"Hey, I met your soul brother," I told him. "The guy takes advantage of people coming *and* going. I need to introduce you two so you can bargain with the devil together."

Josh put a friendly hand on my shoulder.

"Be as cynical as you want, Mike," he said. "You can't ruin my night now. I'm in."

"You're in what?"

"I'm in," he repeated. "They've invited me back." His face was serene. His eyes took on a dreamy quality as though around him now was a quiet meadow filled with butterflies and stacks of corporate bonds. Josh was in his happy place.

"Who says?" I inquired.

He pointed through the crowd to a grey-haired man who had shared our table at dinner.

"Alberto says. He owns a big cement company and Renata says he's a friend of President Endara."

Renata, who didn't speak English, nevertheless understood the gist of Josh's message and nodded her support.

"The man loves me," Josh continued. "Said he would talk to the club chairman about bringing me to the founder's dinner next month. Dude, I'm in. If a personal friend of the president is recommending me then I am made in the shade."

His gaze went long again.

"Well," I said. "I'm happy for you."

And I was, even as I spotted someone in the crowd beyond Alberto who would bring Josh crashing back to earth.

"Hey, there's Jem."

"Yeah, right." Josh didn't even bother to look. The guitarist played a Scarlatti sonata now and Josh hummed along. "You can't ruin my mood, Mike. I'm in."

"I'm serious. Look."

Through the picture window we saw a familiar figure in a cream tuxedo smile and gently squeeze his way through the crowd. On his arm was a statuesque beauty in a silver sarong-style dress. Because Jem was only five-foot-six and the girl at least four inches taller, it was hard to tell if he was leading her or vice-versa. From the look on his face, he didn't care.

All color drained from Josh's face.

"No," he murmured.

"That's interesting," I commented. "Well, at least now we have someone to talk to."

"No," Josh repeated, at a loss for other words. "No, no, no."

Forgetting his date, he hurried up the porch steps into the club. I followed, trying to be more deliberate.

"Where'd he go?" Josh demanded when we got inside the lobby. He stood beneath the shield on the wall and tried to pick out Jem's auburn locks among the crowd.

The lobby curved around the south side of the building and looked out over the front lawn where a light rain had begun to fall. The room was crowded but it took us only a moment to find the one couple moving in the throng: in fact we saw only the head and shoulders of Jem's date, her bright eyes and lustrous hair bobbing above the heads around her like a boat on dark seas. Of Jem himself we caught only glimpses.

Muttering epithets, Josh went in pursuit. We caught up with our quarry on a small balcony overlooking the ocean.

"Jem!" Josh exclaimed. He bit off further words and just stared at our colleague.

Jem turned, surprised.

"Hey, son!" he greeted Josh. "Well, of all the – hello! I didn't know you boys would be here tonight. How the heck are you?"

"Hi, Jem," I said.

"What are you doing here?" Josh demanded.

Jem held up his glass.

"I'm drinking white wine and orange juice. Don't know why but it seems to be a popular drink in this place. It's disgusting but hey, when in Rome...eh, baby?"

He put his arm around his date and she giggled.

"Oh, sorry, sweetie," he apologized. "These are two friends of mine. This here is Josh – don't worry, he always looks like that – and the quiet fellow there is Mike. Guys, this is my friend Lourdes. She's named after a town in France. Isn't that cool?"

"Why are you here?" Josh hissed, ignoring Lourdes. Here he was exploring new frontiers and a beer can named Jem had just showed up on the trail.

"Lourdes invited me," Jem explained, hugging his girl again.

"But...but..." Josh stammered, "this is the Union Club!"

"I know," Jem nodded. "I hear it's kind of hard to get into – you guys might want to lie low. But if somebody gives you a hard time just find me. Lourdes' granddaddy owns the place so we'll make sure you're square with the locals."

Evan walked up just then. He wasn't tall or handsome but he had a natural calm that tonight made him appear distinguished. His tuxedo also fit him like a glove. Instead of the bow-tie he had substituted a cravat that matched the color of Jem's suit. He could have passed for a wealthy banker. Or a wealthy banker's spoiled son.

"Hi, guys. What's up?"

Josh head almost spun off his neck.

"Evan! What are you doing!" Josh looked ready to cry.

"I went looking for beer," Evan replied. "This orange stuff gives me gas."

"But you're not...you shouldn't...!" Josh sputtered. He was overcome. "You guys shouldn't be here. This club is exclusive!"

"Well, they don't have H-B," Evan shrugged. "Just this Pilsner piss-water so it's not that high-class."

"Where's your date?" I interrupted before Josh could blow a gasket.

Evan pointed to the girl with Jem. Jem tightened his arm around her but explained, "Lourdes agreed to share."

Lourdes smiled in agreement. It was the same smile I saw regularly on María Luisa, the one that said, "I'm in control here and I'll do what I want." She clearly hoped I would be shocked but when my reaction disappointed she nonetheless took comfort in Josh's breakdown. At least someone was upset over her choice of date. That was the response she wanted.

"Señor Breitling," a voice behind us said.

We turned to find Josh's companion Alberto standing with a portly man in coat and tails. The stranger was perhaps seventy years old and carried himself with the confidence of a Chicago alderman. He introduced himself as Manuel Luis Mora y Araujo, chairman of the Union Club, and he smiled when Alberto presented him to Josh. But the smile was fixed beneath suspicious eyes. Señor Araujo's face tightened even more when he spied his granddaughter over Josh's shoulder standing in a loose embrace with Jem. The daughter returned the glance with her own look of teenage rebellion but in the next few minutes was wise enough to slip from the room.

"Señor Breitling, my good friend Don Alberto Carrió tells me you have a lost history with our club that we should embrace."

Josh's mind was still fixated on Jem and Evan. He'd gone from high to low in a matter of minutes and now needed to switch back.

"Huh?" he replied.

"Your family," Señor Araujo pressed. "Do I know them?"

"Ahh..." Josh hesitated. I didn't know how to help him so I stayed quiet. María Luisa and Renata appeared just then but held back far enough in the crowd that they could either join us or not as they saw fit. They stood with a crowd that began to gather behind the chairman.

"Well," Josh finally found his voice. "My, ah, family," he said carefully, "has always had an interest in local affairs..."

"*Cómo?* How so?"

"Well, ahh, we...the canal..."

"Who is your father?" Señor Araujo interrupted.

Josh looked at me for assistance but I shook my head. He then tried to re-direct the conversation with a comment about the wonderful dinner and the esteemed company.

"I don't remember the name Breitling," Araujo persisted.

"It's German."

"Ah, are you related to the Brenhoffers?"

"Yes!" Josh enthused. Then, seeing the doubtful response quickly corrected. "Well, no."

"But the Brenhoffers are the only German family I remember being in the Club..."

"Well, we're the east coast Breitlings. Maybe there was another family that..."

"How long have you associated with the Union Club?"

"How long?" Josh repeated.

"*Sí. Pues,* how long has your family been in Panama?"

"Ah, how long...well, uh, you know it's...how long would you say it's been, Mike?"

Yeah, right, my look told him. Don't bring me into your little fantasy. Señor Araujo took a deep breath and Josh, flustered, hurried to pre-empt him.

"You know," he tried again, "my parents used to describe to me how Panama looked in the old days. For example, Calle Cincuenta back in the 1940's..."

"They were here *en los años cuarenta?*" Araujo demanded. "What are you talking about? Calle Cincuenta? Where did they live? Are they on the *Carta Bella?*"

"The what?"

Araujo rattled off more questions but Josh couldn't keep up. With forty people now staring at him his mind went blank. Overwhelmed, he stammered something about his great love for Panama – no reaction from the chairman – his strong interest in the unlimited commercial opportunities of the Canal – still none – and then launched desperately into a discourse about the family insurance business, Spanish classes in high school, the similarities between parts of Panama City and the Puerto Rican community of Hartford, and how his parents had cruised through the Canal on their honeymoon. It was the same babble of generalities that had gone over well at dinner. Now, however, under more direct questioning the details emerged as ridiculous. Alberto visibly shrank.

Señor Araujo, on the other hand, swelled. He had discovered a mole and now reveled in rooting it out. His next question was direct and tinged with retribution.

"Where did you obtain that pin?"

Josh looked down at his lapel as though noticing the badge for the first time. Realization suddenly dawned.

"Uh..." said Josh as Araujo reached forward and removed the piña pin from the twice-borrowed jacket.

"Ah, actually," I interrupted. "That belongs to me." I stepped forward and plucked the pin from Araujo's fingers before he could pocket it. He responded as though slapped.

"Who are you?" he demanded.

"I'm a friend of his," I replied, pointing to Josh. "I'm here tonight with..." I looked around for María Luisa but not surprisingly she was suddenly nowhere to be found. Araujo and his entourage looked with me as I searched but we all came up with nothing. At that I wasn't sure what to say so I just smiled and remarked, "The white wine and orange juice is delicious."

"Who is *your* family?" he asked.

"They're a teacher and a nurse in Chicago," I admitted. "But they may visit next year."

Señor Araujo stopped being friendly. He was now the *patrón*, protecting his beloved club. He snapped his fingers. We observed several waiters move through the crowd toward us. I hadn't noticed earlier how burly they were.

"That pin," Araujo lectured, "is a select item. *Selectivo y selectado.* Members whose families are long-standing in our club *and* have performed great service to its mission wear it as a symbol of pride and of their elite status." He flipped back his own lapel to show an exact replica of the one in my hand. The crowd oooh'ed in admiration as though their medieval king had just unveiled his sword. "I don't know where you obtained that pin," he admonished, pointing at my hand, "but it is not yours."

"I borrowed it from a friend," I explained.

"What friend?"

That threw me. I didn't remember Emma's last name much less that of her ex-husband.

"A...friend," I repeated. "He, ah, might be dead now."

Araujo made a visible effort of stifling his anger. I couldn't fault him. The man ran a club of stuffed-up inbreeds and we were interlopers. There was no way he could tolerate that. Now he had to make a grand display of showing us the door.

He did it beautifully. He stretched his neck as much as his tight collar would allow and stepped aside in a manner that brooked no argument. Everyone in the entourage held their breath.

"*Mozos,*" he commanded. "Escort these gentlemen off the Club premises, *por favor!*"

The waiters stepped forward. I held up my hands to show they would get no dispute from me.

But not so for Josh.

"Wait a minute!" he said, waking up to his plight. "Wait a minute! *Espere un momento!*"

"*Mozos!*"

"No," Josh protested as a waiter gently took his arm. "No, this isn't right. I'm...I'm here, I'm in." He looked around the crowd for support. "I'm like you! Alberto... This is exclusive – I should be here. Take him," he urged, pointing my way. "Not *me*. Take him! Wait!"

We moved toward the door. I whispered to Josh just to call it a night but at the lobby he couldn't take it any more. The exit to him was like a guillotine. Worse, Renata stood by impassive as he passed. Well, not quite impassive: there was disappointment in her eyes, too, and that set Josh off completely. At the door he struggled and pushed the waiters away.

"No!" he shouted. "I'm not leaving! I'm one of you! This club is..."

The waiters picked him up. As they weren't hurting him I didn't step in but accompanied the gaggle as they carried Josh kicking and screaming down the steps and out to the driveway. The only time I moved to intervene was when a few of the club members decided to curry favor by helping the waiters carry him out. One was the tepid boyfriend María Luisa and I had encountered upon entering the club. The other – to my shock – was the effete middleman from the free trade zone. They each stepped into the throng and made a great show of pretending to help hoist Josh airborne. The middleman, at least, did it without actually touching anyone.

That I couldn't accept so I stepped forward to push them away. Josh got to them first. In his flailing he back-handed the boyfriend across the face and then grabbed hold of the middleman's expensive suit and hung on for dear life. In the ensuing fracas the whole crowd lost its way. They staggered across the slippery driveway like an out of control scrum and tumbled headlong into a glistening, muddy flowerbed.

The club attendance gathered at the windows to watch. Some appeared grateful for the excitement.

I hurried to Josh's side and pulled him to his feet. In the darkness the waiters pounced on the middleman. We used the confusion to escape down the driveway and out the gate.

Two miles away Niko's Cafe had fluorescent lights and Formica tables. In our corner the glare highlighted Josh's misery like an interrogator's spotlight.

"Shoot me," he mumbled, his face in his hands. "Please, just shoot me."

The after-midnight crowd at Niko's was the usual mixture of university students and partyers on their way home from clubs. A few homeless seasoned the mix. No one noticed a couple of mud-spattered guys in tuxedos. The smell of gyros and fried rice filled the air.

"It wasn't that bad," I consoled him.

He opened his hands to glare at me then closed up again.

Evan and Jem showed up and slid into the booth next to us.

"Thought we might find you guys here," Evan said. "We thought we'd stop by to see how you were doing." He reached over with a handkerchief and wiped at caked dirt on my shirt.

"Did you see our exit?" I asked.

"A bit. But Lourdes took us out through the kitchen. By the time we got to the gate you guys were climbing into a cab."

"Where is she?"

Jem pointed outside. "In the car. We just stopped to say hi."

"She doesn't want to come in?" Josh inquired, wallowing in pity. "She doesn't want to be seen with the biggest loser ever to get thrown out of her secret, expensive, *exclusive* club?" He closed his eyes and leaned against the wall.

"No," Jem affirmed. "She doesn't want to be seen with Mike, either."

"Don't worry," Evan promised. "We've already figured out how to get even with her grandfather. Having you *picked up* and thrown out is way over-the-top."

"What are you going to do?"

"Well," Jem grinned. "We were going home with Lourdes, anyway. But now we're going to make it even more fun. We're going to take pictures! We'll tag-team her and send the evidence to her granddaddy!"

He cackled and high-fived his cohort. Josh eyed them in disgust.

"She didn't throw us out," he reminded them.

"No, but her granddaddy did. Besides, she's a tiger in the bedroom," Jem assured us. "No reason we can't document it."

They left to continue their conquest. Josh and I bought bottles of Atlas and sat for a while. I wasn't happy with how the night had turned out, of course, but Josh looked destroyed. He slumped in his seat, shrunken within his rumpled clothes. He was famous for rebounding quickly from rejection but this time I wondered if life had kicked him too hard.

"There is a bright side," I tried.

He bent forward and rested his forehead on the beer bottle.

"Forget it, Mike," he said. "This one's a disaster."

"No, seriously, you're better off than I am."

"How so?"

"Well, sure, you looked like a fool getting thrown out..."

"Thanks."

"But remember what your goal was tonight: to get into the club. You succeeded! Ah-ah-ah," I continued before he could interrupt, "you changed goals once you were inside. Once you were inside you decided you wanted to become a member. You wanted them to accept you and let you come back. But you got ahead of yourself. After all, that's not what you've been harping on for months." I wagged a finger in his face as I lectured. "This was about women and crashing the party and showing them you were just as good as they were. It wasn't about social acceptance or membership. So, you succeeded. Give yourself that."

His melancholy was so established that only ten percent of my words sank in. But his brow furrowed as he considered the silver lining.

"How does that make me better off than you?" he demanded. "You never cared about the club one way or the other."

"No," I sighed. "No, I didn't. I only came for that club shield. To tell the truth, I was hoping they would make you a member because then we stood a chance of getting hold of the damned thing. Now I have to go tell Walt I failed. And that's not the worst part."

"What's the worst part?"

"I have to tell Billie that I shredded Emma's suit."

It was true. Not only was Emma's ex-husband's tuxedo jacket slick with the most exclusive mud in Panama City, it was rent down the middle. Someone in the driveway melee had pulled too hard and torn the jacket in half. I pictured Billie's final warning to me and shuddered at the thought of explaining the mishap. I probably had only hours to live.

"Sorry about that, Mike. You're in a tight spot alright." Realizing my peril allowed his own gloom to lighten. As he considered Billie's wrath, he rummaged through his pockets. "Here, it's not much but you can tell her at least we saved her pin."

"What pin?"

"That one with the pineapple," he said, searching through his shirt. "The guy tried to take it but I've still got it. It must be important to somebody." He stood up to pat himself down.

"You don't have it, dude. I do."

I produced the piña pin and looked at it morosely. He was right – it wasn't much. On the other hand, maybe it would keep me from being killed.

"Well, shoot – then what have I got?" He dug into one pocket after another and finally produced an object of his own. As he looked at it his features softened. The old Josh struggled to come back.

"I can't help you with your girlfriend, Mike," he said. "Tell her it was my fault and see if she'll let me make it up to her somehow. But as for Walt, we should have him covered."

He handed over the object from his pocket. It was a cufflink – a gold cufflink with an amethyst inlay across which was inscribed the Club Union crest. The knight looked sideways across the gem and in tiny letters above his head we could read the magic words that were his motto: *Ad Coetum Geniti Sumus.*

I held the cufflink aloft and studied it. Josh chuckled, perhaps considering just how bad our night had to be for us to consider this stupid bauble a success. His giggling grew infectious and soon we were both laughing.

The diners at the next table turned to look. They had no idea what we found so funny. Neither did anyone outside on Via España, nor did Jem and Evan speeding home to have their way with Lourdes, nor did the rest of the guys in my squadron scattered across the city, and neither certainly did the members of the Union Club.

Ad Coetum Geniti Sumus.

Indeed we were.

7. Naked

FASHIONS COME AND GO and for about two months in
our squadron it was fashionable to fly without any
clothes on. Not whenever, not on a regular sortie,
but only on those occasions where circumstances
clearly suggested a more decorous and professional approach, the better to make a statement.

It started when Declan and I landed at a beach-
side airstrip in Salinas, Ecuador one night to pick
up a platoon of SEALs who were practicing water
jumps and swimming infiltrations. We lowered the
ramp and the SEALs ran aboard stark naked. They
didn't have to be naked – they had wet suits. They
just did it as a joke because they thought it would
shock us. As it turned out we weren't shocked,
we just thought they had lost their clothes, but to
reciprocate later in the week we took off our own
clothes before landing at another field to pick up
a different platoon. Those guys didn't have the
same sense of humor as the first team. They ran
up the ramp fully dressed, took one look at us, and
decided we were gay.

Word got around in the squadron of our foolish-
ness. The next thing we knew everyone was looking for opportunities to fly an approach *au naturel.*

Papps and Evan did it when flying supplies into
Terra Preta in northern Brazil to help the locals
when their town caught fire. Flutie and Carl did
it during an exercise in Peru. Mike Vaneya started
disrobing whenever he flew into Apiay, Colombia,
reasoning that if it was fun to get shot at it was more
fun to be shot at while wearing nothing but a smile.
The fun stopped only when Erich Fetterman got in
on the act. Proving once again that fads die when
the wrong people get involved, he decided sponta-
neously during a flight to Swan Island to become
one of the boys. Unfortunately for him, his copilot was Little Bud Blair. Shortly after beginning
their descent from 10,000 feet, Fetterman jumped
out of the cockpit and removed his clothes. Little Bud completely misunderstood the situation.
His horrified "Captain Fetterman, what are you
doing?!" was preserved forever on the Cockpit
Voice Recorder. Worse, when Fetterman made the
rounds of the squadron later to get someone else
to fess up to the activity so Blair wouldn't believe
he was a homosexual, everyone denied taking part
and professed horror at his behavior. It sent the
good Major-select into a spiraling rage.

Eventually Lt Col Rasmussen caught wind of the
aerial nudity. Without demanding confessions and
with minimal eye-rolling, he declared the activity
verboten and threatened action against the next
offender. That was fine with me. After the first

incident I felt foolish, anyway. A joke's a joke, but the fact is that after about thirty seconds of sitting around on a sheepskin seat in the open air with a couple of other naked men, you realize that, well, you're sitting around naked on a sheepskin seat with other men. The half-life of that humor is pretty short.

Sometime later I flew to Bolivia with Major Lou Plunkett. Plunkett was a friend of Lt Col Rasmussen's from our commander's time in the special operations world. He wasn't from special ops himself: Plunkett actually had started out in the B-52 (the "Buff") and then moved to strategic airlift (really big cargo planes) which anybody who looked at him found easy to believe. He was rumpled, overweight, and had a droopy-dog demeanor that gave the impression he was always one nap behind whatever was going on. But Plunkett had an organized brain. He was one of those guys who could look at a hundred independent moving parts and envision how they should all work together, a skill the military loved.

Rasmussen knew Plunkett because of the major's ability to manage large projects. Some years back Plunkett had moved from the cockpit of a C-5 to a tiny office at airlift headquarters on Scott Air Force Base in Illinois where he organized the heavy lifting for special ops missions around the globe. In that job Plunkett went everywhere and met everyone and had his hand in almost every mobility operation the Air Force undertook. Flooding in Nepal? Call Lou. Earthquake in Turkey? Call Lou. Invasion of Panama? Definitely call Lou. No one ever noticed him until he was needed but then he was on the spot, shaking hands and making deals and getting people and things where they needed to go.

Being quiet and hard-working thus earned Plunkett respect. It also got him passed over for promotion. Moving under the radar makes for efficiency but not for glowing performance reports. When his lieutenant colonel's board met and left his folder lying on the table, Plunkett decided it was time to return to the cockpit. The Air Force balked, liking him as a studious drone in a windowless office. But after some phone calls he reached Rasmussen.

Rasmussen agreed to meet Plunkett halfway. For Rasmussen, though a friend, knew where Plunkett's talents lay and they weren't in the cockpit. The special ops world had its eyes on the C-27. So did the Mobility Air Command and so did – implausibly – the Strategic Air Command as it looked to the future and planned its conversion to something post-Cold War. Somebody needed to move among the desks at the Pentagon and keep the C-27 in the budget and out of grasping hands.

Lou was the perfect stateside liaison for us guys down by the Canal. They made a deal: if Plunkett would take on that task, Rasmussen would get him down to Panama as often as possible to fly.

So Plunkett came south from time to time, showing up with little or no notice and appearing suddenly at the ops desk like a disheveled apparition, his droopy eyes and lazy smile enchanting guys like Jake who saw him as a soul brother. He loved coming to Panama. It wasn't the country so much as the squadron that excited him. The 155th TAS was small, the pilots were young, the mission was flexible – for Plunkett it was a college fraternity.

On paper, Plunkett was an ADO, an Assistant Director of Operations. In reality Plunkett's authority derived from the fact that everyone liked him and, further, respected him as the one-deep line of defense against Washington bureaucrats who wanted to slash the C-27 budget in order to buy more boot knives for the Rangers. If he wanted to be on the schedule, he was on the schedule, and nobody – not even Walt – scammed his flights. Besides, he wasn't a bad guy to fly with.

I knew that because halfway through my first year in Panama there was an exercise in Bolivia for which Plunkett was my co-pilot. The planners envisioned it as a series of coordinated raids throughout the country where the Bolivian army – transported and supported by us – would wreak havoc on the coca fields that farmers increasingly turned to to support their families. The "raids" were more police roundups than gun-toting shakedowns. But our job was to take four planes to Santa Cruz, plan with the local forces, and then move to Trinidad where we would help them conduct raids in the Itonomas Valley. Lt Col Rasmussen went along to be the mission commander.

Plunkett was a decent pilot. Because he didn't fly often he was out of practice memorizing ops limits and aircraft systems but adapted by subscribing to the Shiny Switch Theory, which proposes that if a switch in the cockpit is really important it'll be shiny from the number of times that someone has touched it.

He was also comfortable cruising at altitude for long periods of time. That helped out when we went to Bolivia which was twelve hours away. Twelve hours of boring holes in the sky at 20,000 feet, looking at ocean and coastline as far as the eye could see. Worse, we ended up flying down and back twice, doing two shuttles to carry pallets of C-130 parts that the U.S. was donating to the Bolivian Air Force, most of which littered the ramp at the airport in Santa Cruz. Forty-eight hours of flying over four days, almost all of it sitting there looking out the window.

For that I lucked out having Plunkett as my co-pilot. He loved to cruise. He would sit in the

right seat and gaze downward for hours at whatever landscape we happened to be flying over, eyes
fixed on distant things as absently as a bleacher
fan mesmerized by home plate. Ocean, desert, forest, plains, mountains, cities – all inspired placid
satisfaction, a smile of contentment as he remembered what all pilots remember from time to time:
"I can't believe I get paid to do this."

In Santa Cruz the locals were friendly and laid-
back. Our Bolivian Air Force liaison was a short
major with a broad chest and equally broad smile
that showed horrible dental work. We learned
not to tell jokes around him or do anything that
might cause him to laugh. He bustled around
and arranged meetings for us with lots of people
in decorative uniforms but by the time Plunkett
and I returned from our second shuttle no one
still knew anything about the grand plan for drug
raids. Lt Col Rasmussen grew frustrated.

Another challenge in Santa Cruz was to get
accurate information about the places the Bolivians wanted us to fly. It turned out they didn't have
any, that there weren't any maps of the interior of
the country beyond a locally produced road atlas
that was published by an Argentinean immigrant
who had a tendency to draw grass and put the word
"pampas" anywhere he wasn't sure of the terrain.

After three nights in Santa Cruz, Rasmussen pushed the Bolivians to let us move up to Trinidad where we could at least be closer to the Itonomas Valley. The Bolivians balked, content to continue holding pointless meetings, but eventually relented.

In Trinidad the atmosphere was different. There we met a local army commander named Fierosa who belonged philosophically to an entirely different military from the guys in Santa Cruz.

"Here, here, here, and here," he said in Spanish five minutes after we met him, jabbing his pencil into a topographical chart that despite having a worrying number of white spots still was the most detailed picture of the country we had seen so far. He spread it across a plywood board laid on sawhorses in an airport hangar. Outside the wind wailed across a dry landscape. Inside, drafts picked up dust and swirled it into columns that danced past the edges of the chart.

"Four planes, four landings, four raids – all at the same time, every morning." He went on to explain how the farms were laid out and how all but one already had a dirt airstrip that we could use. Mike Vaneya translated for Rasmussen, who stared the local commander in the eye. Rasmussen was grateful to find someone with a penchant for action, even if it was someone who considered a hand-drawn picture of a landing zone the zenith of military intelligence.

"Four raids a day for four days," Mike summarized. "All farms, all with small airstrips. These two in particular are tight."

Rasmussen had a million questions.

"Anyone been to these places lately?" was one he asked Colonel Fierosa.

Fierosa hustled two soldiers into the hangar, explaining that they worked in military intelligence and had traveled the length and breadth of the Itonomas Valley dressed as civilians only one month before. Rasmussen, through Vaneya, grilled the two men at length.

"Are any of these 'farmers' armed?" he asked, turning back to their boss.

The colonel shrugged to indicate that of course, he assumed some of them would have weapons.

"Do they know we're coming?" Rasmussen inquired.

The colonel shrugged again.

To Fierosa's disappointment, our commander agreed to do only two raids the first day. We only had four airplanes, after all. By limiting ourselves to two raids, using one airplane each, that gave us two airplanes to hold in reserve for a Quick Reaction Force. Mike Vaneya and Walt were picked to fly the QRF birds.

Charlie Manson and Little Bud would fly one aircraft into Chilumaniya Farm. Major Plunkett and I would fly the other into a second farm that had no name until we gave it one – the Dust Bowl, called such because workers at a now-abandoned tin mine nearby had scraped the earth bare.

Chilumaniya Farm was a small place and the tougher assignment. Charlie and Bud would have to be on the ball to land there and get back out again. Charlie griped but nobody paid attention. He could land the space shuttle on a Chicago side-street and never touch the curb – and he knew it – so when he complained everyone knew it was just his way of getting ready.

By comparison, the Dust Bowl was long and wide. From the description of witnesses it was in fact a shapeless field of bare earth where wild burros stood around when they couldn't find anything to graze on. Our biggest challenge wouldn't be putting the plane down but the cloud of dirt we would blow up when we did.

Early the next morning Lt Col Rasmussen stood by the nose of our plane and spoke to all of us. The Bolivian ground troops were still assembling at the hangar, the bark of a platoon sergeant audible across the ramp.

"Does everyone understand why we're here?" our commander asked. "We're here to make an effort. That's all. We're not here to win medals. Or prove anything. Or change the world. We're here to get the low-hanging fruit among the local growers. Nothing here is worth losing a plane for. Or a crew. Hell, nothing here is worth the dirt under my fingernails. Understood?"

Everyone nodded at Rasmussen's words. His tone more than anything signified what Rasmussen thought. Our commander had little interest in international relations or nation building. He thought Bolivia was a dump. We would make an effort to help the locals shut down coca farms but as far as he was concerned, the Itonomas Valley and everything it contained wasn't worth the fuel it took to fly over it.

We loaded up the Bolivian troops and took off. The Itonomas Valley ran north-south and was located east of Trinidad. It was hundreds of miles long, meaning it held thousands of square miles of land where anyone with a profit motive and the connivance of local farmers could set up a co-op for coca. It was the kind of place where you could fly for hours and see nothing but forest, plains, and farms – the kind of place that told you the war for drugs would never be won with raids: the battlefield was just too big.

For our first targets Fierosa picked airfields at the extreme limit of his jurisdiction. We watched our gas carefully to get there.

Plunkett flew the take-off and took us up to altitude. High clouds painted the sky grey but the air was clear otherwise. All the mountaintops were visible. A 30-knot wind out of the east gave us turbulence if we flew level to the ridges but even that only emphasized the lack of other weather. Plunkett occasionally made S-turns so he could look behind us and see the other three planes, bobbing his head in excitement.

"Don't see that often, do you?" he asked, pleased by the sight. "C-27s in formation. That's something."

Chilumaniya Farm came up first. After ninety minutes of flying it lay just out of sight on the far side of a ridge that stood 4,000 feet above the valley floor. South of the farm the valley curved and led toward the border with Brazil. Thirty-five miles that way lay the Dust Bowl. Charlie and Bud, Shark 28, entered a holding pattern along our route of flight to wait for Plunkett and me (Shark 27) to get into position. Walt and Tommy Goode followed us while Mike Vaneya and Rolo, with Lt Col Rasmussen on board, stayed with Manson.

Plunkett flew us south along the mountains until reaching our holding point, a dimple of a hill that sat by itself in the plains twenty miles west of our target. We passed over it half a mile up and flew race-tracks at ridge level while we waited for the execution call. Walt climbed in spirals above us. When we made our run-in to the Dust Bowl he would stay high directly overhead and relay radio calls as necessary.

The time to depart our holding fix approached. Two minutes prior Plunkett made a motion for me to take the controls.

"You've got it," he said amiably. "I'm too rusty to trust on this first one."

I took the controls and watched the clock tick down. Exactly on time we heard Rasmussen call, *"Shark flight: execute, execute, execute."*

We had timed our racetracks to be on an outbound heading when the call came. Hearing Rasmussen's voice, all I did was point the nose toward our initial point twelve miles away and keep our speed at 220 knots. I knew that forty miles to the north Charlie Manson was doing the same, maneuvering toward a run-in course that would allow him to put wheels on the ground at Chilumaniya at exactly 0900.

We crossed over the ridge heading east then started a descent into the valley, making a right turn to parallel the forest that accompanied the mountainside on its steep drop to the Itonomas. Below us the floor of the valley was savannah. Open grassland spread between scrub trees and high brush. Stands of trees clung to creeks and the sides of the valley. Farms patchworked the landscape.

"Give the team five minutes," I said over intercom.

In the cabin Bunny Elpole stood by the aft troop doors. He had been there for almost an hour in anticipation. Now he flashed an open hand to the Bolivian team leader and stuttered, "F-F-Five minutes!" at the top of his lungs. The team leader looked non-committal but got up to ensure his troops were ready to run off the ramp.

"There's the IP," Plunkett said calmly.

The initial point we pulled from the map was the end of a ridgeline, backed up by a river bend on the valley floor. Abeam it I hacked the clock, turned sharply to a 168 degree heading, and called for the landing checklist.

"Stand by on the props."

Plunkett nodded. Putting the propellers to their highest speed made a hell of a noise – we wanted to delay that until the last minute.

"There's the field," he said moments later.

"That's it? You sure?"

"A big dirt field. With...what is that? Looks like donkeys at the end. You want to fly past first?"

We were three miles out.

"Give the team one minute," I said.

Behind me Bunny shouted above the engines.

Donkeys? I could see the field. It was really just a big patch of dirt, plenty wide, plenty long...

"No, let's land in front of them."

The land abeam the dirt patch was irrigated and green, the river a few miles to the east. On final I saw individuals scattered through the green. A number clustered by buildings a third of the way up the field. There were trucks, too, but I didn't see anybody with a gun.

"Thirty seconds! Bunny, send the team off to our left."

"To the l-l-left, roger."

We went low over the trees and came in fast. I chopped the power at one mile and pulled the nose up. The airspeed bled off until it hit 110 knots. There I lowered the nose again to let the C-27 swoop down its glide path like a hungry osprey.

"Props to max!"

The props roared as we dove in over an irrigation ditch. At the bottom of the ditch a dozen pigs ran for cover. The nose came up, the flaps were down, the entire mass of the C-27 stretched forward. The ground hesitated...then leaped forward to meet us.

I dropped us in harder than intended. The gear *whoomped!* onto the dirt and rattled the whole plane with the effort.

"Reverse!"

"Reverse," Plunkett confirmed.

The instant the propellers went into reverse they blew into the air a cloud of dust the size of Kansas. We couldn't see a thing out front.

"Crap. Popeye, popeye!" Plunkett called as his world turned yellow.

"I've got it," I replied, a meaningless phrase since I didn't have anything more to see on my side of the plane than he did on his. But the field was huge and if we just rolled out on our original heading there was nothing to run into. So I paused while the plane slowed down, then reached over and threw the props back into Idle.

The propellers stopped shoving dirt in front of us and sucked it behind instead. When they did we drove out of the cloud at forty knots. We had plenty of space out front. The buildings shot by on our left but now we were slow enough for the brakes to stop us on their own. We slid to a halt in the dirt.

Bunny had the cargo door open while we were still rolling. The instant we stopped he lowered the ramp, motioned to the team, and leaped out of the way. We had twenty-five Bolivians on board. The team leader went last, I noticed, making sure everyone exited the plane, but they all ran off with seeming enthusiasm, disappearing into the dust cloud in the direction Bunny pointed.

"C-C-Clear!" Bunny yelled into the intercom.

"Close the ramp, Bunny. Coming left."

Plunkett keyed the radio.

"Shark 27 is Texas, Texas, Texas," he called over UHF.

"Shark 29 copies Texas," Walt replied. We heard him relay the call back to Rasmussen.

The plan was our standard one: infil the team and take off again immediately. Not knowing the length of the field for certain we had planned to turn around on the ground and take off in the direction we had come. But when I spun the plane 180 degrees to the left we realized at once that wouldn't work. The Kansas cloud had spread, fine talc dust floating in the air two hundred feet high from the spot we touched down right up to our tail. With no wind it would take fifteen minutes to clear. I couldn't even see the team anymore.

"Damn, this place is dusty," Plunkett observed.

"You're not kidding. What do we do now?"

Plunkett circled his hand in the air, signaling for me to keep turning.

"Think you can clear the donkeys?"

We faced back to the south. About a thousand feet remained between us and a rail fence at the end of the dirt patch. Through the dust, we saw clustered before the fence a few dozen goats, not donkeys, all standing with heads erect, looking with annoyance at what had just happened to the other end of their field. Their posture suggested they weren't about to move just because an airplane was staring them down.

"Uh, maybe," I answered. "We might have to wait."

"Hey, I th-th-think they're shooting over there," Bunny called from the back.

Plunkett shrugged to indicate, *of course*. So much for waiting.

"In that case," he said, "I suggest we try."

"Okay," I agreed. "Short field take-off. Flaps to ten."

I pushed the power levers up and held the brakes. Once the engines began to spool up I dropped my feet flat on the floor. We started to roll.

"Plenty of room," I said with confidence. A thousand feet was forever, especially since I had the controls almost in my lap, pulling back the elevator as far as it would go so that as soon as we reached flying speed it would get us off the ground. Not far, but into ground effect and high enough to clear the fence. "No problem."

Then I looked out the window.

"What are they doing?"

Plunkett leaned forward and squinted.

"What *are* they doing?" he repeated.

The goats – all 30-40 of them – lowered their heads and started running the instant we began to move. Running – *at us*.

"Is that normal?"

"Maybe something scared them."

"They don't look scared."

"Maybe they're attacking."

"They're charging us? They're charging a plane?"

"More power," Plunkett advised.

I looked at the throttle quadrant.

"We don't have any more power."

"Hit the horn, then."

The goat in the lead wasn't even looking at us. His head was down as though he was searching for a dropped penny – at a full gallop. His horns were short but curved back over his knobby skull. They complemented a white stripe he had on his back to create the image of an arrow pointed right at our nose.

"Jeez, they're fast."

"They're getting closer..."

"Rotate!"

"I can't! The stick's back as far as it'll go. Twenty more knots..."

Plunkett covered his eyes.

Bunny jumped up on the steps and peered over the third seat.

"H-h-hey, are those horses?"

I wondered how much damage a fifty-pound goat could do to a C-27. Then I wondered how much damage three dozen goats could do. The herd was almost on top of us. Airplane and mammals were closing the distance at a combined speed of 150 feet a second. I was so fixated on the mass of approaching horns it never occurred to me to stop.

"Brace!" Plunkett yelled.

But as the lead goat disappeared under the windscreen the nose came up. The picture in the window changed from ground to sky. The wings clawed at the air. I had the stick locked into my lap and would have pulled it right through my seat if I could have. To go with my death grip my eyes were squeezed shut. I didn't want to see my own demise as thirty-six billy goats gruff brought us crashing back to earth. But instead of a series of collisions we heard only one small thump.

The C-27 hopped into the air like a kid playing jump-rope. We skimmed the backs of the goats like a careless reaper, our wingtip vortices kicking up swirls of dust. At the end of the Dust Bowl we shot into the air and cleared the fence with ease.

I looked to my right and saw Plunkett still holding his hands over his eyes. He peered out from between his fingers, not sheepish at all.

"Oldest tactic in the book," he replied. "What you don't see can't hurt you. Want the gear up?"

"I don't know. I heard a thump. Bunny, check the nose gear."

There was a tiny round window beneath the cockpit steps where you could look outside and see the nose gear. We used it to confirm that the over-center lock was in place but in this case it served equally well for determining if goat meat was wrapped around the tires.

"N-n-nothing on the nose," Bunny gasped into his mike, his plump body flopped flat on the cabin floor so he could see through the portal.

It was impossible to see the main gear so we didn't know if those four wheels had any damage.

"Come right," Plunkett advised. "Let's see if the field looks like an Afghan butcher shop."

We turned around to cross the south end of the Dust Bowl. I kept an eye out for the Bolivian soldiers and any signal that they needed help. Plunkett looked for dead goats.

"There!" he called.

"Where?"

"Right where the tire tracks stop. Looks like we nailed him with the right gear."

Sure enough, the white stripe stood out on the brown fur of the goat where it lay with legs splayed in the dust. There was no blood in sight, nor goat intestines mixed into the yellow dirt. Instead the lead charger looked like nothing so much as an overconfident boxer who has received a hammer blow on the chin. His brains were probably scrambled, I figured, his knobby forehead crushed by the force of the Chuck's gear.

"H-h-hey, he's moving!"

Not just moving. Standing up. Like the aforementioned boxer, White Stripe shoved his feet beneath him and staggered upright. He wobbled right, then left, then for a long moment stood in one spot and shook his head.

We made a second turn over the field before he decided he was fit enough to move. As we banked right he made a brave effort to look up. He even kicked his hind feet when the Chuck's props shook the earth beneath him, a stubborn sign that he wasn't averse to a rematch. As we headed up the valley he walked slowly back to the fence to join his companions.

The raids were successful by our modest standards. Lt Col Rasmussen feared the worst but expected that most of the farms would be abandoned as was our repeated experience in Colombia and Peru. The reality came out somewhere in between. The farms were inhabited but not hostile.

Unlike in those countries farther north the farms in the Itonomas had no processing laboratories associated with them. Here the product was the crop itself, pure raw coca plants cut from the field. That's what the soldiers found at both the Dust Bowl and Chilumaniya. Piles and piles of coca cuttings, looking no more harmful than trimmings off a privet hedge, stacked inside and outside the buildings with no attempt to hide them. Somewhere farther up the processing chain – and in a different location – other workers would mix the leaves with water, cement, and lime to extract the juice needed to form a base, a base then shipped as powder or bricks to labs in Colombia or Peru to be refined further into marketable cocaine. But here it was simply a matter of harvesting a crop.

The soldiers rounded up everyone in the area and then set fire to the piles. By the time we returned to pick them up four great columns of white smoke rose into the air over the valley, the valuable cuttings and their oval green leaves on their way to being expensive mounds of ash.

The frustrating outcome of the raids was that no one of any significance was detained. At each location there was one man in charge of plant collection but even he was nothing more than a farmer with a side job. Everyone else was a peasant trying to make a buck.

But in our tiny little world in the 155th it was good to see a tangible result for our efforts. The columns of smoke rising above the Itonomas Valley that first day may not have dented the availability of coke on the streets of L.A. but it made us feel that our 3,000-mile trip from Panama hadn't been a total waste. It was especially satisfying to those of us who almost crashed a plane because of a goat.

"Did you see those kids at the farm?" Plunkett asked me that night in the hangar as we got ready to turn in. He had laid his bedroll on a cot near me. The rest of the squadron along with our duffel bags and flight gear were scattered along one wall of the building.

"The ones cutting the branches?"

"Yeah. Did you see what they were chewing?"

"Gum?"

"No. The leaves from the plants."

"Do they get high from that?"

"Doc Hinnaneman says they can."

"Great. A whole generation in this country has picked up a coke habit."

"Maybe it's cultural," Kurt Norris suggested from his nearby cot.

"No, it's not cultural," Plunkett disagreed. "Bolivia is just a country with a drug problem. They're poor and there's coca lying around. Poor kids who don't know any better, doing something because they've seen adults do it. I hate seeing kids on drugs."

"Then you'd better keep your eyes closed in this theater, sir," Kurt replied. "Honduras, for example. The drug up there is glue. And god knows what the kids in Iquitos are on half the time."

"Oh, I'm no virgin," Plunkett insisted. "I've seen poverty on six continents."

"Maybe what we're doing down here will get some of them away from coke," I suggested.

Kurt snorted his response. "Not a chance. We're down here building hours for the airlines. Anybody who thinks we're having an effect on the drug industry is fooling himself."

"You optimist."

"I'm serious. The only way to stop the supply is to stop the demand and something tells me Hollywood ain't going to be changing anytime soon."

Plunkett stepped over his gear and sat down carefully on the edge of his cot.

"I just hate seeing kids on drugs," he said.

Walt and Mike Vaneya led the raids the next day. Tommy Goode and Little Bud were their co-pilots. Each time the Bolivian troops rounded up a dozen or so adults; each time they burned great piles of coca plants; each time they dispersed scores of worker bees, some of them children, who were there as hired labor. There was no violence, there were no shots fired. The farmers who were arrested even looked ashamed as the Army processed them back at Trinidad.

On the third day, and then the fourth, we continued to raid farms in the Itonomas Valley, each time moving farther north and thus closer to Trinidad. Lt Col Fierosa's intel remained good although by the end of the week word was getting out among the populace. By the time Josh and Evan raided a farm near the village of San Antonio (by doing a nifty landing on a dirt road), the locals had gotten smart enough or scared enough that there was no one there to arrest. The troops still burned a shed full of coca but otherwise came home empty-handed.

"I think we have made our point in the valley," Fierosa announced over the weekend. His troops had Saturday and Sunday off so the airfield was quiet as he discussed his plans in the hangar. Instead we sat around at the airfield on our downtime, studying maps of the area and playing Frisbee on the ramp.

"Does that mean we can go home?" Josh whispered.

"So that means it is time to visit the mountains," Fierosa continued.

The mountains were in the opposite direction from the Itonomas Valley. Rasmussen demurred at first. He didn't have anything against the mountains but in that part of Bolivia the Eastern Cordillera has peaks over 18,000 feet, higher than the Altiplano. Even the Chimore foothills – our real target – were steep and challenging, with verdant valleys and plunging hillsides that were either heavily forested if they faced the weather or arid and rocky if they didn't. It was a great place to hike, a great place to grow coca, and a lousy place to fly.

"This is bull," Charlie Manson advised Lt Col Rasmussen. "There's nowhere in there to land. The lowest safe altitudes are something like eighteen thousand feet, half the valleys you can't turn around in, the weather in that region is very localized and we don't have accurate reports, and it's almost two hours just to get there. By the time we fly back we'll be skosh on gas. Pure bull."

"So what are you saying?" the colonel asked.

Manson laughed.

"I'm saying it's bull, sir. Tell 'em to walk in there if they want the coca. There's a reason all those farms are there – because no one can get to them."

"Actually," a voice spoke up from behind the map table, "the reason they're there is the rain."

It was Mystic Pete, Lt Col Rasmussen's executive officer. Lieutenant Pete Hammond almost never traveled with us when we went off-station but he had begged to come along on this trip. Rasmussen finally brought him in lieu of an intelligence officer that the Wing wouldn't lend us.

Pete actually joined the Air Force to be an intelligence officer but halfway through training had been sent to Panama as an exec because that was what the Personnel office in Texas needed at the time. Just like I was supposed to be flying F-111's somewhere, Pete was a targeting wonk wrapped in admin clothing.

Although he lacked the certificate from the San Angelo intel school, Pete was a good stand-in for a real analyst. He had an eye for detail and a love of history that gave him perspective most analysts lacked. Also, he did research. If he knew we were flying to a particular region of Colombia, for example, he would spend days in the library reading everything he could on that particular region, its people, its economy, and its terrain. He was weird but perceptive and considered his most valuable tool his enthusiasm to view material from the inside out or, in the case of people, to "get inside the heads" of his subjects.

Right now, for example, asked if he thought the Chimore region might hold coca farms, Pete proceeded to give us a five-minute dissertation on weather patterns in south-western Bolivia, annual rainfall levels in the Cordillera Oriental, and the quasi-religious crop rotation techniques of indigenous farmers.

"They consider the cordillera a gift from Mother Earth," he said with a smile, "sacred valleys that give them what they need so they in turn can treat the region with respect. They're not pagans in the traditional sense but a strong animism influences their culture. There are places in almost every valley where no one is allowed to go, just to show respect for the natural state of the land. If they do go there on special occasions, they have to walk on bare feet. Some places they even disrobe entirely. They go naked," he clarified for us.

His speech was met with stunned silence.

"Pete," Lowell asked. "Do you date much?"

"So *you're* telling *me* I can land my plane in those valleys?" Manson interrupted, ready to go full-throttle in his sarcasm when Pete said yes. "Based on the fact that the locals grow soybeans in the off-season and nature-worship in the buff?"

"No," Pete replied, side-stepping the bait. "I'm just telling you that it's a good place to grow coca. And if the coca guys *are* growing there they're not doing it to hide from you or anybody else. They're doing it because the land is, well, special. Soil conditions are good. Rain is plentiful. The gods are happy there."

"It's got great feng shui?" Rolo suggested.

"Exactly. Whether you can get to them or not is the furthest thing from their mind. Which means if you do get there it'll probably be a cakewalk for the ground troops to round these guys up. BUT..." he wagged a finger at all of us, "if you do get there remember to be respectful. Follow local customs and all that so you don't make the natives – the honest ones – hate us. The rains are there because of the mountains. The locals are there because that's where they were born. The coca growers are there because that, my friends..." – he stabbed his pencil into the middle of Rasmussen's map – "...is the Iowa of illegal inhalants, the Napa Valley of narcos, the cornucopia of coca, the Mississippi of mind-altering..."

"Alright, alright. We get the picture," Rasmussen interrupted.

"There are places to land," Walt pointed out.

"Walt..." Charlie sighed. "Yes, there are flat areas. There are roads. There's even an airstrip or

two. But come on, even the low ones are five thousand feet up and we don't know anything about
them."

Walt held up a sheaf of papers.

"The colonel gave me pictures."

The pictures were hand-drawn. Charlie took
one glance at them and looked around for a
wastebasket.

"I looked at the pictures, too," Rasmussen said,
grabbing them from Charlie before he could crum-
ple them into a ball and try for a three-pointer.
"They're not great but I've seen worse. I marked
three that I thought were reasonable attempts.
You guys are the experts: look at them and give me
your honest assessment of the risks and likelihood
of success. You've got an hour."

Putting Charlie and Walt together to negotiate the merits of a landing zone was like pairing
Van Cliburn with Jerry Lee Lewis to discuss how
best to play the piano. Fortunately, Josh mediated.
Despite the odds they reached a compromise.

"These two," Charlie conceded, circling a pair
of fields southwest of Aiquile. "I don't like either of
them and don't think it's worth it to go there, but
they're better than this third target up here. That
one's an abortion of an airstrip. A fly couldn't land
there."

"I could," Walt remarked.

"Whatever," Charlie said. "Sir, if you want us to land up there, here are your choices."

Rasmussen thought about it. He thought about it the next day, too, while he gathered more intel from Fierosa's spies and while a rainstorm pummeled the area around Trinidad and kept us grounded. Finally he approved a launch for the next morning. Walt and Tommy Goode would land at the site near Huanuni. Major Plunkett and I would hit the airfield on the edge of Alta Gracia.

Walt wasn't happy.

"I'd like to swap targets," he told Rasmussen.

"Why?"

"Um, no real reason, sir."

"Then I've no reason to swap you."

"In that case I do have a reason. Huanuni is near a river."

"So? Alta Gracia has a river, too."

"Yes, sir. But Huanuni sounds bigger."

"I beg your pardon?"

"It sounds bigger. There are probably animals all over the place. Pigs and horses and...goats. Mike already has experience on those kinds of fields so he should probably take it. I'll go to Alta Gracia."

Rasmussen leaned forward and sniffed close to Walt's face, searching for the presence of alcohol.

"Say that again?"

"Just considering the risk factors involved, sir. Trying to mitigate them."

"Uh-huh," Rasmussen nodded, not buying Walt's explanation for an instant. "No. The strip at Huanuni is shorter, tighter, and harder to get to. Judging from the skid marks on the runway back home, you like that kind of challenge. Besides, you and Lt Goode are the more experienced crew. Go where you're told."

Later I asked Walt what his protest was all about.

"Alta Gracia," he whispered. "Have you seen it on the map?"

"The village? It's not on the map."

"No, but the location. The coordinates. Look where you're going. Do you see that canyon?"

He showed me a page torn from an atlas. Carefully he traced a finger across the ridgelines.

"Look. Here's the approximate area of Alta Gracia. It's at the opening of a canyon. The canyon connects to this valley."

"So?"

"Follow the valley north."

"It keeps going. So what?"

"Vilcabamba's gold."

"Huh?"

"Vilcabamba's gold! From the list! Remember?"

I remembered the phrase but nothing else.

"Vilcabamba is where the Inca made their last stand against the Spanish," Walt explained. "It's rumored to be a place of great treasure, the place where the Inca gathered all their remaining riches under the last emperor, Tupac Amaru."

"But that's in Ecuador," I protested. "Everyone knows that."

"There's a place in Ecuador by that name, yes," Walt conceded. "A mountain valley where the tourists go and all the local people live unusually long lives, yes. But that's not gold. That's not the Vilcabamba I'm looking for."

"How do you know?"

"The same way I know any of this stuff: my dream! In my dream the hands weren't coming from a valley filled with geriatric tourists. And it wasn't in Ecuador. That place isn't Vilcabamba."

"Then you're saying it's here? Are you telling me there's treasure where Fierosa wants us to fly?"

"No," Walt waved his hand as though the idea were a pesky fly. "No treasure. Far from it."

"Then what?"

For his answer Walt ushered in an expert witness.

"It's a monastery," Mystic Pete explained, leaning on the table we used to brief our assaults. He ignored Fierosa's map and laid out one of his own. "In the hills above Alta Gracia. It's called *La Recoleta*, The Retreat."

"And the monastery was built on the ruins of the real Vilcabamba?" I guessed.

"No, dummy. Nothing like that. Vilcabamba's in Ecuador."

"But he said..." I started to protest, pointing at Walt.

"We're not trying to get to Vilcabamba. We're going to a monastery."

"Why? What does this monastery have to do with the gold in Walt's dream?"

"Nothing," Pete admitted. "Well, everything. See, it's not really a monastery. It was a retreat, someplace the missionaries used in their earliest forays into Bolivia. It's abandoned now and nothing more than a church with a few outbuildings. It's *La Recoletita*," he smiled.

"The Little Retreat?"

"Exactly."

"I'm confused."

"The real La Recoleta has a library," Walt interrupted. "It's farther up that valley a couple of hundred miles. In Peru. It has a library and one of the best pre-Columbian map collections in the world."

"*The* best," Pete corrected. "It shows trade routes and population centers that existed even before the Cuzqueños and the Chankas went to war."

"Who?"

"They were the two tribes in the area up to the 1400s. They had a long war, the Cuzqueños won, and the result was the beginning of the Inca Empire. Unfortunately for them, a hundred years later Francisco Pizarro showed up and kicked their ass."

"And the Inca retreated...where?" I demanded. "Here?"

"Not here," Pete repeated. "Definitely not here. Farther north somewhere. Maybe Ecuador. No one knows exactly. The official word is that valley you mentioned because some archeologist in the 1950s found ruins there. But others disagree. No one ever found gold there, after all. And the monastery at Arequipa won't let me into their library to look at the old maps for myself. You have to be Peruvian, you have to be a scholar, and you have to be approved by the government."

"Wow, you can't just be a treasure-hunter?" I asked, my sarcasm clear.

"Exactly."

"It's not about treasure," Walt insisted. "I mean, I wrote down 'gold' but maybe that's just a metaphor. Maybe the important thing for a bunch of Inca on the run was a spring with fresh water, or a good place to plant crops, or a bunch of fat woolly llamas. Maybe there was a dance hall with hot Inca chicks."

"But what were the hands holding up in your dream? Not a fat llama."

"I don't remember," he, admitted. "There were hands, a guy, a box or bag of some sort maybe... that one wasn't real clear. I just remember the words."

"What does this have to do with The Little Retreat?"

"Ah," Pete exclaimed, returning to his map. "We can't get into the library at Arequipa so we're out of luck on the maps there. Except...a girl at the South American Explorers club in Lima told me that missionary outposts often kept copies of documents that were held at the monasteries themselves. A curator at the *Museo de la Nación* confirmed that. And a geologist I ran into at The Spratley Arms told me about La Recoletita."

"But you said this place was abandoned."

"It is," Pete nodded. "But the curator told me something else. Books the missionaries copied. Maps they drew on walls. He'd never heard of La Recoletita but the geologist knew someone who had been there – according to him, the walls are covered with maps."

"So a guy you don't know has a friend you've never met who said..."

"– that the walls are covered with maps," Pete agreed. He smiled.

I started to get an inkling of what they intended. As confirmation, Walt held up an instamatic camera.

"So, Mike," he said. "Guess what I want you to do?"

"You're going to take a picture of a church?" Major Plunkett asked when we climbed into the cockpit the next morning.

"Not the church," I explained. "The walls inside the church."

"And the walls are going to tell you what?"

"They're not going to tell *me* anything. Supposedly they're going to tell Walt where the Inca used to hang out before they were Inca. He wants a better fix on where they might have gone when the Spanish arrived."

Plunkett laughed. "Why doesn't he just call National Geographic?"

"He did. They don't know."

He taped Fierosa's picture of the Alta Gracia airstrip to the plate holder by his leg. With his finger he traced the outlines of the sketch. Reluctantly, his voice turned serious.

"I don't know, Mike. I know you guys have this search going and everything, but playing Indiana Jones during a raid..."

"Sir?"

"It's irresponsible."

He caught me off-guard. None of us had considered that Plunkett might not go along with the plan.

"Well, sir," I stammered, "we did consider..."

"You're the aircraft commander but as the senior ranking guy I have to rain on your parade. Once these guys get off the plane, we need to be on alert to haul them back out. How can we be on alert if you're gallivanting around the Bolivian countryside? What if somebody gets shot?"

Plunkett was right, of course. We had a job to do.

"Besides," he continued. "A church in the middle of nowhere that Walt wants to see and we happen to be going there? That's a bit of a coincidence. How did he hear about this place?"

"He didn't. Pete did. Walt would never have considered this if Pete hadn't told him about it and then talked him into doing it. Pete's been helping Walt research the stuff on his list and is obsessed with this Vilcabamba business."

"Why, because there's gold?"

"Pete doesn't care about gold. He just likes the challenge."

"And you?" Plunkett asked, looking across the cockpit. "How do they keep talking you into getting involved? What's your motivation?"

I looked out the window toward the southeast where storms were building over the cordillera.

"Me?" I sighed. "I'm just an idiot."

Walt tried one more time to get on my airplane. He proposed having a mission commander on each of the assault aircraft and offered to give up flying in order to come with me. Rasmussen liked the idea of an MC but nixed swapping crews. Instead he added Manny to our plane.

We almost didn't have room for another pilot after Lt Col Fierosa announced how many troops he wanted each plane to carry. Forty-eight soldiers crowded aboard, four squads that crammed themselves into the cabin with some sitting on the floor and holding on to cargo straps. None of us had ever carried that many people on a C-27 before. There was barely room to turn around. We knew that because during the flight Manny tried to get to the latrine and almost didn't make it. He lost his balance stepping between soldiers and in the process of not falling down caught his foot on the pallet-release handle and wrenched his ankle. It wasn't long before it swelled and turned purple.

"Who goes off flying status *during* a flight?" he moaned.

The reason for the troops was that neither Hua-nuni nor Alta Gracia was expected to be a hot LZ.

The strips were near villages while the farms that grew coca lay farther up the valley – far enough that the element of surprise would be limited. Fierosa wanted his troops to have safety in numbers. He ordered a ground element to leave Trinidad the night before and drive to the area so they could arrive shortly after we did. Our troops would leave the plane, march to the farms, capture what they could, then link up with the trucks to carry them home. All we had to do was land and wait to see how things turned out. If everything went well, we would just sit on the ramp until the roundup was complete. Plenty of time to take pictures.

"So where is this place, anyway?" Major Plunkett asked.

"I don't know. I was hoping one of the locals could tell us."

Alta Gracia was surrounded by hills. On three sides they grew in size the farther away you looked until many miles distant the peaks disappeared into clouds. On the fourth side, the side from which we approached, the hills stood only a few hundred feet tall. They were rounded at the top and green all over like giant dimples on a billiards table. Their primary function seemed to be as obstacles for the region's many rivers to flow around. The rivers did just that, creating scores of little islands where cattle grazed on soggy, isolated pastures.

A steady rain was falling when we arrived. Judging from the lushness of the terrain it had been doing so since sometime in the Middle Ages. Besides the roads and the airstrip, almost everywhere we looked was green and wet. The two exceptions were hillsides that stood denuded of trees, cut down for use by the villagers. One was across the canyon; the other loomed over the runway. They were brown and wet. In those places, as on the runway itself, the ground glistened like oil on the surface of a bay.

Our approach was from due east. The plane splashed into a puddle at the end of the strip and then skidded another two thousand feet as we slowed down.

"God Almighty," cried our loadmaster from the ramp as the troops exited the plane. "It's been a long time but I do believe this here mud is what they call Mississippi gumbo."

Junior Flats was an emaciated black guy with a skin condition and an earnest voice. For whatever reason, he wanted everybody to stereotype him as a lazy welfare child from the South. In reality he came from a middle-class family in New York State and his assignment to Panama was the first time he had ever crossed the Mason-Dixon Line. He was also our only loadmaster with a college degree. He didn't mind working hard or getting dirty but to keep the other loadmasters from thinking he was some kind of brainiac he deliberately dumbed himself down and feigned indolence.

"Lord a-mighty, you boys sure made a mess of this plane! Both sides and the tail are coated with mud that's thicker than bacon grease. The rear windows are covered. It's like trying to look through gravy on a mess o' grits."

"Junior," I sighed. "If you keep talking like a Louisiana sharecropper I'm going to come back there and slap you."

"There you go again, boss! It's the same old story: the white man trying to keep the black man down."

"Oh, please. Since when has a pilot ever controlled the loadmaster mafia? Besides, you're trying too hard. Nobody talks like that, not even in the South."

"I beg your pardon, boss. Apparently, a poor ol' field hand like me can't even talk without massah giving him a hard time."

"Field hand? You're a college graduate and a Republican! I'll give you a hard time – I'll strap your college-educated ass to the bottom of the fuselage when we take off and let you taste some of that gumbo for yourself."

"Yessuh, boss."

"Oh, give it a rest."

We weren't in danger of being stuck. The C-27's tires were fat enough that they rode the

mud like a water strider on a pond. We didn't
have any traction, though. When Plunkett goosed
the power on the right engine to turn us around
and face back up the runway, the plane spun 270
degrees before it stopped. He then had to tweak
the left engine to straighten us out. Each correc-
tion picked up gobs of mud and threw it hundreds
of feet behind us onto the corrugated tin roofs of
the nearest village homes. When he finished, the
exterior of the huts looked like the mad experi-
ment of an avant-garde artist. It would take days
for the rain to wash them off. I hopped out of the
plane and faced the unappreciative glares of half
a dozen locals.

"Mike!" Manny called from the ramp. "I've
found a kid who can help you."

He had found a twelve-year-old named Rafael.
Rafael had a long face and wore a wool poncho
with a hood. He was accompanied by a dozen pals
who clustered under the tail to escape the rain.

I knelt down by Manny.

"Major Plunkett ordered us not to go," I
whispered.

"But we have to," Manny replied. "You think he
would tell Rasmussen?"

"I don't know. He might."

Further conversation was cut off when Plunkett
joined us at the ramp. He took one look at the
boys Manny was talking to and cried out.

"For god's sake! What are they doing out in this rain? They should be inside someplace."

Manny proposed the question to Rafael. The boy looked surprised. Helped by commentary from his companions, he gave a rambling response about how the last three rainy seasons had continued for an unheard-of long time. This year in particular if he had waited for a clear day to go outside he would have remained indoors for the last six months.

"It's been raining that long?" I asked.

For an answer Rafael pointed to the denuded hillsides. The villagers, he explained, had cut down trees close by for the first time in generations because it was too difficult to haul firewood from farther away on the muddy roads. Even their crops had drowned. Houses flooded. Cattle washed away. Some families emigrated to Cochabamba.

"He says he knows where your church is," Manny interrupted, forgetting for the moment what I had just warned him. "He says it's right over there."

I looked where Manny pointed. Across the canyon, half a mile distant, was the easternmost house in the village. Beyond it was a meadow, then the other acre of hillside mud. At the top of the hill were trees.

"On the hill?" I asked.

"Behind it," he explained.

Manny looked apologetic. He had planned to accompany me. Now with a sprained ankle there was no chance of that even if I did make the trek.

When Plunkett went back to the cockpit to retrieve some candy bars I quizzed Rafael to make sure his church was the place I was looking for. Rafael shrugged. The chapel in the hills is very old, he told us. It was abandoned long ago.

Old was good. Abandoned was very good.

"Hay mapas?" I asked him. *"Hay mapas en las paredes?"*

Rafael didn't know anything about maps on walls. Neither did the other boys.

Our troops disappeared from view. After we landed they ran down the hill to the main road and moved out to the north. Now, no sooner were they out of sight than Fierosa's ground contingent showed up. The convoy of four trucks came down the road from Aiquile and paused at the base of the hill below the runway.

Plunkett and I walked to the edge of the bluff to look down at them. The drivers met our gaze with a *"Que pasó?"* expression on their face so we pointed to the north. The lead driver nodded. He put his vehicle in gear and the others followed, carving their way up the muddy road. Plunkett and I returned to the plane.

"Now we wait," I said.

Plunkett had made clear that he didn't want me going anywhere to look for Pete's church. Even so, I hoped that once the trucks were out of sight and everything was quiet he would relent. He didn't. He got out the Parcheesi game that was his favorite way of killing time and sat in the cabin moving pieces around the board.

The sound of the vehicles faded away.

The rain fell steadily for the most part. Every now and then a wave of heavier rain swept through, as though a particularly fat cloud had joined the fray above. The squalls always came from the east and arrived in pairs. They swept across the hillside with a companion wind and hit the nose of the C-27 first, causing a high-low-medium chorus to drum across the fuselage as they passed. *SHHH-shoooom-aaHHH*, the rumble echoed through the cabin. Then seconds later, *SHHH-shoooom-aaHHH*. They were brief, only half a minute each, then the echoes faded and it was back to the patter.

After a while Plunkett sighed and folded up his game. He leaned against the left troop door and tapped the board on his leg.

"These kids look like drowned rats," he announced.

He was right, although in truth when Junior let them all run up the ramp into the cabin they looked like drowned, happy rats.

"You say there's no treasure at this church?" Plunkett inquired.

A trickle of water ran off the cabin door onto my head but my seat by the ramp was too comfortable for me to move.

"Frankly, I doubt there's anything at this church, sir," I replied. "I'm not that lucky."

He stopped tapping.

"But there might be?"

"There might be."

"What chance, do you think?"

"It depends how much you believe Mystic Pete."

"Well, he believes it, doesn't he?" Plunkett insisted. "He said there could be something?"

"He said if there's anything, it'll be a map on the wall."

"Just a map?"

"Just a map. Granted, if that map has anything to do with Tupac Amaru it'll be as good as treasure. National Geographic will be all over Walt to get their hands on it."

"Really?"

"Why not? The search for Vilcabamba has been at a dead end for years. Any new information might be worth money. For all we know that church is the key. Maybe that's the 'gold' Walt saw in his dream."

Plunkett walked to the tail and looked off across the valley. Then he transferred his gaze to the kids inside. Manny, nursing his bum ankle, baby-sat them as they hopped in and out of the troop seats and swung on cargo straps hooked to the ceiling.

"This town's got nothing," he murmured.

I shrugged. It wasn't a unique story.

"It's stupid, but..."

"What's that, sir?"

Plunkett looked at me and pointed across the valley.

"If that church does have something like Hammond says, it could be important."

"Important?"

"An important site."

"I suppose."

"Important for National Geographic," he continued. "Important for the Bolivian government. Important for tourists. It could be something for the village."

"What do you mean, for the village?"

"Something they could benefit from. Something besides crops that get washed away."

I must have looked puzzled because Plunkett hopped down into the mud as though to clarify where his allegiance lay.

"I don't like seeing kids suffer," he stated. "If we can find something that gives them a way to make money, a way to eat..." His voice trailed off.

Manny limped back to the ramp, overhearing our discussion. He looked at me for confirmation.

I stared back, stuck on the fact that Plunkett was including himself in the search.

The major stamped his foot in annoyance.

"Let's go!" he ordered.

Fifteen minutes later I wondered if he had lost his enthusiasm.

"This is a sea of mud!" he gasped as we clawed our way up the hill across the valley.

The sprint to the far side of the village soaked us to the skin. We both wore ponchos but they were short and loose at the neck so what rain didn't bounce up from below got in from above. The squalls that blew water sideways finished off the job so that there was no longer a square inch of our bodies that was dry.

The direct route to where Rafael pointed took us up the clear-cut hillside. However, once there we realized we needed another path. Every step up caused us to slide back down almost as far. Worse, once a foot sank into the muck the soil above it slid down in an avalanche of thick, brown pudding. Mud oozed inside my boots and seeped under my pant legs.

"Why is this stuff so slippery?" Plunkett demanded. He tried to climb on all fours but his hands sank in up to his wrists. He ended up belly-flopping into the mud.

"They took the trees," I said loud enough to be heard above the rain. "There are no roots to hold it in place. Now the grass is gone, too. It's a mudslide waiting to happen."

No sooner were the words out of my mouth than it occurred to both of us what I had said. We stopped crabbing across the hillside and turned to look behind us, across the valley to where our C-27 squatted in the mud beneath the village's other denuded hill. It was barely visible through the veil of rain.

"We'd better hurry," Plunkett urged. "Move sideways. Find the grass at the edges. We can keep our feet there."

We moved across the hill to the edge of the clear-cut. There, patches of carib grass still grew in clumps thick enough for us to keep our footing. It was still painful but in time we reached the summit.

"Where now?" the major puffed.

"Through the trees."

We scrambled through a grove of walnut trees, still going uphill. The trees gave way to a field of boulders which in turn stopped before a naturally terraced hillside of waist-high grass. At the top of the terrace was a plateau, a stand of quebrachos, and one sturdy, forlorn, and very old church.

"Is that it?" the major gasped, struggling to catch his breath.

There wasn't a soul in sight. Nor was there evidence that people had been around the building for a long time. There were ruins farther back in the trees but the church was the only solid structure. It looked like it had been alone for decades.

The church was, or had been, white. Bits of an alabaster coat still showed in patches high on the walls, below where the roof hung over and blocked the rain. Everywhere else the plaster had aged to a dirty brown. That was likely the fault of the trees – quebrachos produce a tannin so strong people use it to stain leather.

Other than the white spots there was nothing remarkable about the outside of the building. It was a block edifice in the style of Spanish missions but with a peaked roof covered in clay tiles, no windows, and a single wide door in the west wall. An iron cross stood at the apex of the roof, atop an arch that united two pillars running up from the ground. A second cross was carved into the plaster above the door.

We moved through the trees to the door and stopped, half-expecting someone to yell, "Hey, what are you two doing?" No one did. The plateau continued on the far side of the church but so did the quebrachos and grass. There was nothing to see in any direction except woods, collapsed outbuildings, and pouring rain.

"There's still a door. Someone must take care of this place."

"Why do you say that?"

"Because there's still a door! And it's on hinges."

To prove his point Plunkett pushed on the door just above the large iron ring that served as a knob. The door moved an inch and then stopped, scraping roughly against the floor. Grabbing the ring the major lifted, helping the heavy timber to swing clear. We stepped over the threshold.

"This is a bad time to ask if you brought a flashlight," he commented.

I held up the penlight from my helmet bag.

"Good thinking."

He stepped aside and motioned for me to enter.

The downpour notwithstanding, weather in the southern foothills is usually predictable. Nine months of dry, thin air followed three months of rain. That helped to explain why the inside of the church was in decent shape despite having sat on the mountainside for four hundred years.

The room was empty – the whole building was just one room, with no other doors visible and no separation between nave and chancel other than a short step. Only one small wooden chair, big enough for an adolescent, took up any space. It sat in a corner below the altar railing.

The railing was in one piece although a handful of balusters were either missing or had toppled out of place. The altar itself was empty except for a stone table. A crucifix hung behind it on the east wall. Above the crucifix was a window that we missed from outside. It was small, made with thick lead glass, and smoky to the point that no light came through.

I turned the flashlight up and found the beams still intact. That and the tiles they supported explained why the interior of the chapel was dry. More timbers stretched from wall to wall. They were unfinished but dry and hard as a rock and looked prepared to do their job for another four centuries. Quebracho was tough stuff.

Cobwebs were everywhere.

We stood in silence for a moment, listening to the rain pour outside. Since it was the only thing on the back wall it was hard to keep the crucifix outside the beam of light.

"Okay, this is creepy," I finally admitted.

"I thought there would be more," Plunkett agreed. He stepped around me but didn't stray far from the door. Little light from outside entered the chapel with us.

I cast the beam around. Dust floated in the light. There were water stains high on the plaster and even the cobwebs hung heavy in the musty corners. The air heaved with moisture.

The floor was covered in straw. The piles were moldy and stale, damp with the humidity. When

stepped on, instead of crunching in brittleness
the stalks pressed flat in spongy exhaustion then
sprang back up to cough out little clouds of pollen
and mold.

"Maps," Plunkett reminded us, glancing at his
watch.

I spun the light around and searched the nearest wall with the beam. Nothing. A lot of dirt, some
gouges in the plaster, and more stains.

"Try this side."

The north wall was bare, too. After some study
we were able to make out faded depictions of the
Stations of the Cross but that was all.

Our next stop was the altar where the original
paint was in the best shape of all. However, it too
was blank.

"We'd better go," I sighed.

Plunkett slapped at something on his leg and
started to agree. Then he stopped and pointed to
the west wall.

"There!" he said.

Beside the entrance, in the shadow formed by the
door itself, the wall was a different color. Plunkett
hauled the door closed so I could point the beam
that way. When I did we were both struck dumb.

"He was right," I whispered at last. "That crazy
desk warrior was right."

On the wall on both sides of the door was a landscape painted in beige, green, blue and white. The

beige was a backdrop, brushed onto the plaster with such thoroughness that it could have passed for the same tannin that stained the outside of the building. The green depicted mountains and jungle. The blue showed structures, figures, and a series of lines that I first mistook for mildew. Eventually we recognized a path, one that started low toward the floor on the left side of the door. It wound around various hills identified in tiny writing and forged a sinuous trail that snaked across the wall. Slowly it moved upward in a ladder-like progression as though determined to connect as many locations as possible.

The path moved over the door and high on the wall almost to the beams. Then it descended to where we stood, into a cluttered portrait of valleys, water holes, and animals grazing below snow-capped peaks. Details were hard to read. The colors were faded and the strain of being exposed to the elements showed in the tired plaster where cracks and ridges formed under the burden of gravity. Yet the overall picture was striking. Whoever painted it had crammed a great deal into a small space, smudging alpaca, mountains, and human figures onto the canvas using different shades of the same color and then trying to make it all look vast by improvising a sky and clouds above.

Broad features were clear but the perspective was confusing. Some figures were big, some were small; one forest looked far away although the stream running through it would have had to be the Amazon for that to be true. Snow-capped peaks rose and fell like a bell curve around what looked like a lake. The lake's water was blue but the land near it seemed to be blue, too. A vivid blue, an amazing blue. We ended up not knowing where one stopped and the other began. In the distance was a star but confusingly it sat on the ground in the middle of the jungle. The major and I flashed the light back and forth trying to determine a sense of scale.

"I..." Plunkett started to say, then slapped at his neck and brushed something from his hair.

"Spider?" I asked.

"I don't know. It felt..." He interrupted himself again to scratch at his leg. "Something's biting me. Mosquitoes, maybe."

"Let's get the picture and go," I suggested. "It's been thirty minutes that we've been gone."

I got out the camera and shot almost the whole roll of film, Plunkett moving the door around to allow various amounts of light inside the chapel. One picture after another we took, getting in close and working our way across the wall, then standing back to get wide-angle shots.

"You think they'll come out?" he asked.

"They'll have to," I replied. "Pete can come back himself if they don't."

While taking the last picture my back started to itch. I panicked at first, thinking it was a spider, and slapped so hard the camera flew out of my hand. It buried itself in the straw by the chair. Plunkett and I spent a frantic few minutes digging through the grass to find it.

"There's something in here," I said, holding the camera again. "Ants, maybe. Let's get back down the hill."

I put the camera in my pocket and we hurried outside. Another squall was moving through. It pounded on the roof and bent the quebrachos' branches.

"Good thing we're already wet!" the major laughed above the noise.

We started toward the terrace but almost immediately I had to stop and paw at my back again. My skin was on fire.

"What the heck...?" I muttered.

Plunkett did the same thing. Whatever was biting him was on his legs and into his sleeves. He rubbed himself like he was trying to stay warm.

We walked another twenty feet through the high grass but the itching became worse. Every time I slapped at one body part another stung in response. We forgot completely about returning to the plane and scrabbled at our clothes in agony.

"I didn't see any ants!" the major whined. "And those cobwebs were old..."

"Maybe the dust!" I yelled above the rain. "Maybe it's allergies…"

But then the answer occurred to both of us at the same time. We stopped scratching and stared at each other's rain-drenched face.

"Fleas!"

We whipped off our ponchos to shake them out but that was pointless: the insects were already in our clothes.

"We've got to get to the plane!" Plunkett urged. "We've got to change clothes!"

With that we were off and running. It was easier going downhill so we dashed through the high grass and into the walnut grove. In our hurry we became disoriented. After several minutes of heedless coursing through the trees we broke out onto a brush-covered hillside facing east. We had to re-trace our steps and go back into the grove. There we found the correct path but again had to stop and spend fitful minutes scratching. We were being eaten alive.

"I can't take this!" the major howled.

It wasn't until we stopped for a fourth time, at the top of the mudslide, that we realized running didn't help. Every movement was torture. The itching was driving us crazy. And then I had two thoughts that pushed me over the edge. The first was that we were assuming the itching came from fleas – what if it was caused by some other insect or fungus or worm so small we couldn't see it? How much damage were the little buggers doing?

The second thought was a realization: the itching had spread to my groin.

"Goddammit!" I cried, and tore off my clothes.

"Sons of bitches!" Plunkett replied, and whipped off his own.

Within a minute we were standing stark-naked at the top of the hill, dancing in the rain and trying to wash away the itching in the downpour.

"I look like a smallpox victim," the major whimpered.

He did indeed. His back was covered in tiny red welts that glowed even in the gray torrent. My arms, chest, and legs looked the same. Fortunately, the never-ending downpour did the trick. As we wiped away at our limbs like people soaping up in the shower, the poker-hot prickling died away.

"Well, let's get dressed and get down there," I suggested.

Plunkett's face showed his misgiving. "We're going to have to burn those clothes," he said, pointing at the pile on the ground. "We've washed the bugs off us but there's no way we'll get them out of those rags."

I looked at him and at my muddy, soaking flight suit lying in the grass. Then I looked across the valley to where the C-27 crouched on the opposite hillside. It was almost a mile away.

"Crap."

We tied our clothes in the ponchos and slipped and slid our way downhill. Within minutes we looked like soggy, road-weary, naked hobos.

Then, halfway to the valley floor, we heard the APU on the aircraft start up. The sound of its tiny turbine pushed through the falling rain to reach our ears.

"That's not good," Plunkett commented. We paused for a moment to listen. Was something happening? Were the trucks coming back? Was Manny making a radio call?

As we stood there trying to figure things out, we both heard and saw the propeller on the #1 engine start to turn. At the same time we noticed the mud sliding over itself around our feet, burying us almost to our knees. Suddenly, Plunkett and I remembered our earlier fear.

"Run!"

So far we had sought to avoid the muddiest parts of the hill. Now we gave up trying. Manny was obviously starting up the plane because he feared a mudslide. The thought that he might leave us behind – naked, covered in mud, having to hitch a ride home overland to explain to Rasmussen why we weren't on board our own plane – induced panic such that neither of us had ever felt. Throwing caution to the wind, I gave up trying to stumble down the hillside. Instead I threw myself flat and slid the last hundred yards to the valley floor. Mud coated my body like caramel on an apple.

"Come on! Move!" Plunkett shouted.

I looked behind me but he wasn't there. He had already leaped into the meadow and was now in a full run across the fields. I leaped to my feet and followed him.

The second propeller was turning at full speed by the time we reached the hill below the runway. By then, however, some of Rafael's pals had seen us. They were clustered outside the right wingtip with the adults I encountered on landing. The boys leaped and waved, getting Junior's attention. He peered out the right troop door and said something into his intercom. Moments later, Manny stuck his arm out the co-pilot's window and waved frantically for us to hurry.

We scrabbled up the hill, exhausted. Our bare feet were cut and bruised. Worse, crossing a stream in the valley had made them less muddy than the rest of our bodies, which meant that as we reached the runway we looked like a pair of naked tar babies with albino feet. Helping Plunkett top the final rise, I staggered upright in full view of the locals, too tired to be embarrassed.

The boys laughed. The adults with them didn't. They just seemed surprised. Two of them actually bowed.

Junior yelled above the engines and the rain.

"Hey, massah, we gotta go! This hill's about to come down!"

He didn't exaggerate. The runway we were standing on was slathered in mud that now flowed as quickly as the stuff that Plunkett and I had crawled through on the other side of the valley. The C-27's tires were almost out of sight, buried in the goop. The plane seemed to be resting on its belly.

Seeing Junior point at the ground, Rafael and the rest of the villagers looked down, noticing for the first time the danger they were in. As one, they turned and fled downhill.

Plunkett hurled his clothes bundle through the open troop door. Junior reached down and grasped his hand to pull him inside. I followed immediately.

"We waited as long as we could!" Junior shouted.

I raced past him through the cabin and jumped into the cockpit, mud splattering everywhere as I plopped into the left seat.

"...saw it too late," Manny was saying as I put a headset on. "I was sitting inside and didn't see the tires. We're stuck."

He had the power levers up to 300 ft-lbs of torque, a setting that on a normal runway would have us going forty miles an hour. Right now it did nothing.

I switched on the windshield wipers and looked out front. The soupy dirt runway we landed on two hours earlier now looked like the ford of a river. So many brown rivulets of super-saturated mud flowed across it that the pitch of the strip itself was beginning to change. So much mud was washing down from above that it was only a matter of time before the ledge the airstrip sat on vanished altogether. If we were still here when that happened, we would be carried downhill.

"More power," I proposed. It was the only option we had.

I put my hand on the power levers and together we pushed up. Not fast – we didn't want to pitch forward if the nose wheel refused to move. Slowly, pound by pound, we urged the engines to get us free.

"That's it," Major Plunkett encouraged us from the cockpit steps. "Take her easy, a little bit at a time."

Like me, he dripped mud over everything he touched. Behind him in the cabin Junior stood well clear, his face registering confidence that there had to be a reason why two pilots suddenly

appeared naked from the woods but also his reluc-
tance to find out.

"Easy...easy..."

We alternated power, pushing first one throttle,
then the next.

"There!" Manny shouted.

The right wheels slipped. The nose twitched
left. That broke the suction on the other gear.

"We're sliding...we're sliding..."

I grabbed the steering grip and turned the
nose wheel into the hill. Increasing the power, we
rolled/slid at an angle down the runway.

"I can't push the rudder," Manny apologized.
He had the controls in his lap to keep the nose
wheel up but couldn't help me steer because of his
twisted ankle. I motioned for him not to try.

"Get flying speed. Then I'll take it."

The C-27 accelerated slowly. Though I couldn't
see the tires it felt like they were wading through
the mud as much as rolling on top of it. It was good
we were empty.

The mud outside slid faster. It came down from
high on our left as though pushed. We barreled
through but the slide picked us up as we did. It
washed under the tires and lifted them, tilting us
to the right. We heard the left prop dig into the
sludge and throw it against the side of the plane.
Fighting the current, I twisted the nose another
ten degrees to the left. Our sideward progression

stopped but now I was looking out Manny's window just to see where we were going.

"I can see behind us!" Junior reported from the back where he was glued to the left troop door. Then, realizing what he'd said, he added, "That ain't right. Why can I see behind us?"

Nobody answered.

"There ain't no runway back there, either," he mused after a moment. "How'd that happen?"

It happened because the C-27 was causing chaos on the hillside as it rolled along, knocking free soil that was about to be washed away anyway. As we hydroplaned sideways down what was left of the runway, the ledge collapsed behind us and slid onto the road below. If we ever did get airborne, coming back to land again was out of the question.

"Seventy knots," Manny called. "We need more!"

I released the steering grip and grabbed the controls, mashing on the left rudder as I did to keep our crab into the hill. Our vector outside drifted to the right again; we weren't keeping up with the mud. Though we were basically moving east, we were pointed upriver like a ferry trying to cross in a swift current – and the current was moving faster than we were. Inexorably we were being pushed to the side of the ledge. In seconds, if we didn't get airborne, we would be washed down the hill. Manny pushed the throttles as far as they would go.

Then a squall hit. Though I had the wipers going the rain outside abruptly drove sideways from our two o'clock and obscured our vision completely. *SHHH-shoooom-aaHHH.*

Manny threw the wipers to high-speed but as he did so I realized an ugly fact: we were trying to fight the current and get airspeed at the same time. It wasn't working. We were about to crash.

The second squall hit just then and that's when I had my epiphany: *if what you're doing isn't working,* a little voice said, *do the opposite.*

For us, the opposite was to stop fighting the slide and go downhill. Downhill, which made no sense at all except that for the next few seconds that's where the wind was coming from.

SHHH-shoooom-aaHHH.

"Right turn!" I called.

Before anyone could object I took my foot off the left rudder pedal and jammed on the right.

The C-27 pivoted as though on furniture coasters. The tail spun to the uphill side and was immediately pushed upward by the wave of mud there. For two seconds we surfed with the avalanche, gaining speed. For two seconds...then we ran off the ledge.

"Woah-ooahhh!"

The nose tilted down. The windscreen filled with mud and we all got light in our seats – me especially, since I hadn't bothered to put my seat belt on yet. My butt rose off the cold, damp sheep-skin. I clutched the yoke in terror, convinced I was about to die.

At that exact moment when I should have been contemplating the afterlife, instead I suddenly realized why the locals outside had bowed to us with such deference. Pete had said they considered some of their lands so sacred they rarely visited them, and if they did they left their clothes behind to emphasize their purity. Those simple, honest people thought the major and I were merely show-ing reverence for their culture. They bowed to us because we were naked.

Suddenly the nose came back up. It was shoved up hard and the tail pushed down as we slammed head-on into the next wave of the squall. We dropped into our seats again. The blast of air caused a wind shear across our wings that added forty knots to our airspeed in the space of a few seconds. The C-27 caught the blast and rode it, sucking up the added lift like a thirsty man tak-ing a drink. Our ground speed dropped to almost nothing but we were flying, powering into the wind and flying.

The plane dipped below the ledge and then rose again, soaring out over the valley and clearing all the fences, cattle, and billiard-table dimples on the way. By the time the squall petered out we had climbed to six hundred feet. We were flying.

We climbed to the east until clear of the rain, then found a patch of blue sky in which to draw a wide circle. Only then did I look around.

"Sorry we were late, guys," I mumbled.

Manny climbed carefully out of his seat, tending his ankle.

"I'm just glad you made it," he groaned. "I hate to fly alone. Especially when one foot doesn't work. Of course, you guys have no clothes on. Maybe being alone isn't so bad."

I hastened to mention the fleas but then gave up. There would be time for details later. Besides, Major Plunkett squatting in the cabin and spraying our clothes with a can of pymethrin pretty well summed up the situation. I just hoped the chemical would have its effect before we landed back at Trinidad. Landing without the troops would be easy to explain. How my clothes wound up in the cabin, how a mountain tried to kill us, and why a village now considered the US Air Force to be a culturally-sensitive organization would be harder to elucidate.

"Done!" Plunkett exulted. He reached into the cockpit and spread Junior's poncho across the right seat, then climbed up to plop himself onto it. He looked over the glare shield with undisguised glee and even wiggled to watch his belly shake in front of the yoke. "They'll be dry in a bit. Until then, it's flying in the buff. Not in a Buff, but in the buff! Hee-hee! I never did this even in pilot training! It's not bad! The floor's cold but I've got to admit when you put these gaspers on you in the right direction it's quite an invigorating experience!"

"You're covered in mud," I reminded him.

"True, but Junior says we now look like him and that's a step up."

He chuckled but I didn't see the humor yet. I had cheated death and my heart was still racing. Plunkett, on the other hand, was already putting the incident behind him. He made light of the situation by using the rest of Walt's film to take pictures of his ass. When I still didn't respond, he sat back with a contented smile, looked out the window, and summed up his feelings in the only way that mattered.

"Well," he said. "We almost died. And we almost ruined our careers. But we got the pictures, we helped some kids, and you did some spot-on flying. Not exactly regulation but it sure beats a day in the office." He crossed his arms over his belly and giggled. "Hee-hee! Flying naked. I can't believe I get paid for this!"

Flying Naked continues in
Flying Naked 2: The Hunt for Vilcabamba's Gold

The List

1. One vicuña pullover
2. A case of Kunstmann lager
3. Dirt from the collpa de Guacajayos
4. A stele (Jaguar Paw, from Copan)
5. Two Brazilian lottery tickets
6. A skull
7. A petroglyph
8. A pizote
9. A Monarch butterfly
10. A flute
11. Tagua nuts
12. A sisal
13. Wings
14. A coconut
15. A coat of arms
16. A Korubo war club
17. A rainstick
18. Warekena pitcher
19. The branch of a carob tree
20. A cayuca
21. The wheel of a paddleboat steamer
22. Tapir fishhooks
23. Lotus fiber sleeping mat
24. Maximón

25. The Sol of Antofogasta
26. A blue gentian
27. Vilcabamba's gold

GLOSSARY

Albrook AB – Albrook Air Base, the second largest American air base in Panama. It sat on the east side of the Canal, right next to Panama City.

ADO – Assistant Director of Operations. The #3 officer in a squadron.

AOC – Air Operations Center

DEA – Drug Enforcement Agency

DNIF – Duties Not Involving Flying (meaning a pilot is too sick to fly but can be assigned to desk work)

DO – Director of Operations. The #2 officer in a squadron.

DZ – Drop Zone

FAIP – First Assignment Instructor Pilot

FOD – Foreign Object Damage

Group – The next level in the chain of command above a squadron. Above the Group is a Wing.

GPS – Global Positioning System

Howard AB – Howard Air Base, the main American air base in Panama. It sat on the west side of the Canal, away from the city and along the Pan-American Highway leading out into the countryside.

INS – Inertial navigation system

LZ – landing zone

NCO – Non-Commissioned Officers (sergeants)

Popeye – pilot shorthand for not being able to see out the window

Soto Cano AB – an American air base in Honduras, about 800 miles from Panama City. It was used during the 1980s to support the contras in Nicaragua but by 1990 was almost deserted. A small Army detachment called Task Force Bravo was stationed there but except for the occasional cargo plane passing through the runway and ramps there were usually a ghost town.

TAS – Tactical Airlift Squadron

TDY – Temporary Duty (a short trip to a location other than one's normal air base)

Stan/Eval – Standardization and Evaluation Office (the senior pilots who give check rides to everyone else)

VVI – Vertical Velocity Indicator (a needle that points up or down to tell you how fast the plane is climbing or descending)

ABOUT THE AUTHOR

Michael Bleriot is a military and civilian pilot. For several years he flew tactical airlift missions in Central and South America, supporting local militaries and U.S. forces in their attempts to limit the production and distribution of illegal drugs.

Made in United States
Orlando, FL
21 April 2023

32324871R00202